TopGear
SUPERCARS

SUPERCARS

Edited by

Jason Barlow

BOOKS

The content of TopGear's Supercars consists of edited stories that appeared in their original form in BBC TopGear magazine. The publishers are indebted to all the contributing writers and photographers. In particular, we wish to thank the following for their sterling efforts: Charlie Turner, Jack Rix, Oliver Marriage, Tom Ford, Vijay Pattni, Paul Horrell, Chris Harris, Rowan Horncastle, Ollie Kew, Pat Devereux, Sam Philip, Stephen Dobie, Tom Harrison, and Matt Jones. Special thanks to Andy Franklin, Pete Barnes, Craig Jamieson, Elliott Webb, Esther Neve, Tom Cobbe, Owen Norris and Chris Rowles.

BBC Books would like to thank Andy Franklin and Peter Barnes
for their help and contribution to this book.

1 3 5 7 9 10 8 6 4 2

BBC Books, an imprint of Ebury Publishing
20 Vauxhall Bridge Road,
London SW1V 2SA

BBC Books is part of the Penguin Random House group of companies
whose addresses can be found at global.penguinrandomhouse.com

First published by BBC Books in 2019

www.penguin.co.uk

A CIP catalogue record for this book is available from the British Library

ISBN 9781785944819

Edited by Jason Barlow
All images © Top Gear

Printed and bound in Italy by L.E.G.O S.p.A

Penguin Random House is committed to a sustainable future for
our business, our readers and our planet. This book is made from
Forest Stewardship Council® certified paper.

CONTENTS

"Life moves pretty fast. If you don't stop and look around once in a while you could miss it."

Ferris Bueller said that in 1986, before 'borrowing' a Ferrari 250 GT California Spider that belonged to his best friend's father. Interesting that this famous movie day off should involve the most celebrated supercar maker of them all, but if Ferris thought things were moving rapidly back then, he wouldn't recognise 2019. At all.

He certainly wouldn't recognise the cars. These are crazy, crazy times, and it's a job and a half keeping up with developments in the world of fast automobiles. However, we are led to believe that three things are happening. Firstly, that it's two minutes to midnight for the motor car. Secondly, that the hypercar world is being completely rewired by a new generation of pure-electric ultra-machines whose batteries are so powerful they're producing close to 2,000bhp. (If that sounds like science fiction, that's because it pretty much is.) Thirdly, that some of the nuttier elements in the hypercar firmament have set their sights firmly on smashing the 300mph threshold.

On TopGear we tend to think that the second and third of these three statements nullifies the first…

Supercars are here to stay. We know this because human beings are incredibly resourceful when it comes to facing down the challenges we routinely face, and a big chunk of us love beautiful looking, thrillingly engineered cars. If you learn anything as you leaf through the pages of this new A to Z of supercars, aka the collective thoughts from the best team of automotive writers on the planet, it's that cars are faster, cleverer, and more compelling than ever. Cleaner, too. Nowhere else does design, innovation and performance intersect with such explosive results as it does in this sphere.

In fact, some of the best cars within these pages are the ones that have squared up to the demands of a changing world, and manage to combine blistering high performance with incredible efficiency. Of course, plenty of the others just want to entertain, and go for hell for leather in pursuit of pure hedonistic thrills.

So jump in, and enjoy. There isn't a moment to waste.

Jason Barlow

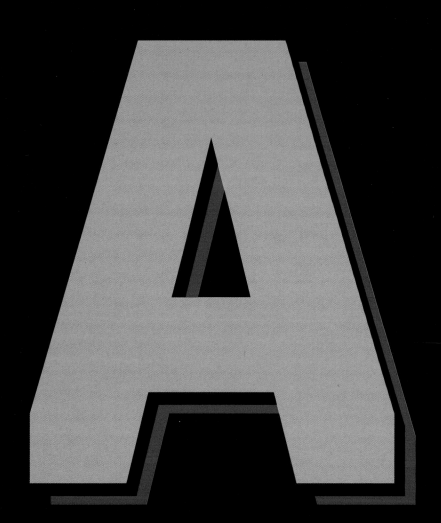

"THE NOISE IS GLORIOUS –
A PROPER SOARING
LAST-NIGHT-OF-THE-PROMS V12"
....

ASTON MARTIN VANTAGE GT12

Only 100 were made, and they cost £250k each

The GT12 gets busy with the composites: it has carbon fibre front wings, bonnet, door casings, sports seats, and centre console. Weird then, that a carbon fibre roof is on the options list. As is a polycarbonate rear window. An all-up kerb weight of 1565kg ain't bad, and as it's fitted with a 595bhp V12 it's not like the GT12 lacks the necessary grunt to punt itself up the road. The standard 6.0-litre has been fully upgraded: there's magnesium inlet manifold, magnesium torque tube, titanium exhaust. That's mated to the familiar seven-speed sequential manual gearbox. It doesn't have the same intricate alliance between chassis and engine that allows Porsche's GT3 RS to find and use every last available scrap of traction and grip, to convert every ounce of internally combusted energy into forward motion. If you absolutely need to get round a circuit as fast as possible, the Porsche would be faster. And probably by some margin. But don't for a moment think that makes the Aston irrelevant. This is a very special car, the kind you go out and drive and just completely revel in. It has real depth, the GT12, because it's so rich and textured that it carries you along with it. But mainly because it's chuffing loud. The noise is glorious, a proper soaring, cackling, last-night-of-the-proms V12 that makes an F-Type sound like a damp fart in the Albert Hall. Other V12 Astons feel mellow and lazy, but this is angry, fast-reacting and challenging, a noise projected and magnified by the titanium exhaust into something much more than just the clash and flare of cylinder explosions. If you want proof of why we love V12s so much, look no further. The GT12's response, muscle, pick-up and potency are all fabulous. The engine seems to be operating within itself, not over-reaching, just giving you everything effortlessly. It's all matched by a chassis that's not ultra-edgy or precise, but has the mother of all sweet spots. A modern classic.

PRICE £250,000 **0-60** 3.5 SECONDS

TOP SPEED 185MPH **POWER** 592BHP

DID YOU KNOW? THIS CAR SOLD OUT BEFORE IT WAS EVEN ANNOUNCED

ASTON MARTIN VULCAN

**How to take left-overs from another project
and turn them into one of the best cars *ever***

Power figures are disruptive. They condense everything about a car's performance into a solitary, web-digestable, easily repeatable number. But it's what that horsepower feels like that really matters. So no, even with brave pills swallowed and dial twisted its final click into position three, the Vulcan's 820bhp isn't as much muscle as mustered by a McLaren P1 GTR or Ferrari FXXK. So if you think those cars are better as a result, move on. This isn't as simple as good, better, best.

The Vulcan started life when Fraser Dunn, chief engineer of Aston's Q Advanced Engineering division, and David King, director of advanced operations and motorsport, got chatting about some old One-77 development prototypes that were kicking around. Unsurprisingly, their first thought was to make a faster one. They envisioned a One-77 R. The trouble was that the project that interested and excited them also brought out the small boys in almost every other department at Aston Martin. Design wanted a piece of the pie, and when they got the go-ahead to make some sweeping changes, including shaping the bodywork in carbon instead of aluminium, every other department started pushing to make equally significant changes.

So the plan to use the existing 7.3-litre V12 was abandoned. Aston Martin Racing pointed out it had a very potent 6.0-V12 running in the Vantage GT3, that, with a significant amount of modification (including gaining a litre of capacity), would deliver on one of the key parameters – over 800bhp.

Whether another parameter was the ability to drive upside-down is doubtful, but, given the right location, at 190mph the Vulcan would glue itself to the ceiling. Since it weighs 1,350kg, you get an idea of just how much use the Vulcan makes of the tortured air that beats over its surfaces. And under. The single most effective aero device on the car is not the rear wing that's big enough to taxi a Boeing on, but the diffuser underneath. Look at the size of the front splitter and imagine how much air it channels beneath the car. And, because it's front-engined, once air is slicing along the diffuser can be opened out earlier, generating more suck further forwards.

But it's not just the big aero components that count. Those vents aft of the front wings extract the high-pressure air that builds up in the front wheelarches. The race-minded engineers wanted them to expel upwards through the bonnet, but Marek

"THE VULCAN IS THUNDEROUS,
DEMANDING AND ADDICTIVE.
THAT'S NO SURPRISE, BUT
IT'S ALSO APPROACHABLE."

Reichman, Aston's chief creative officer, wouldn't permit that – he wanted an expanse of bonnet – so they vent onto the flanks. The compromise turned out to have an unanticipated benefit: the extracted low pressure air draws higher pressure air from the bonnet down on to the sides of the car, improving the flow.

Look at the Vulcan and tell me you don't want to drive it. Check out the low rear-three-quarter angle where the view is mostly wing, the carbon bazooka that passes for a side-exit exhaust, lollipop-stick rear lights and a rear haunch that appears to be forcing its way forward into the back of the driver's head. That's Marek's favourite angle, by the way.

We get to drive the Vulcan at Yas Marina. It's mostly made up of tight 90s but it has one or two ballsy corners – Turn 3 is fast and cresting, and the double-apex right that brings you face on to the hotel. The backdrop is what sets it apart. The hotel, the people on bridges, the boats in the marina, the vast grandstands, the sheer inclusiveness of racing in semi-urban surroundings. You're on display, an actor on a stage. It's a kind of motorsport utopia, a Middle Eastern Monaco. It's got a tunnel as well as those yachts. There are also no noise restrictions – none – during running hours that can extend beyond midnight.

We're on Michelin Cup 2 road tyres to start and with the three-position power dial wound to its base setting. Just 550bhp – it's good enough for over 150mph on the long back straight. The Vulcan's door closure is precise, the bonnet rises on gas struts, the precise feel and click of the paddles, the power of the aircon blower, the leather, toggle switches… the design and execution is stunning. But you don't care about 550bhp mode, nor 675. All you need to know is that each time I flick the dial onwards, the Vulcan kicks forwards. One-fifty on the back straight becomes one-six-five, becomes one-seven-five. At the 200-metre board I hit the brakes with everything my left leg has. The power I can put into the carbon Brembos will make my left hip ache for days afterwards.

It's an addictive business, mashing the brakes, knowing you'll never lock them, that your leg is the weak link, pummelling down through the gears, trying to remember to lift off as the aero grip bleeds away and the car lightens, carrying braking all the way to the apex to keep that nose locked on line. The forces on your body change direction, the push forward into the harness arcing round your body as the lateral grip takes hold, your neck muscles give way and your helmet-weighted head falls sideways to meet the welcoming arms of the headrest. It's akin to a self-inflicted fairground ride.

As the power comes on, it's V12 time. Naturally aspirated, ultra-responsive, wondrous, strident and sonically magnificent.

It howls. Shrieks almost. The sound pulses pile on top of each other, the detonations more densely packed than in a V8, coming faster and harder and more urgently, each forcing speed from the car. When they're not gobbing out fire, each exhaust is an entrance to Hades, glowing orange in its depths.

Downshifts shock the car, the flames lick about, the side pipes pop, rumble and crash, shift lights flash, gears whine – it's a mashing, roaring mechanical melée. Something you feel awed to be in control of. Every so often I have to go back into the pits to recover. Driving the Vulcan is a brutal, exhausting business. Five laps and I'm spent – I get a headache, I need to drink, sweat gathers, ears ring. I haven't heard a word from my man on the pit wall, because even with the intercom turned right up, he's fighting an unwinnable battle against the V12. When someone else goes out, you hear them around the whole circuit, each gearshift, each lift. The sonic shockwaves batter the stands.

The Vulcan is thunderous and demanding and addictive. This is no surprise. But it's something else as well: approachable. You have to drive it properly. If you're late with your downshifts, each will kickback through the drivetrain, jolting the car. The brakes squeal madly, tauntingly, if they're not used hard enough. The traction control isn't that sophisticated. Try as you might to hold the throttle steady as you process down the pit lane, it'll kangaroo and lurch. It feels truculent until you get up to its pace. Then it's simply staggering.

Just as with McLaren's P1 GTR, Aston has got the balance between aggression and suppleness spot-on. When I eventually work my way up to pushing the Vulcan about a bit, I discover that it will understeer mildly wide of the apex if you're too greedy or too early with the throttle; it'll also oversteer if you attempt to nullify that with extra throttle. Too much brake, and the back will step out when you put some steering on. The lateral grip, even at three-figure speeds, will eventually run out, pushing the front out of line.

As it is, it's deliciously neutral: small throttle adjustments, particularly at high speed, having marked effects on your trajectory and line. You can also alter its behaviour – it's a racing car after all. You can change the dampers, toe angles, caster, cambers, gear ratios, fuelling, tyres, whatever. Just come in, have a word with your engineer, maybe go over your data traces. It's the ultimate track-day car and you've paid enough for it, so play around with it, indulge yourself. That's what it's there for. It can change and develop with your talents and experience.

Forget the price – the Vulcan is a pulse-pumpingly, chest-thumpingly, ear-thrashingly, intoxicating machine that lets its owners indulge themselves in a fantasy. It's absolutely magic.

PRICE £1.8 MILLION **0-60** 2.8 SECONDS **TOP SPEED** 205MPH (APPROX) **POWER** 820BHP

DID YOU KNOW? THE VULCAN WAS NAMED AFTER BRITAIN'S COLD-WAR ERA STRATEGIC BOMBER

"ADRIAN NEWEY HOMED IN ON A CAR THAT WAS TRACTABLE. IF IT HAD SIMPLY FELT LIKE A RACE CAR ON THE ROAD, HE WOULD HAVE VIEWED THAT AS FAILURE"

ASTON MARTIN
VALKYRIE

The greatest technical innovator in 21st century motorsport creates a road car

I am shoeless in the middle of Aston Martin's design studio, peering through a porthole into a dark capsule. Surrounding me is the senior design team, all of whom are silent, fixated on how I'm planning to contort myself into the driver's seat. Maybe a head-first Klinsmann dive would work, or bum-first, leaning back and hoping for the best. In the end I lead with the feet, standing on the measly padding and clinging to whatever carbon-fibre extremities I can while lowering myself into a position I last experienced during a root canal – feet way above my hips, heavily reclined, mouth agog. One thing is obvious, the Valkyrie isn't a road car jacked up on F1 power figures, it's an F1 car with its edges chamfered for the road.

But then what would you expect from a project born of one of the great F1 minds, a titan of the sport, the man with a freakish understanding of how to make fast things go faster? I'm in his office now at Red Bull Racing HQ. A wall of glass bathes his desk and vast drafting board in sunlight, a stack of hand-drawn sections and calculations sits casually on the side. I sense I'm about to be schooled, drowned in engineering complexity and shown to be the charlatan I am, but Adrian Newey – dressed down in a checked shirt and jeans – isn't interested in any of that. He pours a glass of water and asks if he can tell me a story.

"The whole thing came about in 2014. I felt as if I needed a new challenge beyond Formula One and something I'd always wanted to do was to design a road car. In the process of renewing my contract at Red Bull I spoke to Dietrich Mateschitz, our Austrian owner, and Christian Horner about the idea and in the August break I started sketching out some ideas. I thought, OK, clean sheet of paper, what would we like to produce?"

What Newey homed in on was something that was "tractable" on the road. "If it's simply a racing car on the road and feels as such, I'd view that as a failure." It also needed to be capable of extreme performance therefore small and light (he calls the McLaren P1, LaFerrari and Porsche 918 "big, clumsy and heavy") and intimidating like the very fastest superbikes. It also needed to be, in his words, "a piece of art." He tells me about one customer, an American lady, who's designing her entire house with the Valkyrie as its centrepiece.

Then, in the winter of 2014/2015, Newey started spending a lot more time in his garage. "I started, almost as a weekend

hobby, developing drawings from those basic principles – coming up with the spec sheet if you like." Around this time he assembled a small team of trusted Red Bull F1 colleagues to turn his drawings into a computer model and start working on the trickier technical aspects, such as the active suspension and bespoke single-clutch gearbox.

This takes us to Autumn 2015. Newey now had an early stage research car with a broad mechanical package including cabin dimensions and where the "big bits" would go. "We had a package that looked as if it worked and we had a rough weight estimate of around 1000kg," he explains. "The big decision then was do we find a private investor or do we go with an OEM? If you think about the OEMs we could partner with, with the right image, Aston was clearly the one. We already knew Andy Palmer from his Nissan/Infiniti days, so it was fate."

As it turns out Aston had already been working on a hypercar of their own, and had a quarter scale model in the studio. "Their car was quite a lot bigger, let's say LaFerrari-sized, ours was narrower and lower. Our car, from a looks point of view, effectively had a lineage with the Red Bull X1," Newey tells us. And it was Newey's proposal that progressed. Aston "did a styling job on it" keeping all Newey's aerodynamic surfaces below the waistline, his canopy shape, but restyled the painted bits. "If you look at the first styling model we showed – the green bits were Aston, the rest was ours. It was rather thrown together to amalgamate our ideas and theirs, and then we started developing from there." It was given the codename Nebula - an abbreviation of Newey, Red Bull and Aston – but it didn't stick, because "Aston like their 'V' names".

Newey describes how there were a few "points of contention," aka big fat arguments, with Aston along the way. "They didn't believe two people could comfortably sit side by side in it, so they went away and made a seating buck and were completely shocked that you could." Because he wanted to keep the front bulkhead as narrow as possible for aero, Newey's solution was to angle the driver and passenger inwards by five degrees – there were mumblings from within Aston that this would be disorientating. Newey used the simulator to disprove that.

Another sticking point was the powertrain. There were only ever two contenders for Newey: a V6 twin-turbo and a naturally aspirated V12. "I did some homework and came to the conclusion that weight wise there's wasn't much between them, in terms of cooling requirements the turbo was worse, in terms of sound the V6 is worse and it would vibrate too much if you solid

mounted it to the chassis. Technically and emotionally the V12 was the better solution.

"Some at Aston liked the idea of a V12, but wanted to use a derivative of the One-77 engine, but it wouldn't produce the power we needed. The other group said it should be a V6 twin-turbo. It almost broke the deal, because we said we wouldn't do it unless it was a bespoke V12, made by Cosworth."

By piecing together conversations with Newey, Reichman and CEO Andy Palmer, here's what we know – one mouthwatering engineering subdivision at a time. We'll start with aerodynamics because, well… have you seen it? At the front an active front wing is suspended low beneath the flat nose section. Its efficiency is governed by holes cut into the bodywork next to the front wheels to release the pressure, holes that weren't there on the first Valkyrie model, holes that also reveal the gorgeous wishbones beneath. F1-style brake cooling ducts sit on the inside of the wheel, while the wheels themselves won't be flat Chris Boardman-esque discs as per this model. "We need to get air from the internal brake air duct to the outside, so there has to be porosity in the wheel design somewhere to let that air out," says Newey.

The roof, originally punctured with a NACA duct, is now home to a scoop that scoffs air into the engine. Most would stop there, but Newey was troubled by the 'spill' - air that leaks out the scoop when you lift off the throttle. Carefully shaped channels, either side of a dorsal fin, ensure any spill is sent on its way smoothly – making it more useful when it arrives at the wing. If you've got your specs on you'll also notice the Valkyrie's rather unique CHMSL – rather than a metre wide LED bar, the 'centre high mount stop lamp' is in fact a single piercing LED on the point of the fin.

Round the back a two-part active rear wing hovers dangerously close to the exhaust exit – an area than can reach up to 800 degrees. Oh yes, and then there's a diffuser inspired by Crossrail. And making this all possible is an active suspension system that reacts to the lateral G-loading with the aim of keeping the car perfectly level to let the aero do its thing. Body roll will not be in the Valkyrie's vernacular.

There are still secrets buried in the powertrain, such as where the rev limit will fall and what the magic bhp figure will be, but we can have a good stab. The 6.5-litre V12 is a new design loosely derived from the CA2010 18,000rpm 2.4-litre V8 used by Williams in their 2010 F1 car, and currently on the test bench at Cosworth. It will be "high-revving" and immensely powerful.

How powerful? Well, Newey's original weight target for the car was 1,000kg; he admits they've slipped over that a bit but will still "comfortably eclipse" a one to one (1000bhp-per-tonne) power-to-weight ratio. So a total system output, V12 and e-motor combined, that's easily north of 1000bhp.

The electric motor itself is fed by a flat lithium-ion stack, fitted low and centrally under the fuel tank. And the motor isn't just there to torque fill at low revs or to augment straight line performance, it's there, in Newey's words, to give the car a "milkfloat feeling" in traffic – expect a small EV-only range. Rumour is it'll act as a reverse gear, too, saving weight and space in the gearbox – a Newey-designed, Riccardo engineered, single-clutch unit driving the rear wheels. It had to be bespoke for this car not just to meet the performance demands, but leave enough space for those monster venturi tunnels.

As for the sound it will make when it first clears its lungs… shrieky should cover it. Newey insisted that it had to be a twelve-into-one exhaust system, rather than two six-into-ones because "that makes it sound like it's revving twice as high as it actually is." Remember when F1 cars used to sound good? Yea, that.

Ah yes, lest we forget, this is still a road car and therefore has road car chores to fill. The wiper blade sticks out immediately, although Newey is convinced owners will just unscrew it the moment they get it home. Placing a number plate is also particularly tricky – suspended somewhere below the exhaust tips appears to be the consensus for now – and the badge is now laser cut and just 0.07mm thick, so it weighs 99.4 per cent less than Aston's normal badge.

Newey admits that climbing into the passenger compartment won't be glamorous for anyone in a miniskirt, but the size of the aperture was unavoidable "because it's quite a narrow chassis and there's no room for pontoons, so it needs to be high-sided." The gullwing doors were necessary so the driver and passenger can pull their feet back and stand straight up when they're getting out. As you'd expect, the interior itself is ruthlessly efficient, but relatively comfortable once you're in. In front of you is an F1 style wheel riddled with buttons, a central touch screen, and two other screens either side – your in-board, camera-fed wing mirrors. The cameras themselves are hidden out of the air stream in the side gills behind the front wheels – taking advantage of new legislation allowing digital wing mirrors pushed through by the VW XL1.

There are two seating options – padding stuck directly to the sculpted tub for taller customers, such as the 6ft 3in Reichman, or a removable padded carbon fibre shell a few inches proud of the tub for the more vertically-challenged, like me. As in the Ford GT you can adjust the wheel for reach and rake and move the pedal box, and that's your lot.

Performance? I wouldn't dare to speculate, but I ask Newey to position it for me relative to the P1, LaFerrari and 918. "We have done lap time simulations and yes it'll be significantly quicker around a lap than any of those." He also dismisses an assault on the Nurburgring record: "It's a dangerous place in a Mini, let alone a Valkyrie. If a customer wants to take their car and get the lap record then that's up to them." He hints that setting a time around a modern F1 circuit like Silverstone holds more appeal. Indeed, we have heard rumours of lap times in the Red Bull simulator that would keep the F1 car on its toes.

It's clear Newey doesn't care about so-called rivals, how the project is perceived or how convention dictates he should demonstrate the Valkyrie's extraordinary attributes. He's not interested in benchmarking or scoring points – it's only about staying true to his vision and making this the fastest and most satisfying road car he possibly can. He's unflappable in other words, but perhaps my final question can unstick him.

Like Gordon Murray and the McLaren F1 before him (Newey owns an F1 GTR), this is Adrian Newey's road car, it could make or break his name. Does he feel the weight of expectation? "Maybe a little bit, I'm human so I want my first attempt at a road car to be looked upon fondly. If it's a flop then I'll feel I've failed myself and potentially damaged my name, but it's not something I spend a lot of time worrying about. Aston talked about benchmarking other cars, but we haven't bothered really – we want to do it our way."

PRICE £2.5 MILLION **0-60** 2.5 SECONDS (APPROX) **TOP SPEED** 250MPH (APPROX) **POWER** 1,160BHP
DID YOU KNOW? ASTON'S BUILDING A LIMITED RUN OF 25 TRACK-ONLY VALKYRIES, WHICH'LL GO EVEN FASTER

"THE VALKYRIE'S 6.5-LITRE V12 IS
IMMENSELY POWERFUL AND HIGH
REVVING. ADD IN THE E-MOTOR AND
THE TOTAL SYSTEM OUTPUT IS WELL
NORTH OF 1000BHP"

. . . .

ASTON DBS SUPERLEGGERA

Aston has a long history in creating well-bred GTs, but rarely as powerful as this one

"It's all about torque. Power numbers are interesting, but you drive torque." So says Paul Barritt, Aston Martin's vehicle line director for the DB11 and DBS, as he talks about the new DBS Superleggera, before going on to mention that it not only has 147lb ft more than the regular DB11, but 111lb ft more than the mighty One-77. Oh, and half the fuel consumption of the latter.

The DBS Superleggera, then, is the ultimate Aston Martin. At least until the Valkyrie rocks up. And even when it does, this is the car that epitomises Aston's brand values better than any other. Massively potent twin-turbo V12 up front, rear-wheel drive, 2+2 layout inside. How potent? 715bhp. Aston calls it a "brute in a suit". Yes, really.

It sits above the £120k Vantage ('Hunter') and £140k–£175k DB11 ('Gentleman') at the summit of the three-strong model range, features carbon body panels to help lower weight by 72kg and justify the £225,000 asking price. It's been sportified and in the flesh it looks properly muscular, the anti-roll bars are stiffer, it has greater acceleration, it rides 5mm lower, and its suspension features bespoke geometry settings with increased camber front and rear to sharpen cornering and firmer bushes.

But the biggest single change is the gearbox itself. It turns out that what limited the DB11 wasn't the engine, but the ZF gearbox – it couldn't cope with much more than the DB11's 516lb ft. But it also turns out that ZF makes a high-torque version of the eight-speeder, able to tolerate more like 700lb ft.

So now there's 663lb ft available from 1,800rpm to 5,000rpm. Aston is keen to point out that a Ferrari 812 Superfast falls 134lb ft short and makes you wait until 7,000rpm to get it. Consuming a continent? You'd have the Aston every time. This is a long-legged machine, pulling just 2,000rpm at 70mph in top. At that speed, the engine is a sophisticated purr of noise, wind no more than a rumour, the ride so impressively damped you don't notice the work it's doing. Then you can play with the different chassis modes to explore the other aspects of the car's personality.

But the aspect to really focus on is the 4.2secs it takes to make the 50-100mph leap in fourth gear. That's deeply fast, supercar fast but with gentler manners. And it sounds lovely while you do it. Aston claims it's 10dB louder than the DB11, but it has just the right amount of burble on the overrun. Gorgeous.

PRICE £225,000 **0-60** 3.4 SECONDS
TOP SPEED 211MPH **POWER** 715BHP
DID YOU KNOW? SUPERLEGGERA MAY MEAN
SUPERLIGHT, BUT THE DBS STILL WEIGHS 1,840KG

PRICE £1 million (EST) **0-60** 2.5 SECONDS (EST)
TOP SPEED > 220MPH **POWER** 1000BHP (EST)
DID YOU KNOW? JUST 500 OF THESE SUPER
CARS WILL BE BUILT... AND ARE PROBABLY ALREADY
SOLD

PRICE N/A **0-60** N/A
TOP SPEED N/A **POWER** 700BHP (EST)
DID YOU KNOW? IT'S ASTON'S FIRST SERIES
PRODUCTION MID-ENGINED SUPERCAR... SOUNDS
GOOD TO US

ASTON MARTIN
VALHALLA
& VANQUISH

A glimpse into the future, as Aston Martin goes mid-engined and chases Ferrari

Not one but two all-new mid-engined Astons, wrapped in bodies that draw heavily on the skeletal form of the Valkyrie, that use their configuration to propel Aston Martin into a different sector of the market. The Valhalla will run to 500 units only, at a proposed cost of £1m each, a son-of-Valkyrie entry into the territory most recently staked out by the LaFerrari, McLaren P1 and Porsche 918. It will have an all-carbon-fibre chassis. The Vanquish (Vision Concept) is mostly aluminium and will be pitched against the Ferrari F8 Tributo and McLaren 720S. Both cars will use an all-new twin-turbo V6 engine, hybridised in major and minor forms in the now familiar supercar manner, taking advantage of the technology's low-end torque-fill to enhance performance and drivability, with the added benefit of optimising efficiency and reducing fuel consumption. The engine is currently under development, guided by Joerg Ross, lately of Maserati, but with Scuderia Ferrari and Ford also on his CV. It's the first V6 in Aston's history, and the first all-new engine since Tadek Marek's V8 in the Fifties. Max Szwaj, Aston Martin's chief technical officer, arrived at the company a few years ago following stints at BMW, Ferrari and Porsche; he worked on the Noughties Mini, Carrera GT and LaFerrari, among others. Chris Goodwin, seemingly a McLaren lifer, jumped ship 18 months ago, and has spent the 18 months in the Red Bull simulator honing the Valkyrie. He'll work on the mid-engined cars' chassis integrity, with Matt Becker across the hallway sprinkling his magic dust on the GTs. It's a formidable line-up. The Red Bull collaboration, says Aston's chief creative officer Marek Reichman, has been critical. Expect F1/aeronautical tech like FlexFoil, which allows wing composites to alter shape without hurting their structural integrity, to feature. Like the Valkyrie, the 003's underbody is ruthlessly aero-optimised, but this time it's fuller. "We've learnt about crash structure, packaging engines amidships, downforce, things we didn't have here, from simply the best in the world," Reichman says. Its cockpit also posits a new minimal approach; all you need to do is dock your smartphone for entertainment and connectivity. Roll on 2021.

A

PRICE £2.3 MILLION **0-60** 2.7 SECONDS

TOP SPEED 208MPH **POWER** 769BHP

DID YOU KNOW? THE CHIEF DESIGNER, RESPONSIBLE FOR
ALL THAT SLASHY BODYWORK, IS A BRIT. WELL DONE, LAD

APOLLO IE

A supercar that looks like something from the Marvel Cinematic Universe? Step this way

Limited to 10 units priced at a tasty €2.3m a pop, the Apollo IE – *intense emozione* – is a track-only, road-illegal supercar that's here to launch Apollo into the boutique exotica scene. Risen from the ashes of Gumpert, the company has been bought out and reimagined by Hong Kong businessman Norman Choi, and he's created a nostalgic GT1 racecar for the 21st century. Where the Gumpert Apollo cloaked a tubular steel chassis in slab-sided carbon panels, the slashed-up IE is all carbon fibre – carbon tub, carbon crash boxes front and rear(the whole chassis weighs just 105kg) and carbon body panels on top, from Pagani's supplier. The whole car rocks up at 1,250kg. And thanks to a monumental 1,350kg of claimed net downforce at 186mph, the Apollo IE can use the same party trick as the defunct Gumpert. Yes, it could drive on the ceiling, theoretically. Motive force comes from a mid-mounted 6.3-litre V12, driving the rear wheels via a six-speed Hewland pneumatic racing dog-ring gearbox. The V12 is naturally aspirated, and gets no electro-hybrid boost, unlike a certain Italian hypercar we could name (which also has a 769bhp 6.3-litre V12). Apollo's guys clam up pretty quickly when you start to ask where the engine has come from, especially if you use the F-word (no, not that F-word). We're told the engine isrelated to Ferrari's (whoops) F150 project, but has been thoroughlyreworked by Italian engineeringpartner Autotecnica Motori. There is no prancing horse branding to be found. Sodon't dare go thinking it's a Ferrari engine… Thanks to a 9,000rpm red line and 560lb ft, Apollo claims 0–62mph in 2.7 seconds, and a top speed of 208mph, sounding evil. The triplet exhaust is a 3D laser-printed item that costs, in Choi's words, "more than a whole BMW M4". The material attention to detail everywhere is nuts, using lacquered, symmetrical carbon andanodised metalcomponents. The engine compartment? Yeah, that'slined with heat-reflective gold leaf. The pushrod suspension is fully adjustable. There's a built-in airjack. The seats are cushions stuck directly to the carbon tub, and the button-covered steering wheel and pedal box adjustto meet the driver's limbs. It's all rather silly in the grandest supercar tradition, but there's nothing wrong with that.

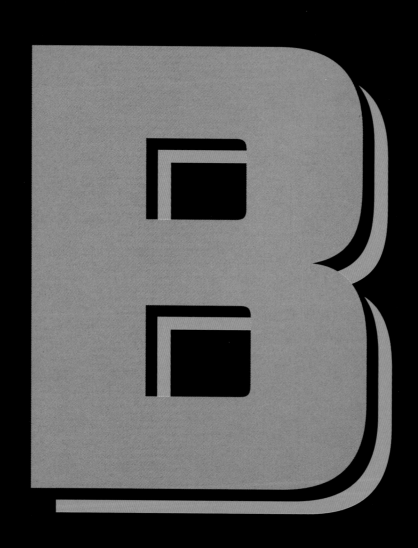

PRICE N/A 0-60 < 2.5 SECONDS
TOP SPEED (86MPH (EST)) TORQUE 1,106LB FT
DID YOU KNOW? THE ANCIENT OAK USED IN
THE EXP INTERIOR IS MORE THAN 5,000 YEARS OLD

BENTLEY
EXP 100 GT

What will luxury look like circa 2035? This...

Ettore Bugatti referred to the original 'Blower' Bentley as the 'fastest lorry in the world', a back-handed compliment if ever there was one. It was a big thing all right, but still fast enough to trounce its rivals in the formative years of the Le Mans 24 Hours endurance race, bequeathing us the infamous Bentley Boys in the process. The EXP 100 GT is the company's celebratory centenary car, but more important is what it says about the next 100 years. 'What's the future of luxury? What's the future of Bentley? What's the future of mobility?' Bentley CEO Adrian Hallmark asks. This vast machine also ponders what grand touring might look like come the year 2035. The conversation began around two years ago, which partly explains why the EXP 100 GT is an uncommonly well executed concept car. At 5.8m long and 2.4m wide, it also has enormous presence. Even its doors – two metres long themselves – arc upwards to a height of three metres. Its structure is a mix of aluminium and carbon fibre, which keeps its weight down to 1.9 tonnes, no featherweight but not bad given the car's size. It's also Bentley's first pure electric car, and the shiny, techy bits underneath aren't light. The batteries power four motors, producing the equivalent of 1000bhp-plus, and propel the EXP 100 GT to 60mph in 2.5 seconds and a top speed of 186mph. Bentley claims a range on a full charge of 435 miles, and also says they can recharge to 80 per cent capacity in just 15 minutes. A new exterior paint finish called Compass, derived from recycled rice husk, uses a special sustainable pigment to evoke a spectrum of autumnal colours. Copper proliferates, too. The grille is made of a clear acrylic and together with the enlarged headlights communicates with other road users. The illumination in the grille matrix alters according to the car's driving mode. The 'Flying B' mascot glows as the owner approaches the car, and the illumination continues throughout the car's exterior. Interior highlights include 5000-year old copper-infused river wood, 100 per cent sustainable organic textiles that use grape pulp leftovers from wine production, and wool carpets. Fibre optics mix with hand-embroidered fabrics. Nor is there a conventional dashboard: the Bentley Personal Assistant is the centre piece of the main cabin console, and anticipates the owner's preferences. Biometrics are used to track head and eye movements, and measure blood pressure. For all that, this car is still about creating and curating a truly human experience.

BUGATTI CHIRON

If the Veyron was the car that changed everything, the Chiron has to do it all over again

To fully understand where Bugatti has taken the Chiron, we really do need to spend a few minutes understanding the Veyron, because its significance transcends its obvious performance qualifications. Yes, it was the fastest, most complicated, most expensive thing available at the time, but it also prefaced a new technology language– one that virtually all modern fast cars have now adopted: turbocharging, all-wheel drive and perhaps most significant of all, the dual-clutch gearbox. The Veyron was essentially Volkswagen's then-boss Ferdinand Piëch showing the world what his vast conglomerate could achieve. It was his Saturn V moment. And nearly as costly.

Yet the world never fell in love with the Veyron. It was never a poster car in the mould of a Countach or an F40 – somehow Piëch created a kind of million-dollar Audi Quattro that we respected but didn't crave or desire. If the Chiron has two unenviable tasks, the first is perfectly obvious – it must out-number the Veyron in every single area. The second is more subtle and perhaps more difficult to achieve: it has to become a poster car. It has to make those of us who could never afford such a machine desperately want to drive and own one. To want a poster of one. Because that is how legends are made.

I had a day to drive the Chiron at my own pace. Just a day. It seems churlish to insert the word "only" into that sentence when so few people will ever be so lucky, but hey-ho, I suppose I just love 1500hp cars and can't really get enough of them. We were in the Middle East, and the car needed to be delivered somewhere and the seemingly simple exercise of nominating a location to drive and learn about the new Chiron brought home the key paradox of this type of car.

Should I have it sent straight to a race circuit? That's surely the best place to test a car that will accelerate from rest to 186mph in a claimed 13.5secs? Absolutely not – this is no more a track car than a Citroen 2CV. Even the vast 420mm-diameter carbon silicon carbide front brakes would succumb after a few laps shouldering 1,995kg, and I have no doubt that the Michelin Cup 2 rubber would suffer a similar fate.

Maybe a road? That's a good place to begin testing a road car. But this bought back memories of my day in a Veyron back in 2006, a time when we were a little less worried about instant incarceration for small speeding indiscretions. Anything more

B

than three seconds of full-throttle acceleration left me wondering if it was the sheer motive force or the consequences of the law discovering what speeds it created that bothered me the most. VW had built an engineering masterpiece; there just wasn't enough space to use it.

And then someone said there was a wonderful place on the border between Dubai and Abu Dhabi, the Jebel Hafeet road. I google-mapped the location and swallowed hard because it looked like just the kind of technical nightmare to undo a big, heavy machine like this one. But what is the point of this car if it can't be used and enjoyed on such a road?

I didn't much like the way the Chiron looked when I first saw it in pictures, and that opinion didn't change when I clapped eyes on it in the flesh – the nagging proportional similarity to the Veyron left me thinking it was just a clumsy facelift. Expectations were low enough, but when Bugatti told me the car was painted gold I packed a precautionary sick bag, and when they unloaded it I winced and then – well, I underwent something of an epiphany. Either that or I finally went loopy, because it looked superb. Almost square thanks to its vast tracks and low roofline, despite being 52mm taller than the Veyron. Is there something about Middle Eastern light that draws a honey-like warmth from the colour gold? Maybe I've just stumbled into taste Hades, but I stood there and gawped.

Pre-drive warming duties were left to Andy Wallace, a man who won Le Mans when the cars were terrifyingly powerful.

Asked just how potent it felt, he proffered one of those jokey-but-serious nods: "Ridiculously." OK. Gulp.

The Veyron wouldn't have worked on Jebel Hafeet. The strange Michelin PAX system tyre would have squidged and squirmed, the steering would have given the driver little idea of what was actually going on underneath and by the time the four turbos had exerted maximum pressure those poor brakes would have been straining for the next turn.

Within a few minutes the Chiron had totally shredded those preconceptions. This is a road best suited to something the size of a Boxster and it felt superb. It's the steering that gets you first – stop and consider for a second just how special your steering must be to outswagger a 1,479bhp engine. But you just never think twice about where to position the car; within minutes you find yourself threading this vastly expensive machine the way you would a £10k used M3. The rack is electric, and some large-foreheaded genius from Molsheim has managed to make seven algorithms communicate with each other to the extent that this might be one of the best electric steering systems on sale. Though you'd expect it to be pretty good given its cost.

Michelin has ditched the PAX system rubber for a Cup 2 design developed especially for this car. On a twisty road it's night-and-day superior to anything we experienced in a Veyron. There's big front grip from the 285mm section on turn-in, and then the 4WD system juggles things around so you can experience the full slingshot. And believe me, the first time you

B

"THE THRUST FROM 100MPH IS INSANE, BUT THE WAY IT BULLDOZES ITS WAY THROUGH THE NEXT 100MPH IS SPOOKY. HOW FAST WILL IT GO UNLIMITED? THERE'S TALK OF SOMETHING IN THE 270S"

give it full afterburner from a second-gear turn in a Chiron is a moment to remember – up there in my top 10 memorable motoring moments (and other alliterative criteria).

You see this 1,479bhp claim in itself means nothing if it can't be accessed or effectively deployed. For example, a Veyron Super Sport has 1,183bhp, but once traction and clumsy electronic intervention and gearshifts and fear and other factors have nibbled away at the process the number of times you actually get to use that 1,183bhp are negligible. In the Chiron, the full madness is available most of the time. Even on the Jebel Hafeet road's dusty cambers, I could just bury it in second and the thing flew. No traction control warnings, no hesitation, just acceleration and instant gearshifts of a type I have never before experienced – not even in some zapped-out tuner GT-R.

I drove up and down the Jebel Hafeet road not believing what the Chiron was capable of. In terms of direction changes, braking performance and cornering ability, it was like a very, very powerful Audi R8. And that's a huge compliment. As for the big W16 – it sounds more aero than automotive, it's never musical, more a rumbling presence whose pitch alters as your peripheral vision greys-out under g-loading. There isn't time to judge the noise, you're too busy managing the speed. From zip to a tick under 4,000rpm, just two of the turbos spool, and then the other pair arrive with a delicious kick to send you up the road faster than you'd think possible.

The road was good, but a few extended bursts of acceleration left me asking the only question of interest to most people – at what point does the Chiron's acceleration dissipate? For me, the difference between your averagely fast supercar, your cooking Aventador or vanilla F12, and a Bugatti is the way it pushes beyond 200mph. The ordinary ones hit a wall at the double-ton and the numbers only creep onto the dashboard thereafter.

So we headed north to the Al Maktoum airport, 4.8km of asphalt where we could run between the cargo-spec 747s as they landed. The journey was two and a half hours of tickled-throttle, carefully avoiding Dubai's new obsession with the speed camera and enjoying the extra silence in the cabin.

Slacken the dampers and the ride is pleasantly supple, the audio is strong and the cabin is so, so special. I love the minimalist approach. The thinking is that large infotainment screens would quickly date the Chiron, so all the information and controls are parked around the central speedometer.

The Veyron was noisy at speed, but some extra sound-deadening materials and, most importantly, double-glazed glass make the Chiron much quieter at a cruise. The glazing is so effective that when you drop the window the turbochargers' whooshing and chattering is quite alarming. And quite gratifying – windows down, this thing sounds very naughty.

But you can't run with the windows down at 231mph – the cabin becomes a little blowy. Not 261mph? They wouldn't hand me the extra key because this is the first time anyone's driven the Chiron and, rather sensibly, Bugatti feels that she shouldn't put out on a first date.

Tyres are everything in the world of 200mph-plus motoring. Andy checks them with a rigour I find slightly alarming, but then he's the man who did 240mph in a McLaren F1, so he knows how to de-risk high speeds. The rubber needs to be fresh; if the treads are too worn, you can't head beyond 210mph. If the pressures are too low, the same applies. The stats generated at speed in this car are more NASA than automotive.

Aerodynamically, the Chiron is way more advanced than the Veyron. It channels air aggressively down its flanks, keeping it attached to form a stabilising pressure either side of that carbon skin. The rear wing switches for the best blend of slipperiness, downforce and air braking. The Chiron even has a separate pair of downward-facing exhausts to create a blown diffuser.

But it cannot cheat physics, and that means the Chiron has a curious battle to overcome as it hurtles towards 231mph – the acceleration is so brutal that the air flow over the tyres cools them to the extent that they lose pressure. And too little pressure could lead to very bad things. This is why you always run with the car's tyre-pressure monitoring system on the dashboard – it runs to two decimal places and you watch it like a hawk.

I had to abort my first two runs because the front right dipped below the recommended 2.8 bar, but on the third attempt the Chiron kept pulling. The thrust from rest to 100mph is insane, it must take around 4.5secs – but the way it bulldozes its way through the next 100mph is spooky, and it just keeps going; much more aggressively than a Veyron Super Sport. It hits 231mph a little over 2km down the runway, nudging into its soft limiter with nary a hint of drama. How fast will it go unlimited? There's talk of something in the 270s. In its lifetime, it is mooted a Chiron variant may exceed 300mph.

It all sounds unreal. And that's why the Chiron is so enigmatic – it goes about its everyday business with a competence that belies just how much engineering has been thrown at it to be able to travel at such remarkable speeds. I expected to come away questioning the Chiron's reason for being. Instead I drove a car that does things no other car can; one with a distinct personality. And yes, I want a poster of it on my office wall.

PRICE £1.9 MILLION **0-60** 2.4 SECONDS **TOP SPEED** 261MPH **POWER** 1,479BHP

DID YOU KNOW? AT TOP SPEED, THE CHIRON WILL DRAIN ITS 100-LITRE FUEL TANK IN NINE MINUTES

BUGATTI
DIVO

Custodianship of the most exclusive car brand in the world confers a high degree of responsibility

It takes a special type of mind to stroll in on your first day, poke around the quickest production car in the world, and decide item one is to make it a quantum leap faster. But on 1st January 2018, that's precisely what Stephan Winkelmann, the new president of Bugatti, did. The Divo is the result – a car that takes its ingredients from the same allotment as the Chiron, but cooks them up into something with a bit more kick.

This is the genius of Winkelmann. A man who knows his customers better than they know themselves, who can take a relatively shoestring budget and turn one car into many, keeping the buzz going while, behind the scenes, he ponders his next move. At Lamborghini, he mastered the art, recasting the Murciélago as the Reventón, the Gallardo as the Sesto Elemento and the Aventador as the Veneno and Aventador J, while the Urus's lengthy development process bubbled away. The Divo is born of the same philosophy.

Over to Achim Anscheidt, design director, the man tasked with turning Winkelmann's brainwave into three dimensions: "The brief for the project was very clear, to design a car that is completely different from the Chiron, but make it recognisable, instantly, as a Bugatti. That's why we have the horseshoe grille, the centre line accentuation and a modified Bugatti side line."

A tough assignment, then? "Sorry, it was easy for me. I've been burning all these years to do something like this, and who better could you ask for than a president that's gained so much experience, knowledge and brand awareness in his former life."

It's also around a full eight seconds faster than the Chiron round Nardò's 6.2km handling circuit But why go down the route of a road-legal racer at all? Isn't it at odds with Bugatti's hard-fought reputation for building cars that bend physics, but have the ease of use of a well-specced Rolls-Royce?

"We started in this direction already this year in Geneva with the Chiron Sport, which is already a bit lighter, a bit sportier," Winkelmann explains. "But in the performance part of the cake, handling is something which we feel could be highlighted more in a Bugatti. That's what we concentrated on here."

Winkelmann wasn't about to push the green light without first consulting the history books. It's from there that the name was plucked – Albert Divo – a two-time Targa Florio winner in the late Twenties and a Frenchman of Italian descent, like Ettore

B

"THE DIVO TAKES ITS INGREDIENTS FROM THE SAME ALLOTMENT AS THE CHIRON BUT IT COOKS THEM UP INTO SOMETHING WITH A BIT MORE KICK"

Bugatti. The Divo also builds on Bugatti's history of in-house coachbuilding, an idea driven through by Ettore's son, Jean.

We meet the Divo in a dimly lit Hamburg studio, and a gloomy lair is where it belongs, for the way it shapeshifts depending on the shadows, the sheer spectacle of its new light signatures and because pure evil belongs in the dark. There's inspiration from the Gran Turismo concept that spawned the Chiron, in its colour palette and extravagant aero, but every vent, duct and wing is there to work. In total it produces 456kg of downforce at top speed – 90kg more than the Chiron.

The rear pulls its weight via a wider and deeper diffuser that splits either side of the retrimmed quad exhausts, and a 1.8m-wide hydraulic wing (23 per cent wider than the Chiron). On the roof, fresh air is rammed through a NACA duct before being cleaved by the fin and fed smoothly over the engine bay and square onto the wing. The front mucks in with a huge chin spoiler, air curtains to tidy the air as it passes over the wheels and four separate vents channel air to cool the front brakes.

Really it's a car of two halves, an imaginary line drawn horizontally along its midriff. On the top, organic shapes and smooth slipperiness, below is something more brutal, designed to slice and bully the air. It's still a Chiron under there, no question, but this feels like something sketched after two-dozen espressos early in the Chiron's development and binned in favour of a more sensible physique. It's the front that's the biggest departure. Impossibly thin headlights bracketed by LED running lights that swoop upwards and right to the outer edges of the bonnet, widening the car and defining it. The tail-lights are made up of 44 3D-printed fins that light up individually.

You can see the push and pull between engineering and design departments playing out in front of your eyes.

Unsurprisingly, it wasn't all plain sailing: "The days are gone when you just draw something and throw it over the fence at engineering. Of course there are arguments – it's like talking to your wife," says Anscheidt, grinning.

Inside, the architecture is familiar, but that doesn't make it any less impressive. There's more padding on the centre console and deeper sculpting on the seats but otherwise it's all Chiron.

Where the real shift has occurred is where the eye can't see. Stiffer springs, dampers and anti-roll bars, an extra degree of negative camber on the wheels and 35kg of weight saved though the carbon-fibre wiper blades, grooves cut into the wheel spokes, less insulation, a lighter sound system and deleted storage in the doors and centre console. Hardly a crash diet, I admit, but every little helps. Lead engineer Stefan Ellrott insists: "The step we've taken with the Divo in terms of agility... can be compared with the overall development from the Veyron to the Chiron." That's a seriously ballsy claim.

The 8.0-litre quad-turbo W16 produces the same 1,479bhp, the seven-speed twin-clutch 'box is identical, 0–62mph is still 2.4 seconds... but the top speed isn't. While the Chiron is capped at 261mph, the Divo slams into its limiter at 236mph. That's because the extra downforce and negative camber increase the load on the tyres, hence this nod to self-preservation. Essentially there's no top-speed mode, unlocked with an extra key in the Chiron, just EB, Autobahn and Handling. Could it take on the Nordschleife? "Not for the time being, no," says Winkelmann.

"We're working on a lot of things, but do we have resources to do more? I will say no today because I don't have the people and money. Already, people are telling me to slow down, but I don't think that's the way to act. If you're ever satisfied, then something is wrong."

PRICE €5 MILLION **0-60** 2.4 SECONDS **TOP SPEED** 236MPH **POWER** 1,479BHP

DID YOU KNOW? ALBERT DIVO WON THE TARGA FLORIO – TWICE – IN THE EPOCHAL BUGATTI TYPE 35

"IN THE PERFORMANCE PART OF THE CAKE, HANDLING IS SOMETHING WE FELT COULD BE HIGHLIGHTED A BIT MORE IN A BUGATTI. SO THAT'S WHAT WE CONCENTRATED ON WITH THE DIVO "

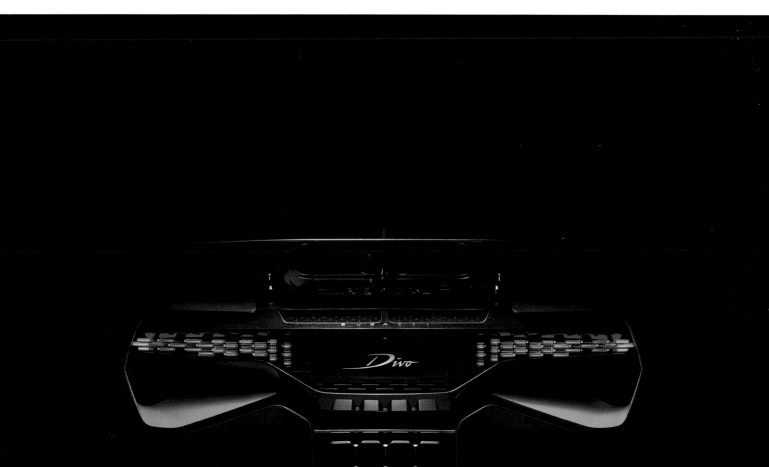

BUGATTI
LA VOITURE NOIRE

Drawing on the most mysterious Bugatti of all is a good way to create the most expensive new car ever made

Imagine being paid to rifle through the Bugatti back catalogue before choosing a car to completely re-imagine in a manner appropriate for the 2020s. But while Ettore and his son Jean Bugatti were responsible for a truly outrageous group of cars, there is one that nudges above the others, for a whole bunch of reasons – the 1936 Type 57 Atlantic. 'When the team and myself started to design this car,' says Bugatti designer Etienne Salomé, 'we really wondered, "what if Jean was still be there, how would he translate the timeless elegance of his own private Atlantic onto a modern-day Bugatti?"' 'La Voiture Noire' is the result, an extraordinary looking machine that uses the Chiron as its basis

seam that runs the length of its body. Jean's friends and many of Bugatti's racing drivers regularly borrowed the car. So as well as being unutterably beautiful, it also has incredible provenance. Or it would if anyone knew where it was. When the Germans seized Bugatti's Molsheim factory in 1940, the most important company property was quickly gathered and put on a train to Bordeaux. This included 'La Voiture Noire', but when the train arrived at its destination the car had vanished. Given that Ralph Lauren reportedly turned down an offer north of $100m for his Atlantic, the status of the original 'La Voiture Noire' would likely make it the most valuable car ever – if only it could be found.

BUGATTI
CENTODIECI

Bugatti celebrates its 110th anniversary in style, as well as honouring an important part of its history

Although the Chiron is quite the halo car, things move fast in the hypercar sector. Bugatti President Stephan Winkelmann figures that regular internet-breaking one-offs – like 'La Voiture Noire' – are a way of keeping the focus firmly on the brand, not to mention lucrative business. Better still, how about a run of 10 'one-offs', at £9m each? The Centodieci, though, is more than just a cynical revenue generator. When VW bought and reactivated Bugatti in the late Nineties, there was zero recognition for the achievement of the brand's previous custodian, Romano Artioli, or the car he created, the EB110. Remember, that was a contemporary of the McLaren F1, powered by a 3.5-litre quad-turbo V12, with a carbon fibre chassis, and active aero, manufactured in a superb, state-of-the-art facility in Campogalliano near Modena. Hell, Michael Schumacher celebrated his first F1 title by buying one in 1994. Bugatti is 110 in 2019, and as part of that it's bringing the EB110 in from the cold. The Centodieci may be Chiron based but it's a clear visual homage to its Nineties forebear. "We faced a number of technical challenges in terms of the development and design of the Centodieci," says Achim Anscheidt, Bugatti's head of design. "The EB110 is a very flat, wedge-shaped and graphically quasi two-dimensional super sports car of the late 1980s. Transporting this classic look into the new millennium without copying it was technically complex, to say the least. We had to create a new way of combining the complex aerothermal requirements of the underlying Chiron technology with a completely different aes-thetic appearance." Though hardly a continuation car, the Centodieci evokes the EB110 via a clever headlight treat-ment, and the signature horseshoe grille is smaller. The Chiron's bold C hoop line is replaced by five round air intakes in a diamond shape that reference the EB110, there's a glass panel over the engine, and a huge rear spoiler. Imagine the effort expended optimising the cooling and aero. The Centodieci is 20kg lighter than a Chiron, and the mighty 8.0-litre produces 1578bhp. Yes, it's rather expensive, but a) we need cars like this and b) they've all been sold so the cost is irrelevant…

PRICE €8 MILLION (PLUS VAT) **0-60** 2.4 SECONDS
TOP SPEED 237 MPH **POWER** 1578BHP
DID YOU KNOW? CENTODIECI STANDS FOR '110', CELEBRATING BUGATTI'S 110th ANNIVERSARY AND THE EB110

BMW I8 ROADSTER

As one of the cleverest cars in recent times, we have no problem pronouncing it 'super'

The i8 has its roots in a 2009 concept car, and in earthly production form has been with us since 2015. It still looks as good if not better than anything else that's appeared since then, although McLaren's 570S Spider is cut from similar, jaw-dropping cloth. But, faced with an onslaught of EV rivals, the i8 recently had to double down on its mission. The lithium-ion battery pack now has a 11.6kWh energy capacity, increasing the electric motor's output by 12bhp to 141bhp, a fully integrated boost for the i8's synthetic but still characterful 1.5-litre, three-pot turbo petrol engine. We're talking a healthy rather than seismic 369bhp overall, an increase slightly offset by the Roadster's 60kg extra bulk, mostly in windscreen reinforcement, from which the doors are now hinged. Hot air at the front is also re-routed out the sides to protect the occupants with the roof down, and the engine bay is reworked for cooling purposes. BMW claims almost 134.5mpg combined for the Roadster, just 49 CO2s, and a range of 33 miles on e-power alone on the NEDC. Updated 360° charging software works in tandem with a beautifully designed 7.2kW i station, promising an 80 per cent charge in under three hours. While the Roadster looks similar in profile to the Coupe, the fabulous origami of the i8's rear deck is even more impressive in open form. There are shades of Seventies motor show concept car, especially in the floating buttresses, which are more pronounced thanks to the deletion of the coupe's rear windows. The fabric roof folds away in 16 seconds in a complex Z shape, and BMW claims 3D printing was used to realise areas of the mechanism. The i8's CFRP tub is unaffected; the source of its structural rigidity, it's still an impediment to graceful entry and egress, though less of an issue with the roof stashed. Inside, you now get a central touchscreen. More than ever, this is a car with a genuinely unique set of talents. It summons up just as much magic out of a virtuous 20mph fully-electric commute as it does when the ICE wakes up with a sonorous thrum and there is a great road ahead. None of its various drive modes will melt tarmac, and the suspicion persists that this is the genetically modified work of Munich boffins rather than a red-blooded engineer's car. As to the supercar question, well, unless you absolutely insist on 1000bhp, then the i8's pace and precision is up there with the very best. This has all the makings of a quirky modern classic.

PRICE £126,935 **0-60** 4.6 SECONDS
TOP SPEED 155MPH **POWER** 374BHP
DID YOU KNOW? THE BMW'S 1.5-LITRE
TURBO WON WORLD ENGINE OF THE YEAR IN 2015

CONCEPT CAR
MAYBACH
VISION SIX

Concept cars can be super, too. Especially when they look like this...

When the automobile was young, the world's rich preferred to take a chassis and have it clothed in a bespoke body. *Carrozzerie* such as Henri Chapron, Figoni et Falaschi, Vignale and the incomparable Zagato created nothing less than art on wheels.

Now feast your eyes on the Mercedes-Maybach Vision 6. This may take a while because it's only a few millimetres shy of six metres long, and has a hood that occupies a different zip code to the trunk (we get to see it in America, please keep up). There are definite shades of Marvel cinematic universe in its execution, while the gullwing doors, tapered bottom, and split rear window all serve up supreme visual entertainment.

Like the Rolls-Royce Vision Next 100, the Vision 6 also junks tired old internal combustion in favour of fully electric propulsion. There are synchronous electric motors on each wheel, while the batteries live under the floor. Mercedes claims 550 kW (equivalent to 750bhp in old money), enough to power this flamboyantly attired behemoth to 62mph in less than four seconds and deliver a range of 200 miles, though probably not at the same time. The Vision 6 can be replenished wirelessly or via an electromagnetic field, and quickcharging can pump enough energy back into the system to deliver 65 miles of range in just five minutes. All this stuff is rapidly evolving.

Both subjectively and in pure sales terms, the v2.0 iteration of Mercedes' Maybach adventure is proving to be vastly more successful than the creatively impoverished original. So this epic super coupé isn't just a narcissistic internal high-five, it signals the company's ambition to go beyond sticking quilted leather and silver-plated Champagne flutes in the S-class. In fact, expect Maybach to develop an identity as a Mercedes luxury sub-brand to match the self-determination of AMG in the high performance realm. If this is anything to go by, bring it on.

The Vision 6 also suggests that automotive luxury has at least one eye fixed on the rearview mirror as it accelerates forward. It was conceived specifically for Pebble Beach, partly because the world's car-loving mega-rich colonise the place come mid-August, but also because it explicitly references those fashionable

"DRIVING HAS BEEN FUN FOR THE PAST 130 YEARS, AND IT WILL BE FUN FOR THE NEXT 130. A GOOGLE POD ISN'T A CAR YOU WANT TO DRIVE YOURSELF, BUT THE MAYBACH VISION SIX DEFINITELY IS"

1930s scene-sters. Check out the Mercedes 540K – now a hugely valuable collector's eternally awesome SSK if you want proof. Strident of grille, long of nose, these machines were as priapic as they were purposeful or elegant. They were also cars that everyone could aspire to but almost nobody could afford.

Which brings us back to today, and a private tour of the Maybach with Mercedes's design director Professor Gorden. Wagener – who, unlike any other car design boss I know, goes surfing with Beastie Boy and all round dude Mike D – has successfully reversed Mercedes out of its bewildering design cul-de-sac and done a J-turn. He calls his ethos 'sensual purity'. This is car designer-speak for cleaning up a mess. 'We like pure surfaces,' he says. 'If there is a line on a car and we take it off and still really like the shape, then we'll take another line off.'

Wagener recruited ex-Ford and erstwhile Seat man, the affable and talented Stefan Lamm, to head up Merc's advanced design wing, and the Maybach Vision 6 is his first effort. Not a bad place to start. 'We've had a fantastic response so... it might change something,' Wagener says with a slightly camp sense of mischief. 'I've certainly bumped into a lot of people in the past few days who want to buy one – $3m each, no problem. But it also gives hints of what we might do with the design language at the top end of the brand.'

Although projects like this can be done much faster nowadays, Lamm tells me that the Vision 6 was still rendered as a full-size clay model. This probably explains why its proportions are so beautifully managed, a significant achievement on a car that could have collapsed under the weight of its own ambition. Wagener and Lamm agree that the chrome line that runs virtually the entire length of the body is their favourite element, not least because it keeps the tension together. 'It was very challenging to do, and difficult for our supplier to get right,' Lamm says. 'If it hadn't been perfect all the way through, it would have compromised the entire car.'

'Getting a car this size under control is difficult,' Wagener adds. 'The Vision 6 has an aero "drop" shape, inspired by 1930s streamlined coupes. The coachbuilders who stretched the skin over a chassis were creating a form that is as good as luxury gets. Streamlined shapes aren't just beautiful, though, they're intelligent and efficient, too.'

If you think the Maybach's vast acreage of bonnet on a car that doesn't even have a conventional engine is a trifle indulgent, you'd have a point. Then again, what is luxury if not deliberate indulgence? Just don't call it retro. 'We invented the automobile, so no one has a heritage like us,' Wagener continues. 'We're inspired by it, but rather than repeat it we prefer to reinterpret it. Looking back is nostalgia. It's a tempting thing to do – after all, life seemed easier and more fun when you were young. But looking forward, well, that's more difficult, because you don't know what's coming.'

Of course, that's not strictly true. Fully autonomous driving isn't just on the horizon, it's already here, and it's Mercedes that's leading the charge. 'It's only autonomous if you want it to be,' Wagener insists, a little impatiently. 'A Google pod isn't a car you want to drive yourself, but you will want to drive the Maybach Vision 6. As digitalisation becomes more prevalent, you'll also see a counter movement – we call it "hyperanalogue". Chronographs, cameras, 10 songs on a treasured vinyl record not 10,000 on an MP3 player or a billion being streamed... I'm talking about stuff you want to keep, that maintains its value.'

Inside the Vision 6, the occupants are treated to a 360° lounge experience. The seats wrap into the IP (instrument panel) in a seamless flow – 'it reminds me of a manta ray,' Wagener notes – and the digital display flows across the windscreen and into the sides of the doors. The interior also uses psychometrics; while the inlay on the seats mimics the buttons on a Chesterfield sofa, they actually house body sensor displays to monitor the occupant's vital functions. In other words, the Vision 6 knows if you're having a difficult day, and automatically adjusts cabin temperature or starts the seat massage function. This is car as digital companion. But that doesn't mean an end-of-days, Terminator-style takeover; it's warm and witty, too.

PRICE N/A **0-60** < 4.0 SECONDS **TOP SPEED** 155MPH **POWER** 740BHP
DID YOU KNOW? EVEN THOUGH IT'S A CONCEPT, IT USES ACTUAL MERCEDES ELECTRIC DRIVETRAINS

AUDI PB18 E-TRON

Another ultra-futuristic autonomous electric car determined to keep the driver front and centre

This 23rd-century rollerskate is the Audi PB18 e-tron. Details include a low, mid-mounted 95kWh solid-state battery, capable of accepting a 310-mile charge in 15 minutes, thanks to 800-volt charging. Or, if you're less stung by range anxiety, a claimed 0–62mph sprint of two seconds. That comes courtesy of three electric motors: one shared between the front wheels, and one each for the rears, developing a combined 661bhp, but capable of short 'overboost' spurts up to 753bhp. So far, so 'generic electric supercar concept study'. What makes the PB18 different is its love for you, the driver. Audi wants you to enjoy yourself. This is the first battery-powered hyperpod we can remember which doesn't twin its bowel-bothering urgency with visions of a self-driving, computer-controlled utopia. There's none of that 'you enjoy the twisties, then let the microchips take over for the commute' rhetoric. In fact, Audi says the skunkworks codename for the PB18 was Level Zero, to ram home the fact it couldn't be further in philosophy from the Level 4/Level 5 grades of self-driving autonomy it's currently scrambling to offer in flagship models. So, there are no self-driving guardian angels on board. But you can alter how you experience the ultimate in Vorsprung durch Elektrisch – as long as you're happy to trust a machine with no mechanical connection whatsoever between its brake pedal and the carbon discs, nor its steering wheel and those 22-inch front tyres. Thanks to the wonders of drive-by-wire, Audi's designed the entire cockpit of the PB18 to slide from stage left to dead centre. Bucket seat, pedals, steering wheel and OLED head-up display all shuffle as one. jump seat. There's a Professor Brian Cox brain's-worth of physics going on too: magnetic conductive charging, corner-hungry torque-vectoring, laser headlights and so many lightweight construction elements the car only weighs 1,550kg – Lotus-like for a full EV. Can you build it please, Audi?

PRICE N/A **0-60** 2.0 SECONDS (APPROX) **TOP SPEED** N/A **POWER** 670BHP

DID YOU KNOW? THE CENTRE-MOUNTED DRIVER'S SEAT CAN MOVE LEFT OR RIGHT, SO YOU CAN BRING A FRIEND

RENAULT TREZOR

Having reimagined the Clio, Scenic and so on, Renault's design boss kicks back and has fun

Renault's brilliant Dutch design director, Laurens van den Acker, sums this car up in one memorable phrase: 'It's about falling in love'. Inspirations include that famous 1960s shot of Steve McQueen climbing into his Jaguar XKSS, minimalist furniture, but also a shot of a wooden buck around which the body of one of the most famous concept cars of all time was formed. That's Pininfarina's 1970 masterpiece, the Modulo, as recently restored and turned into a fully running car by Jim Glickenhaus. 'Every car designer loves that thing!' Laurens says. Having arrived at Renault in 2009, it took him and his team a while to steady the company's design, before they could stretch out a bit, which is what the Trezor represents. 'I think it's a beautiful object,' van den Acker says. 'We're a popular brand, and we need to make cars that are easy to like.' The Trezor has an old-school concept car vibe to it, but a hi-tech carbon fibre chassis underpins its bodywork. It's 4.7m long, 2.1m wide, a little over 1m tall, with a 2m-wide front track and a rear track that's wider still. The occupants access the cabin via a massive single-piece canopy, which hinges forward on beautifully engineered struts. The rest of the body is covered in tiny little hexagons; they actually change form as they flow into the car's curves. Citing bespoke bicycle manufacturer Keim as an influence, the Trezor also uses wood as a major structural element; under that vast bonnet, you'll find a stunning, naturally finished wooden frame that houses sumptuous leather luggage. Renault, like all other car companies, knows that the age-old GT narrative is about to be wholly rewritten, and the Trezor does it magnificently. Its cabin has reconfigurable OLED instrument panel but the mood manages to be both modishly digital and appealingly analogue. There's saddle leather and plump carpet. There are no A-pillars, so the screen wraps around in an uninterrupted flow. The cockpit is entirely red. The electric powertrain architecture is real, though. The Trezor's 260kW (350bhp) motor works. A proper concept, like they used to do.

PRICE N/A 0-60 < 4 SECONDS TOP SPEED N/A POWER 350BHP

DID YOU KNOW? THE TREZOR HAS THE SAME KERS SYSTEM AS RENAULT'S FORMULA E CARS

ROLLS-ROYCE VISION 103EX

Even a company as venerable as R-R is getting ready for the next 50 years

If your toddler's football skills are already showing Premiership potential, this is what they could be driving come their 25th birthday. It's called the Rolls-Royce Vision Next 100, and for a company not normally concerned with such vulgar pursuits as "thinking about the future", it's a big deal.

For starters, it's Rolls' first-ever visionary concept, and easily the most out-there thing it's ever done. Designed to reassure oligarchs and captains of industry that they will have somewhere to sink their wads of cash for decades to come, it portrays a very different vision of ultra-luxury to the petrol-guzzling land barges we've come to love.

Well, not that differently. The 103EX is still the size of one of Jupiter's moons – at 5.9m long and 1.6m high it pretty much fits the same cut-out as the extended wheelbase Phantom, but being powered by batteries and four in-wheel electric motors, there's

no need for a torquey V12 under the bonnet. In its place is a luggage compartment, complete with two bespoke cases that emerge from a side flap, personalised to CJ Rolls and FH Royce. Nice touch.

Not keen to let go of the past entirely, the Rolls design team have kept the long bonnet and an interpretation of the bluff "Parthenon" grille, topped by an enlarged Spirit of Ecstasy statuette carved from glass. And then things all go a bit mental. The wheels, covered save for a semi-circular cut-out, are 28 inches in diameter, while the entire canopy is a stargazer's fantasy – fashioned front to back from tinted glass.

Leveraging the fact that there's no longer any need for driver and front passenger seats, the cabin is set back creating a slippery profile to go with the enclosed wheels. In fact the overall look has more than a hint of catamaran about it, while

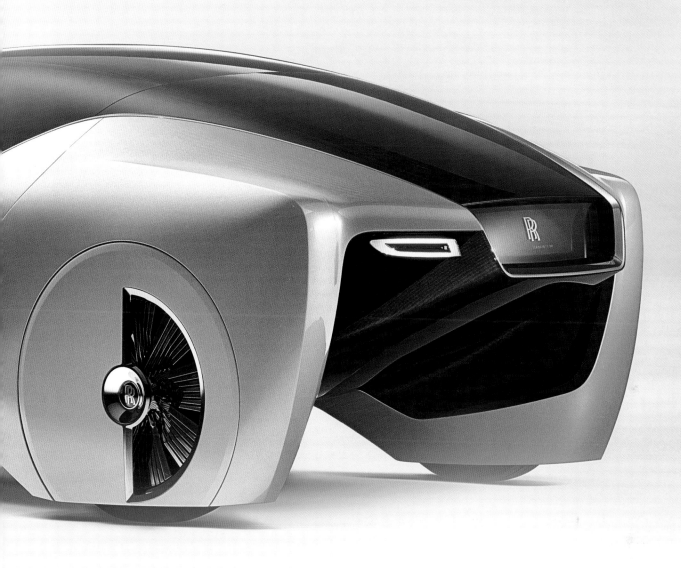

the whole car appears to float several inches off the ground.

In the future you'll also be able to design the entire car to your personal specification. Rolls says it plans to harness modern manufacturing techniques to bring back the all-but-lost art of coachbuilding. It will make the chassis and zero-emissions powertrain, but what goes on top is up to you. The car you see here then is just an example cooked up by the design team, and what do they know, really? It's the interior, though, sorry "Grand Sanctuary", where things start to get freaky. The entire glass canopy, hinged on the left of the car, opens, and a step emerges from beneath the side sill allowing the passengers to step in without having to concern themselves with bending down. Safely aboard, you're encircled by wood panelling and sit on a sofa, trimmed in a curious blend of silk and wool. Or, in Rolls speak, "a beautifully textured, ivory-coloured luxurious throne upon which our passengers are conveyed, and from which they command." You will notice there is no dashboard, no steering wheel and definitely no tape deck. That's because whatever you need, or wherever you want to go, you simply ask Eleanor, your own virtual assistant and chauffeur, and she'll whisk you there autonomously. "Would you like to cancel all your meetings and relax in your enormous mansion?" Yes, we would. Cheers.

PRICE MANY MILLIONS **0-60** PROBABLY QUITE RAPID (ROLLS DOESN"T RELEASE FUGURES) **POWER** LOTS **DID YOU KNOW?** ELEANOR IS THE NAME OF THE CAR'S ARTIFICIAL INTELLIGENCE (AND SHE KNOWS EVERYTHING)

BMW VISION M NEXT

When is a BMW concept car not really a concept car? When it's previewing the new i8

If we invited you to a magical world where the BMW M8 and i8 were mashed together, you'd surely come along with us. Imagine the i8's planet-saving disposition, and its exotic looks, construction and layout. And the M8's thundering performance. Meet the Vision M Next. It was unveiled strictly as a concept car, but someone who knows told us something like it will go on sale as a standalone M car in a few years. "It won't be exactly like this. But remember how the Vision EfficientDynamics turned into the i8." It's a mid-engined wedge, futuristic as you like. But at the same time it's slyly looking in its rearview: we're seeing the 1978 M1 and, come to that, the 1972 Turbo concept, as well as the i8. When it's in full angry mode, there's a strongly turbo'd four-cylinder behind the seats. That's assisted by an electric motor at each end. Totalled up, BMW is talking 600bhp. BMW's R&D chief Klaus Fröhlich says it has more performance in pure-EV mode than the i8 does in all-systems mode. The top speed is claimed to be 186mph. The 0–62mph time is more impressive, at 3.0secs. We suspect those numbers are theoretical, not test-track verified. "BMW M is not just about acceleration, so weight is important. It would be 1,600kg to 1,700kg. If we made it pure-EV it would be 2.1 tonnes." Fröhlich also says the electric motors allow clever traction control. "You can do a drift mode, up to 45 degrees." But it's also friendly: plug it in and charge the battery and you've got a claimed 62 miles in electric drive. And unlike the i8, there are electric motors front and rear, so it's true electric AWD. He says the underbody aero has been worked out already, and the cooling (of which it needs much more than an i8). In fact, he says it has almost no parts in common with the i8, though it has the same sort of carbon-fibre tub, made from recycled material chopped and moulded. Approach, and face-recognition tech lets you in. Gullwing doors admit you to a sparse interior, scooped as if from a solid block. The steering wheel's a butterfly shape like a dragster's. Mounted on the skeletal column is a curved glass display covering all the usual instruments and infotainment, plus a heart-rate display. It even has gyroscopic cup-holders.

PRICE N/A **0-60** < 3 SECONDS
TOP SPEED 186MPH **POWER** 592BHP
DID YOU KNOW? COMPOSER HANS ZIMMER CREATED THE VISION M'S UNIQUE SOUND

MERCEDES SILVER EQ

Lewis Hamilton's racing car, assuming he ends up in a retro futuristic parallel universe

The EQ Silver Arrows exists to shine a light on Mercedes' EQ pure-electric sub-brand, but also references the W125 Rekordwagen, the legendary stream-liner that Rudolf Carracciola drove into the history books in January 1938 when he achieved 268mph on a public road. That car's 5.6-litre, 725bhp V12 is now – and necessarily – a distant memory, the concept car showcasing Mercedes' MEA (modular electric architecture), its single-seater configuration hiding an 80kWh battery and electrical architecture good for the equivalent of 738bhp. The giant half-covered wheels use rose gold, and the thing measures a mammoth 5.3m in length. Once you've managed to climb inside, Mercedes-AMG F1 boss Toto Wolff appears in hi-def on the display intoning, 'good driving'.

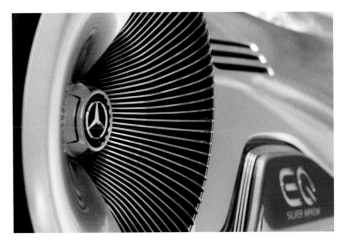

PRICE N/A **0-60** < 2.0 SECONDS
TOP SPEED N/A **POWER** 750BHP
DID YOU KNOW? THE ONBOARD COMPUTER HAS GHOST CARS TO 'RACE', SUCH AS LEWIS' F1 CHARIOT

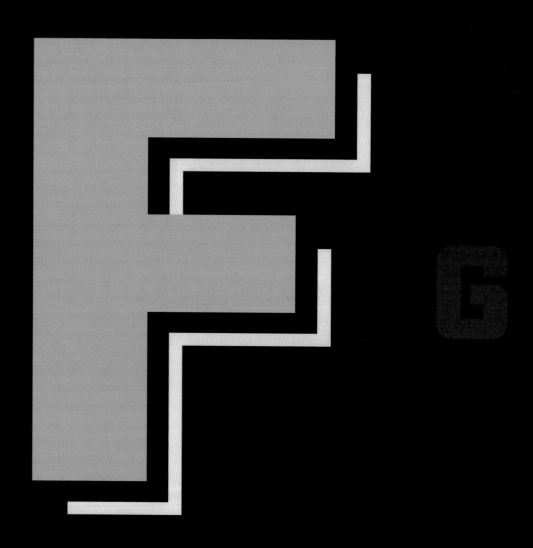

FERRARI SF90 STRADALE

Into a shiny new hybrid future we go, Ferrari softening the blow with approximately 1000bhp

The SF90 is a production car, not one of Ferraris limited-edition hypercar series. It's got as much power as a LaFerrari or a Porsche 918, but it doesn't need one of those mysterious "friend of the brand" handshakes or an unobtanium loyalty card just to get the invitation to buy.

Its colossal output puts it in the power-ballpark of the Aston Martin Valkyrie and AMG One and some of the Koenigseggs. They're about five times the price of this Ferrari, which, costs £375,000. The SF90 seems to have created a new slot: in power it's north of the supercars, but in price it lies comfortably to the south of the limited-edition hypercars.

Ever since the mid-Seventies 308 GTB, the first of the V8 mid-engined two-seat Ferraris, they've had a certain recognisable proportion. Not this time. The cockpit has moved forward, the overhangs are shortened, the silhouette of the tail has risen even as the height of the engine below it has dropped. The rationale is aerodynamics, but the emotional effect is knee-trembling.

The twin-turbo V8 is a further development of the one in the F8 Tributo. Which itself is the same as the one in the 488 Pista. Now I'm thinking back to the time I drove the Pista and trying to figure out how it could be further developed. It felt like some kind of historic pinnacle. Not to these guys though. It's now been bored out from 3.9 to 4.0 litres, and gets new induction and a lightweight Inconel exhaust system. The turbos are modified and injection pressure raised. The new parts are shaped to drop the centre of gravity too.

The result is a staggering 195 horses per litre, for a total of 780. But not, you will have noticed, actually 1000. Nope, to get to the full total, the SF90 also has three electric motors. One rotates with the crankshaft like a formula one MGU-K. Another drives each of the front wheels. So, yes the SF90 is four-wheel drive, and it has torque vectoring to help you through corners.

Those electric motors add another 220 horsepower, arriving at our four-figure total. The front motors can operate independently of each other. If your line is running wide, the outer one will draw you inward, and vice-versa if you're on the way to a spin. If you're aiming straight they'll both give their all. That's how it'll

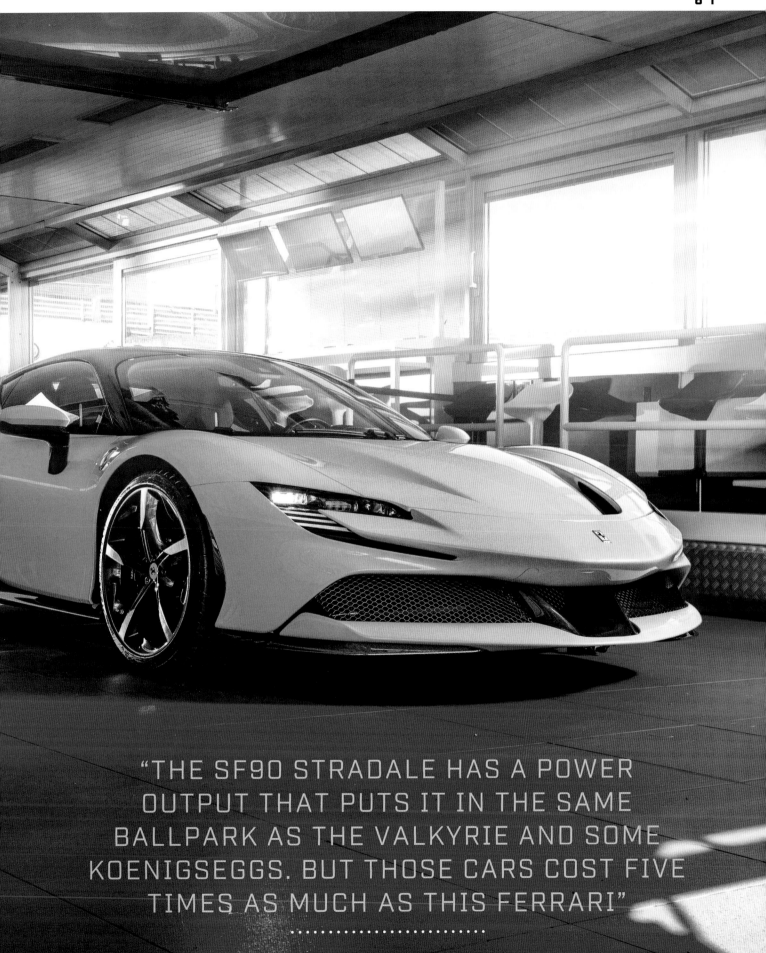

"THE SF90 STRADALE HAS A POWER OUTPUT THAT PUTS IT IN THE SAME BALLPARK AS THE VALKYRIE AND SOME KOENIGSEGGS. BUT THOSE CARS COST FIVE TIMES AS MUCH AS THIS FERRARI"

"BETWEEN THE TAIL LIGHTS, AIR EMERGES FROM UNDER THE FIXED SECTION OF THE REAR WING. BUT IN CORNERS OR UNDER BRAKING ELECTRIC ACTUATORS RAPIDLY LOWER THE FORWARD SECTION" do 0-62 in 2.5 seconds and 0-125 in 6.7, up there with LaFerrari. And yes, it'll also lap Fiorano in shorter order than the six year-old hypercar, at 1 min 19 secs. Of course Ferrari has employed every one of the voodoo electronic systems that make the Pista such a vibrant, responsive and heck driftworthy track machine. Then it's added this extra measure of front torquery-sorcery.

The gearbox, by the way, is entirely new, and has an extra gear – now eight – but is lighter than the old one partly because there's no reverse. This isn't because Ferrari sends a white-gloved factotum to push you every time you want to go back. The SF90 simply uses its electric motors for that job.

Indeed it'll operate on those front motors alone for up to 15 miles if you've plugged in and fully charged. That's the eDrive mode, and the parents of nearby sleeping babies will thank you. The next notch is Hybrid, when the engine cuts in and out in pursuit of economy with performance. All modes use blended regenerative braking, naturally. Then Performance. Does what it says, and the engine stays on, but the power is managed to make sure the battery doesn't deplete far. So you can go like that all day. Finally Qualify, where the thing will deploy all the power whenever you ask, even if it means draining the battery and finding a slight tail-off when that occurs.

Of course there is weight in these motors, and in the 7.9kWh battery, and the power electronics and the cooling for it all. Dry weight is 1,570kg, and that's with the Assetto Fiorano pack fitted, which saves 30kg. Let's say 1650-odd at the kerb. About the same as a 918, despite having turbos, and twin instead of single front motor/gearboxes. It's also a mostly aluminium tub, not carbonfibre, although carbonfibre is used for the engine bulkhead. It's a new structure, not borrowed from the F8. It has to be, to make room for the hybrid systems, the new aerodynamics, and the fresh proportions.

They call it a fighter-jet style cockpit. Of course they do. Honda said the same of the first NSX. Can we quit with the killing-machine analogies? But yes, this enigmatically gloss-black bubble is mounted well forward, and it's narrow so as to present as little of itself to the air as possible. Trailing obliquely behind it are a pair of flying buttresses above the engine's greedy air intakes. The engine itself, by being mounted lower,

doesn't only benefit the centre of gravity but also the aerodynamics over the rear deck. Between the tail-lights, air emerges from under the fixed section of the rear wing. Well, normally it does. But in corners or braking, electric actuators rapidly lower the forward section of that wing. That staunches the flow underneath, creating a new high-downforce Gurney.

Out front, radiators at either side manage engine coolant, and the central one does the motors and high-voltage electronics. Above the bumper, that indented step compresses the flow, working with the front diffusers to create downforce at the nose. The headlights can be slim because they all-LED, and the slit-intakes below them feed the brakes, which themselves have calipers actually shaped to improve their cooling airflow.

Look into the wheels and you see little helical bumps on the rims themselves. they're pretty but they do more, drawing air out of the arches, which reduces lift, but also shaping this flow so it attaches neatly to the side of the car, cutting turbulent drag. The driver's heels are 15mm higher than in the other Ferraris, because the floor is stepped upward at the front, improving the effect of the vortex generators mounted there. Their job is to disturb the local boundary layer and delay airflow separation, further improving front downforce to match the rear. All of which aero work means an equivalent of 390kg extra downward push on the tyres at 155mph compared with the static weight.

The SF90 Stradale has a new instrument setup, whose design will influence the future range. The main pod is a 16in curved-glass configurable screen. There's also a touchpad on the steering wheel, a trick even Mercedes can't make work properly so let's see how Ferrari does. One amusing and sentimental touch is the transmission selector switches, which resemble a tiny version of the old open-gate manual gearshift.

Perhaps as a way to PR its way into a hybrid future, Ferrari is keener than ever with the SF90 Stradale to emphasise that principles it learns on track actually feed into the road cars. SF90 is the name of this year's F1 car, named in honour of the team's anniversary year. Stradale means road, even if of course this isn't a roadgoing race car. That'd be a frightful nuisance. Whereas this sounds like a rather useable thousand horsepower, if you can imagine such a thing.

PRICE £400,000 (EST) **0-60** 2.5 SECONDS **TOP SPEED** 212MPH **POWER** 986BHP

DID YOU KNOW? THE SF90 IS FERRARI'S FIRST PLUG-IN HYBRID. DID YOU EVER THINK YOU'D SEE THE DAY?

FERRARI 488 PISTA

The ultimate version of Ferrari's mid-engined V8 reaches stratospheric new heights

Its specification reads like something that could have won Le Mans a few years ago. The engine is lifted from the 488 Challenge race car, and is substantially different from the GTB's twin-turbo V8. The big numbers are 710bhp and 568lb ft of torque, although that last figure is only available in seventh gear, such is the extent of the calibration to make the car feel as unturbocharged as possible.

Weight has been reduced by 90kg through the usual blend of lightweight components and a barren interior – carbon-fibre wheels are also an option for the first time on a Ferrari. The front cooling package is taken from the Challenge car too, allowing for the large bonnet scoops, and the whole aero package has been revised to create a downforce figure that is, as usual, difficult to fathom. Interestingly, the vast side intakes no longer feed air into the plenum like they do on the GTB; that is now ducted from two new scoops on the deck lid.

The latest version of Ferrari's traction and stability programme has added abilities and acronyms, but majors on juggling a variable locking differential with single brake disc applications to make the car turn more effectively and to make owners feel like superheroes. And they'll feel pretty good about this car, because it is shockingly fast. The 50bhp increase over the GTB doesn't make it profoundly different to the "base" 488, but I can only judge these things according to my trusty swear-ometer, and, from the moment I gave it full beans, the vernacular flowed in much greater quantities in the Pista. The motor pulls from below 2,000rpm, and the effects of the reduced torque in the lower gears can be felt but is never a frustration, because even the fancy Michelins – specially developed for this car – simply cannot cope with how potent this motor is.

The systems are something else, though. You really can place yourself in the hands of the Pista and let it carve its way around a circuit. It helps if you stop in the correct places and aim for the odd apex, but otherwise it manages the available traction to perfection, and the interventions are so seamless, the juggling of differential and brakes so smoothly deployed that, at times, you have to remind yourself it's actually happening. In fact, you can only fully appreciate how much work the systems are doing by switching them all off – at which point the Pista becomes one of

the most outrageous motor cars I've ever driven.

Because there comes a point when pure motive force overwhelms even a delicate mid-engined Ferrari chassis At Fiorano, corners that were full throttle in second gear in the old 458 Speciale are part throttle in third, and if you push any further on the long-travel throttle pedal, the car moves into big oversteer. And it will do this everywhere, even into fifth gear. It's completely ridiculous and also totally addictive and quite unlike anything I've experienced from Ferrari before.

Of course, you can drive the car neat-and-tidy, manage the torque yourself and rely on what must be the most approachable mid-engined chassis on sale. The set-up is very conservative, with a good chunk of understeer on a constant throttle to stop the thing looping around on itself. Grip is actually very good, but because the rear is so easily unstuck if you want to be silly, it gives the sensation of actually not being that grippy.

In fact, this is the paradox at the core of the Pista. It deploys the very latest in sports car tech, is probably making more calculations per nanosecond than a spacecraft, but with all the systems switched off, the resulting driving experience sits somewhere around the mid-Sixties. And I mean that as a huge compliment. The torque-to-grip ratio is actually very similar to an old sports car in that drivers really can choose to overcome traction whenever they want to.

The brakes are monstrous carbon-ceramics, and they need to be, because the Pista arrives into braking zones at such silly speeds that they take a pasting – you spend most of your time thrumming into the anti-lock and praying it will stop. The steering is typical modern Ferrari: pretty inert and fantastically quick – you just steer between your wrists.

Ferrari has worked very hard to make this turbocharged engine want to rev all the way to the 8,000rpm limiter. The GTB always feels breathless over the last 1,000rpm and that dulls the excitement factor on a circuit, but the Pista keeps pulling all the way to eight grand. What I didn't realise was that the base car has a soft limiter that tapers power away gradually as you near the cut-out and that obviously hurts the sense of aggression even more. The Pista does away with that, so it offers far more zing at the top end. No, it doesn't scream like a Speciale, but it is so much faster that the two can't really be compared. I'm probably the wrong person to ask about the quality of the noise because I've always found Ferrari at-plane V8s (apart from the 355) to be rather tuneless and shouty, especially the Speciale. This thing is less shouty and still pretty tuneless.

So, as a driving device, this is Maranello at its best. On paper, a 710bhp twin-turbocharged, mid-engined Ferrari should be approximately as approachable as a Victorian headmaster with a cracking hangover, but this thing is a complete honey to slide around. However, as an object, I have a few reservations. The cabin design is now eight years old and it looks it. There are so many different materials and textures that the whole thing is a bit of a mess. And much as you have to admire the use of underbody aero as it means no ugly rear wing, there's an unfortunate fussiness to some of the details.

The Pista is a stunning achievement. In a marketplace that seems to be increasingly obsessed with track-focused machines, it's a very fast track toy that can be used perhaps even more effectively as a road car. The lucky few won't be disappointed.

FERRARI
F8 TRIBUTO

In the face of intense competition from old foes, Ferrari ups its game. Again...

This is the new Ferrari F8 Tributo. Not only the most powerful mid-engined V8 Ferrari supercar in history, but also a rosso-liveried haymaker aimed at Woking. Watch out 720S: the 488's successor is here. Ferrari tells us this car is the first to wear a new design language exploring the company's high watermarks of aero excellence and being batsh*t quick. Mission accomplished, we'd proffer. So, the F8 Tributo houses the same 3.9-litre twin-turbo V8 as that 488 – an engine Ferrari doesn't hesitate to remind us won International Engine of the Year Awards three years on the trot, and last year took the title of best engine of the last two decades. It's really quite good.

It pumps out 710bhp – just like the 720S – which is 50bhp more than the 488, "without the slightest hint of turbo lag". Understatement there: it'll record 0-62mph in 2.9secs, 0-124mph in 7.8secs and a top speed of 211mph. Elsewhere, Ferrari's ability to flatter yet more ham-fistedness continues with the latest version of 'Slide Slip Control' and 'Dynamic Enhancer', the latter acting on the 'Race' position, making "performance on the limit easier to reach and control for a greater number of drivers". The manettino is now mounted on a smaller steering wheel, too, and the interior quality continues to improve. To think that this used to be the entry-level Ferrari is to boggle the mind.

FERRARI 812 SUPERFAST

The big GT is a very specific sort of Ferrari, and the Superfast may be the end of the line

Progress is measured empirically, and Ferrari is more interested in what is possible rather than what might be necessary. If you leave a bunch of engine nerds with a 730bhp 6.3-litre V12 it's inevitable that they will increase the capacity, add the variable intake from the tdf, the highest-pressure injection system ever fitted to a petrol-engined car (350 bar) and change pretty much all of the internal components. Shortening the gear ratios is a good idea, as is the adoption of the tdf's rear-wheel-steering hardware. The steering system itself is now electrically powered. The styling changes are largely a function of the complicated aerodynamic revisions over the F12. A pair of front intakes manage underbody flow – they're actuated through air pressure. This means the car can stall a good deal of its lift-reduction flow to reduce drag (211mph isn't too bad) but can use a much more prominent rear spoiler and larger diffuser when needed for medium- and high-speed cornering. So, yes, the 812 Superfast is a facelifed F12. But this is much, much more than a nip 'n' tuck. The short gearing allows that more potent V12 to spool even faster, and the result is a car that leans on its chassis electronics more than any other. Remember it's a street car and so the standard P Zeros need to work in deep standing water and freezing temperatures. In Race mode with all the systems on, you can open the taps before the apex and just let the electronics manage all the dangerous stuff, but the tyres become hot so quickly that at times the interventions seem unnecessarily harsh. The brakes are strong and the pedal feel pretty good. There is much witchcraft occurring within this chassis. The electronically variable differential is linked to the traction and stability control and now the rear steering too. The change from hydraulic to electric assistance doesn't alter much about the Ferrari's big V12 Berlinetta because theold rack was pretty inert, and so is this one. It's a car you steer through your wrists and one I still feel has too fast a rack for this type of machine. But it's consistent and the 4WS system has one neat trick up its sleeve: if you get some understeer it can tweak the rear toe-angle to help the car rotate. Given the insane power, this big, front-engined, normally aspirated beast just shouldn't be so amenable. The 812 isn't perfect, but it drips with personality and seduces with vast performance. It might well be the last of its type; if so, it is a fitting celebration for the end of an era.

"NO ONE ELSE MAKES A CAR LIKE THIS –
A SUPER GT IN THE GRAND TRADITION,
FRONT-ENGINED, NORMALLY ASPIRATED
AND INTERGALACTICALLY FAST – YET IT'S
SOMEHOW SO VERY DIGNIFIED"

PRICE £262,900 **0-60** 2.9 SECONDS **TOP SPEED** 211MPH **POWER** 789BHP

DID YOU KNOW? THE SUPERFAST NAME ISN'T AS SILLY AS IT SOUNDS – IT DATES BACK TO THE SIXTIES

FERRARI FXXK

The ultimate Ferrari road car, track optimised

Why would anyone make a LaFerrari any faster? "Because they could". Normally I just swallow that line and grin at the results of the man maths, but this time I have to think back to the last time I drove a LaFerrari, at Portimão circuit, where it was so fast I had to stop every few laps to consider my own mortality. Most who've driven the LaFerrari would agree it simply doesn't need to be any faster.

Well, stripping out what was left of the interior creature comforts, ensuring that everything is fashioned from either carbon or some desperately exotic metal, has done just that. The energy recovery and hybrid system has also been changed to the same unit used in the company's Formula One racer, which is lighter, more efficient and more powerful. All of which means the FXXK is 90kg lighter than the LaFerrari.

Now this alone, plus a little more downforce and some slick tyres would be enough to make a track-only machine capable of terrifying your average billionaire. But the FXXK goes a step further. The aforementioned KERS system gives an extra 176bhp and the big 6262cc V12 has new cams, intakes and a few other detail changes to bring power to 860bhp. And we all thought this base engine was running at its maximum when they rated it at 730bhp and plonked it in the F12. The combined output in the FXXK is 1,036bhp. The claimed kerbweight is 1,495kg. Two. Wheel. Drive. You do the maths. As for the name, Ferrari sensibly opted to use the most versatile word in the English language.

You don't just jump in and drive the FXXK. First you walk around it and gawp at the aggressive beauty of the whole thing. The minute attention to detail that has released over 500kg of downforce at a smidge over 130mph. The active rear wing is carried over from the street car, but the rest is all new, and that includes a front splitter and rear diffuser that wouldn't look out of place on an LMP1 racer. In fact, scratch that, they wouldn't be allowed on any current racecar – they're too big. This car does have the look of being a part of some unlimited category; Can-Am for the hybrid generation.

On top of the roof are two lights, one red, one green. If the red one is illuminated, you cannot touch the vehicle. There's enough electricity to kill a human being if you manage to provide a human-shaped earth source. It somehow makes the FXXK seem even more exciting knowing even when it's lurking

"THE FXXK'S COMBINED OUTPUT IS
1,036BHP, ITS CLAIMED KERBWEIGHT
1,485KG. TWO. WHEEL. DRIVE. YOU DO THE
MATHS. AS FOR THE NAME, IT'S THE MOST
VERSATILE WORD IN ENGLISH'"

stationary in a garage, gimlet-eyed, it can still kill you.

Like the LaFerrari, the driver's seat is scalloped into the carbon tub, so each driver has a set of cushions made. I'm borrowing some today, which reminds me I really must do some more jogging. But the driving position is superb. The basic shape of the LaF dashboard remains as, sadly, does the weird square steering wheel. But everything else feels like a mix of WEC and NASA. Your eyes dart around the place drinking it all in, but they eventually rest on the single large rotary knob that offers the following options: Long Run, Fast Charge, Manual Boost and Qualify. The last of these is the real eye-opener. This is the full depletion mode: no harvesting, just full-power deployment for a single lap of an average-length circuit.

Once comfy, I jump out, squeeze on some racing threads, put on a helmet and wriggle back in. Is a Plexiglas side-window with a little slide-open aperture considered motorsport cool or a bit cheap on something costing £1.85m? I think it's pretty cool. I also wish I'd squished in some ear-plugs the moment I press the starter button. Dear Lord, this thing is LOUD. The starter sings a brief shriek and then it catches with a bark so powerful the camera crew take a step back. The last time I heard something so gloriously musical and noisy was a V12 Ferrari F1 car, but I suppose with the exception of some batteries and pneumatic valves, this isn't too far off being just that.

The gearbox is the same as the LaFerrari's dual-clutcher, bar running a shorter set of ratios. I'm sure several kilos could have been saved by fitting a full race sequential, but the way these cars will be used and the complicated nature of all those ECUs trying to communicate with each other probably explains why that didn't happen. Turns out that doesn't matter, because from the moment you pull the right lever into first and trickle out onto the circuit, the car is so easy to drive. Push the right pedal and it moves. Visibility is a bit tight, but the steering is light and the brake pedal doesn't take much of a shove, even when the Brembo ceramics are cold.

But there isn't much sense of connection at first. Like all modern Ferraris, the steering is light to the point of making you wonder what actual connection there is. The transmission is almost too smooth, and then there's the tyres. The FXXK runs a Pirelli slick that's not too exotic or sticky, but like all slicks, until it's fully up to temperature the lack of tread blocks squishing around gives the driver a sense of inertness that isn't especially helpful when one prod of the right pedal can release 1,036bhp.

Things quickly improve with temperature. Physics tells you that the rear tyres should warm up quite quickly, and they do. This allows you to start leaning on the electronic chassis systems,

and it takes all of two laps to confirm that they're the best I've encountered. They allow you to push the car to its absolute limit of grip, but rather than aggressively cut the power or apply unsubtle braking inputs to individual wheels, a seamless blend of electronics somehow holds you at the limit. With the manettino in Race mode, you really can just clog it out of second-gear turns and let the software divvy up the mayhem.

The normally aspirated V12 always sounds perfect, but the integration of the electric boost never leaves you anything but gasping with surprise. It's the perfect combination – massive, instant torque from virtually no revs and then a V12 that sings beyond 8,000rpm at the top end. And it makes for a much more flexible driving experience than you'd ever credit from something that looks so otherworldly. I just ran a gear up everywhere: your brain tells you that Daytona's slower turns should be second, but third still gives enough instant urge.

The handling is approachable and sensible – and by that I mean it would be ridiculous and probably suicidal for Ferrari to make these things too knife-edgy for Clienti customers. Once the slicks are warm, there's a decent wall of understeer on turn-in, but frankly you could have any amount of front-end push and one dose of 1,036bhp hybrid-V12 will prove to be an effective antidote. Things become even more interesting in the faster turns because then the aero really does begin to take effect. This car does have proper downforce – you can feel your face tighten with the g-loading.

When you consider who will actually end up driving these things – rich amateurs rather than professional racers – it quickly becomes the most impressive aspect of the machine. And that says a lot when you have that engine at your disposal.

What's it like if you switch all the electronics off? Potentially expensive, and also very, very rewarding. Oh and completely irrelevant because slick tyres really weren't intended to be used that way. But you can hold big smokey slides in the FXXK, balancing the throttle and trying to make sure that when you react with the right steering input you don't grope for fresh air in the space where a round steering wheel might once have been. The brakes are immense; I pounded lap after lap and they never faded or gave any impression of getting tired.

Perhaps the cleverest thing about the FXXK is that it feels like the fastest street car you'll ever drive. The controls aren't heavy, and the grip certainly isn't limitless. It gives the car a unique quality and makes it a challenge for sure, but doesn't leave it being *too* challenging. I'm sure the 40 owners already know how lucky they are, but I'll just reassure them that they really do own one of the greatest driver's machines ever built.

PRICE €2.5MILLION **0-60** < 2.9 SECONDS **TOP SPEED** 217MPH **POWER** 1,036BHP

DID YOU KNOW? FXXK NOT MAD ENOUGH? TRY THE FXXK EVO, WHICH IS LIGHTER AND HAS EVEN MORE DOWNFORCE...

"THE F12TDF SEES FERRARI DABBLING IN AN AREA INSPIRED BY STATE-OF-THE-ART AVIONICS IN PURSUIT OF ELECTRONICALLY ENHANCED SUPER-MANOEUVRABILITY. IT'S A TECHNICAL TRIUMPH"

PRICE N/A **0-60** < 2.9 SECONDS **TOP SPEED** 211MPH **POWER** 710BHP

DID YOU KNOW? THE F12TDF IS PRETTY MUCH A MOBILE TEST LABORATORY FOR FUTURE FERRARI TECHNOLOGY, AND A RATHER EXTREME ONE

FERRARI
F12TDF

Question: is this the craziest Ferrari ever?

We bump into Sebastian Vettel at Ferrari's Fiorano test track just before we drive the F12tdf. The car's party trick is its four-wheel steering which, Ferrari says, works in-phase with the front axle to dramatically improve high-speed stability and agility. Vettel is no stranger to these things, of course, but at 1415kg (dry) the F12tdf is roughly double the weight of his F1 car. 'Its high speed stability and balance are incredible,' he tells us, grinning. 'It's incredibly fast, but it's the way it feels through turn seven [Fiorano's infamously fast sweeping right/left] that is so mind-blowing...' Given that the new F8 Tributo pumps out 710bhp and has easily enough real-world performance to seriously harass the LaFerrari hypercar, the F12tdf is on an intriguingly different mission – Ferrari on ultra fast-forward. It's exploring some pretty far-out thinking, taking Ferrari into territory in which it's actively challenging itself as well as its clients. Following the deliberately tricky and frankly almost bipolar 599 GTO, the F12tdf sees Ferrari dabbling again in an area inspired by state-of-the-art avionics in pursuit of electronically enhanced super-manoeuvrability. 'We're at the frontier of new automotive technology,' chief test driver Raffaele de Simone tells us. 'It requires a clever driver to get the best out of it, not in terms of pure "feel", but in being able to get the maximum out of the car. You cannot just jump in the F12tdf and go straight to the limit. You have to learn about what it can do. And you have to drive it in a very linear and precise way.' You can definitely feel the active rear axle – Ferrari calls it 'passo corto virtuale' or 'virtual short wheelbase' – do its thing, and initially it's distinctly weird, to the point of being rather unsettling. In 'Race' mode, it is just amazingly fast and stable. Switch the guardians off, though, and it can be spikey until you've got your hand properly in. The engine is the F12berlinetta's 6.2-litre V12, whose entirely unshabby 730bhp power output has been hiked to 770bhp. It can now rev to 8900rpm, and shovels out 520 torques at 6750rpm. The dual-clutch 'box has new tdf-specific ratios; upshifts are 30 per cent faster, downshifts 40 per cent quicker. It accelerates to 62mph in 2.9 seconds, 124mph in 7.9 seconds, and it'll keep going until 211mph. It has the neutrality, poise and agility of a smaller, lighter, mid-engined car, with all the thunder and colossal force of a large, normally aspirated V12. All in all, a technical tour de force. But a handful.

FERRARI MONZA SP1/2

Another limited series car, only this one dispenses with a roof. And windscreen

You don't have to wear a helmet to drive Ferrari's new Monza SP1 or SP2. We would, though, unless you enjoy the very specific sort of pain which can only be inflicted by a pigeon to the face. Maranello will build "less than 500" examples of this latest limited-edition. Yep – despite appearances, this is not some hyper-exclusive ten-off. A few might even get driven on a somewhat regular basis. Wouldn't that be a thing? The SP is the first in Ferrari's 'Icona' series of cars. Sitting above the sports (F8 Tributo), GT (GTC4 Lusso) and 'Special Series' (488 Pista) models in its line-up, these cars will be targeted at its most loyal customers and inspired by iconic models from the past. In this case, the 166 MM and 750 Monza that delivered wins for Ferrari in the World Sports Car Championship back in the Fifties and Sixties. As you might have guessed, the SP1 is the single-seater. Besides a 20kg weight saving from eliminating the second seat and added rollover protection, it's identical to the two-seat SP2. The powertrain and platform come from the 812 Superfast. It's a 6.5-litre, naturally aspirated V12 that borrows know-how from Ferrari's F1 programme, running through a 7spd dual-clutch transmission. With 799bhp, it's the most powerful engine Ferrari has ever made, and can propel the 1,500kg (dry, and that's only 25kg lighter than the 812) SP1 to 62mph in 2.9 seconds, to 124mph in 7.9 seconds and on to a top speed of over 186mph. Bodied entirely in carbon fibre, the SP features bespoke forged wheels, LED headlights and a full-width light bar across its rear end. The doors are small, almost pointless items that open upwards and outwards, while the bonnet is a huge, front-hinged piece like a Jag E-type's. Meanwhile a 'Virtual Wind Shield' sits ahead of the instrument panel, aiming to disrupt airflow to "maintain driving comfort". In the SP2, the passenger gets no such luxury. Speaking of "driving comfort" – the SPs feature the 812's all-wheel-steering system. We're told that despite the power output, and promises of the SP's speed, that it's "not in any way challenging". We'll be the judges of that, with our fists of ham and feet of lead, thanks very much. Ferrari has also partnered with some Italian fashion brands, so each SP will come with a bespoke "Pilot Suit" we guarantee none of its owners will ever wear. They're all allocated, but pricing will only be revealed at a later date.

"THIS IS THE FIRST IN FERRARI'S ICONA
SERIES OF CARS, TARGETED AT THE
COMPANY'S MOST LOYAL CUSTOMERS AND
INSPIRED BY SOME OF ITS MOST ICONIC
BACK CATALOGUE MODELS"

PRICE £1.6 MILLION (APPROX) **0-60** 2.9 SECONDS **TOP SPEED** > 186MPH **POWER** 799BHP

DID YOU KNOW? FERRARI ONLY BUILDS ONE A DAY, SO IT'S GOING TO BE LATE 2020 UNTIL THEY'RE ALL DONE

"IT MIGHT BE A ONE-OFF BUT THIS IS NO VANITY PROJECT. THE P80/C IS FIVE PER CENT MORE EFFICIENT AERODYNAMICALLY THAN THE 488 GT3 IT'S BASED ON. FERRARI REALLY PUSHED THE BOUNDARIES"

FERRARI
P80/C

The P80/C is a 488 GT3 race car in a bespoke suit. The greatest one-off Ferrari ever made?

Time with any racing car tends to be fraught. Fraught in terms of the track window, of ensuring that all the temperatures are optimal, that you're comfortable both physically in the car and mentally with its myriad operating systems. The variables are almost endlessly... variable. Yet somehow we've added a few more today, and they're biggies. As the man from Michelotto, the Paduan specialist that has prepared and run Ferrari GT race cars since 1969, adjusts the belts on a seat designed for someone rather more snake-hipped than your correspondent, the Monza pit-lane beckons.

Monza. The heartbeat of Italian motorsport. Home to some of the most romantically oil-flecked looking dudes ever to climb into a racing car. Stomping ground of the tifosi. Ahead lies one of Formula One's most notorious chicanes, the variante del Rettifilo, which flows into the breathtaking curva grande, and then the curve di Lesmo... This place is hugely fast and hugely historic. On a warm Spring day, the light has a liquid quality and strafes the trees in poetic shards.

So we have the location. We also have the car, the Ferrari P80/C. The what? It has fabulous front wings, prominent rear buttresses, a visor cockpit, and enough aero to retard a rocket. But it's also as enigmatic as the guy who commissioned it, a true flight of fantasy, one of one, with a price tag to match (Ferrari keeps the exact figure quiet, but think multi millions). It's based on the 488 GT3 race car, so it comes with a 'takes-no-prisoners' default setting and some fat Pirelli slicks. The paint finish is called Rosso Vero – true red – and has a ceramic finish that requires above-average valeting skills.

P80/C might not be wearing the SP nomenclature that denotes its status as the latest from Ferrari's Special Projects division, but that's what it is. This is the skunkworks that sits at the summit of the company's product hierarchy, and invites Ferrari's top clients to create their own car. According to former Ferrari CEO Amedeo Felisa, SP clients 'effectively embody the marque, and [go] beyond just being a collector'.

This is an elite club. There have been approximately 40 since Ferrari activated the programme in 2008, from Japanese Ferrarista Junichiro Hiramatsu's SP1 – a restrained ode to Pininfarina design great Leonardo Fioravanti – via Eric Clapton's SP12 EC BB 512 homage, to last year's SP38 'Deborah'. These are

F

highly personal expressions, on which basis some are, let's just say, more convincing than others.

Then there's the P80/C. This isn't just the best SP car, this is one of the best cars to emerge from Maranello in aeons – and that's saying something, given Ferrari's 21st century run of form. Its owner, Hong Kong-based publishing entrepreneur TK Mak, is representative of the new breed of Ferrari owner, which tends to be younger, hipper and more innately fashionable than the established adherents, something Ferrari is keen to cultivate as the car world shifts on its axis, geographically and geo-politically.

TK is no arriviste, though: he knows more about Ferrari and its history than pretty much anyone. The P80/C is remorselessly now, but also a love letter to Ferrari's best-loved endurance racers, in particular the 330 P3/4 that saw the company avenge its drubbing at the hands of Ford's GT40 at Le Mans by winning the 1967 Daytona 24 hours.

'Like many Ferraristi, I've been enamoured of the 'Sports Prototipi' of the Sixties and Seventies since I was a child,' he tells me. 'A time of trial and error, a world without computer assisted design, where engineers would travel the lengths of their imagination and experience to try and claim those milliseconds, driven by a sink or swim mentality, and when races were sometimes won on grit alone.

'To survive, you had to win – and the result was some of the most beautiful racing cars ever made, even to this day. For P80/C, the goal from the get go was to recreate the feeling of that era – of aesthetics meeting engineering, of equal parts beauty and performance. I wanted to use this as a way of projecting my vision for a future GT Prototipi – my interpretation of a future design language for Ferrari, a brand that lies very close to my heart.'

TK's team is making a film about the car, and it's enjoying something of a world tour. A couple of Ferrari GT drivers have shaken it down during its development and another, Maurizio Mediani, is here today. In total, maybe three people have driven it – not including its owner. Now me. Kid gloves have replaced the racing variety.

Such are the complexities of GT racing that the 488 GT3 is less powerful than its road-going sibling, and runs approximately 600bhp according to the series' 'BOP' – balance of performance – regulations. This drives Maranello's top people crazy and seems retrogressive to say the least, but it levels the playing field. Ferrari has race-proved hundreds of these cars in various global championships, and they're robust and usefully fuel efficient.

The engine is the 3.9-litre, twin turbo V8, with modified, lightweight internals and an Inconel exhaust, but as the race-spec engine is only running 0.7bar of boost there's way more potential. Which is where today's assignment gets slightly political: the P80/C is running a more aggressive engine map, but no one will confirm how much more aggressive. There's talk of 800bhp, though, and on the simulator it's apparently doing some eye-popping times round Fiorano. In the midst of the conjecture, all I can think is: one-off, slick tyres, high speed track, nothing to prove, bring it back in one piece…

It fires up with an extended push on a surprisingly small starter button, and settles into an even, unexpectedly high-pitched idle. The digital display ahead of me monitors the vital signs with hyperactive intensity. The central console is a single wodge of carbon fibre totally unrelated to the road car, though a big vent and air con issues a welcome blast of cool air. Nor is the wheel even a full wheel; its alien form should feel odd and it's festooned in buttons, but of course it's brilliant to hold. Race car. Amongst others, there are dials for fuel mode and engine map, and the switches to adjust traction control are top left and right. We won't be troubling them today, although no amount of fast-acting algorithms can help yaw on stone-cold slicks.

The transmission is the ubiquitous six-speed unit from Xtrac. Engage first and release the weighty clutch pedal for an easy getaway. The car is instantly straining its muscle and sinew like a newly enraged Bruce Banner, but it's also amazingly well-mannered. We have images to capture, so I use the time stuck behind the intrepid Richard Pardon to familiarise myself with the car and the track.

Monza is spiritual. No wonder the F1 guys all rave about it. Sure, it's not particularly technical and doesn't have the banzai elements of Spa or Suzuka, but it's still so rewarding. How do they get through that first chicane, or overtake in the middle of the Lesmo? Physics and impregnable self-belief, I guess.

Halfway round the first lap my patience expires and I give the P80/C the beans in second gear. Honestly, it doesn't reel in the horizon like a LaFerrari, but it's not a hypercar, it's a racing car, and it feels alive in a way no road car ever can, not even a loony one, an audible riot of buzzes and zings, shorn of sound-proofing and utterly fit for purpose. I'm staying well away from Monza's sadistic sausage kerbs and rumble strips for obvious reasons, asking little of either the aerodynamic or mechanical grip. But it doesn't matter: this is a one-off Ferrari freaking racing car.

Unencumbered by any of the usual road or indeed competition

"IT WAS A CHALLENGE, BUT WHATEVER PLATFORM WE CHOSE WE WERE ALWAYS GOING TO EXTRACT THE MAXIMUM MECHANICAL AND AERODYNAMIC PERFORMANCE OUT OF THE CAR"

homologation regulations, the team that created the P80/C enjoyed an exceptional degree of creative freedom. The 488 GT3's underpinnings mean the wheelbase is 50mm longer than the standard 488, and it only weighs 1260kg. The new car is reportedly five per cent more aerodynamically efficient overall, and although elements of the rear diffuser are shared with the GT3, the front splitter and all the external surfaces are unique. For Ferrari to be pushing the aero boundaries on a one-off underlines how how far the company was prepared to go.

Although the innermost workings of the client/Centro Stile relationship remain closely guarded, TK is able to shine some light on the process. 'We sat down with Flavio and the design team and carefully described the raison d'etre behind the car. That was very important to me – that they understood why we wanted to build this car,' he explains. 'It wasn't for vanity nor was it a chance for us to dictate to them what to do – this was an opportunity for us to make something truly special that we can all be proud of for years to come.'

The freedom they were given was startling. 'Ferrari gave us an almost open slate to work with once everyone was on board the project. We needed to make sure that both parties saw eye to eye with our vision for the car so that I knew they were as enthusiastic as we were to commit to bringing this to life. In all,

it took us over four years to see this car from sketch to metal – but that was a reflection of the commitment I made to them in our first conversation.

'We worked closer with Flavio, the design team, engineers and aerodynamic specialists than any other SP project to date,' he continues, 'and we wanted to be sure that it was absolutely perfect to all parties involved before we showed it to the world.'

It wasn't always going to be a racing car, though. 'At one stage we considered a 458 GT2 base, but in the end, we chose the then in-development 488 GT3 platform in 2014 to ensure that the car was built on the most modern race chassis available at the time. That allowed the designers access to the latest tech available and to push the boundaries.'

Naturally, this presented some challenges. 'Certainly, there were aspects that were difficult to execute due to aerodynamic efficiency, engineering or proportions given the base that we selected to work with,' TK says. 'But no matter what platform we chose, we were going to try to extract even more mechanical and aerodynamic performance out of it.'

It worked. TK is a serial Ferrari owner and collector, but the SP experience has sharpened his resolve to do more. The first man to build a Ferrari one-off based on a racing car is looking into singular multi-cylindered possibilities. Watch this space.

PRICE £5 MILLION (APPROX) **0-60** N/A **TOP SPEED** N/A **POWER** 660BHP (UP TO 800BHP)
DID YOU KNOW? THE 488 GT3 (ON WHICH THE P80/C IS BASED) DOMINATED THE 2017 BATHURST 12 HOUR

FITTIPALDI EF7

One of the greatest names in motor racing
finally creates a road car to match

Sharks. A McLaren P1 GTR. Love of a Brazilian homeland. There's a selection of the ingredients that were poured into the creation of the Fittipaldi Motors EF7 Vision Gran Turismo by Pininfarina. OK, the name needs a trim, but that's an intriguing mood board, you must admit.

The EF7 exists because of the most mouthwatering foundation a supercar can be conceived upon. An F1 world champion cherry-picking suppliers to build him the ultimate no-compromise machine. And, just maybe, a chance for the godfather of Italian supercar style to settle a professional score. In 2011, after half a century of marriage, Ferrari cut ties with Pininfarina and established Centro Stile Ferrari – its own in-house design studio. The first Ferrari road car to emerge without the hand of Pininfarina forging its bodywork was quite a vehicle: the LaFerrari. So, Fittipaldi's EF7 is the opportunity for Pininfarina to show Ferrari how it would have gone about the ultimate air flow-harnessing hypersexy two-seater.

Where Ferrari aims to put F1 know-how on the street, Pininfarina wanted a great white shark with wheelnuts. "We always like to design shapes inspired by nature," says CEO Paolo Pininfarina. "Shapes that are fast in water are fast in air. That front wing? It's the mouth of the shark."

Emerson himself is now 70 years old. When he was just 26 he became the youngest man to win the Formula One world championship, taking five wins in the 1972 season perched within the flimsy black and gold bodywork of the John Player special Lotus 72. Two years later, the São Paulo-born upstart who'd previously shown promise racing motorcycles and hydrofoils before winning the British Formula Vee and F3 titles, took McLaren's dominant M23 to his second F1 crown. After a sabbatical and switch to American oval racing, Fittipaldi won the 1989 and 1993 Indianapolis 500. One of the all-time greats, he always wanted to create his own car.

"It is a dream", says a friendly, enthusiastic Fittipaldi. "And now I have done it, using German engineering, because they are the best, and Pininfarina design, for the same reason." Paolo, grandson of company founder Battista, stands unmoved next to Emerson. "When I first left Brazil", continues the F1 champ, "I thought one day it would be my dream to have my own GT car. A car for the track: the lightest car possible."

He stops short of actually quoting Colin Chapman's mantra, but says, "When you drive F1 or Indycar, you need good agility and braking to make up time. When you drive a GT car after that [he's using 'GT as shorthand for a closed bodywork car with a fixed roof], it feels heavy and sluggish."

Lightness being an obsession, Fittipaldi and Pininfarina drafted in German engineering firm HWA to build the EF7's carbon core. Their track record includes the Le Mans-winning tubs in Porsche's 919 Hybrid prototype, giving immense strength and contributing to the EF7's kerbweight of an even 1,000kg. Which means the car produces 592bhp-per-tonne. How it delivers 592bhp was up to Emerson… "When you have a normally aspirated engine, you're able to drive the throttle and steering together", says the Brazilian. "Anyone who drives cars fast knows this. So a normally aspirated engine was part of my dream." He relates this to a recent experience driving McLaren's P1 GTR ("beautiful car – a very heavy car – but with a lot of downforce.") Emerson wanted the aerodynamic performance of his car to be that competitive, but to do without the weight of battery packs or turbochargers and intercoolers.

"Our engine is all bespoke. It is a 4.8- litre, naturally aspirated V8. We have 600 horsepower [that's European PS, or 592bhp in Anglospeak] at 9,000rpm." I note that the power and rev band is identical to a Ferrari 458 Speciale's engine. Could there be some carryover there? Emerson twins a firm shake of the head with an adamant denial. "The engine is brand new, has done a lot of dyno testing, the gearbox casing is ours, and the rear wishbones are bolted straight onto it like an F1 car". The transmission is a seven-speed paddleshift unit, chosen for lightness and ease of use, because the whole point of the EF7 is it'll be easy to drive, and safe. Emerson namedrops 'safety' five times more than power and twice as often as he mentions his baby's lightness.

Intrinsic safety won't matter to the countless petrolheads who'll get to drive the car virtually (it's a downloadable bonus for the Gran Turismo PlayStation simulator), but it will encourage the 39 lucky (and rich) people who'll own an EF7 for real – each daubed in a bespoke colour and unique racing numeral – to actually get out and thrash the thing. Thirty nine, incidentally, is to commemorate one for each of Emerson's international motorsport victories. We suspect they'll enjoy themselves.

"FITTIPALDI AND PININFARINA DRAFTED
IN HWA TO BUILD THE EF7'S CARBON CORE.
ITS TRACK RECORD INCLUDES MAKING
THE TUBS FOR THE MULTIPLE LE MANS-
WINNING PORSCHE 919 HYBRID"
....

PRICE $1.5 MILLION **0-60** < 3.0 SECONDS **TOP SPEED** N/A **POWER** 592BHP
DID YOU KNOW? JUST 39 WILL BE MADE – ONE FOR EACH OF FITTIPALDI'S VICTORIES IN F1 AND INDYCAR

"IMAGINE WHAT THE AIR IS DOING AS THE
FORD GT HEADS INTO IT. IT ISN'T SHREDDED
OR TATTERED, BUT CAREFULLY ARRANGED
AND PROCESSED, PEELED APART AND TEASED
INTO THE RIGHT SHAPE"

FORD GT

With this new incarnation, one of history's greatest cars gets a stunning sequel

Today's lesson is bonkers aero. Stand right behind the Ford GT and what you see in front of you are the menacing barrels of the twin exhausts. Imagine you're behind it while it spears along this coast-draped masterpiece of a road, hot gases being blasted into your face. Either side of that, torrents of ambient air sweep through those gaping channels, ducted under wing-profile flying buttresses, compressed and shaped and then flowing off the back.

Your eyes are at the taper point, where the air flow fuses itself back together. From here you see up and through the car; it looks hollow. It looks like nothing else. Except maybe a pod racer. Or the Starship Enterprise. Those filmic teases are only enhanced by outriggers that house the rear wheels and lights.

And what fresh madness is this? Peer inside those round LEDs and you'll see radiators – they vent air from the intercoolers behind. More air passes over the turbos and around the engine bay, subtly channelled in and out. Now look lower down, to the 11 carbon bars of the under floor diffuser, extracting and organising air that's been sped up to reduce underbody pressure.

So as you sit there, imagine what the air is doing as the Ford GT heads into it. The air isn't shredded or tattered, but carefully arranged and processed, peeled apart, teased into the right shapes and places, morphing through and around; used then discarded. But discarded as carefully as it was collected in the first place, the various streams flowing back together, probably a bit hotter, but as uninterrupted from their original path as possible. Free once again to be used to nature's purpose out over the California coast.

So, lesson one: the Ford GT is not about downforce, but aero-efficiency. You may now stand up and dust yourself down.

Have a wander around the GT, look at the shape of the central canopy – get it from the right angle (nose on, high up) and you'll see the teardrop shape: two passengers ahead of one engine. It explains the V6, it explains the fixed seating position. Those allowed Ford to shrink the greenhouse, lower the frontal area, reduce the drag. How weird would it be if this bleeding-edge aero work was teamed with an old school big-banger V8?

You push a flap, the door pops up, you pull a toggle and the pedals slide back to meet you. The cabin is bare, naked carbon, the luxury layer is absent, two levers under the steering wheel

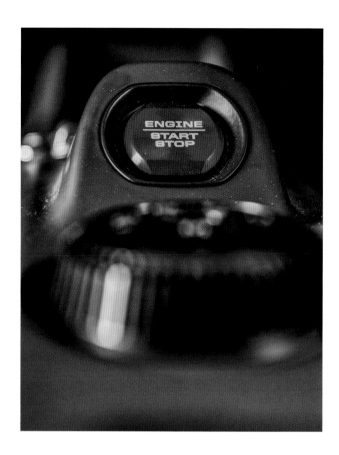

control macro and micro adjustment, all of which says "racer". But the seats are slightly soft with shallow thigh bolsters and mounted a touch high in relation to the rest of the cockpit. As an initial message it's slightly confusing. I'd expected hard, sculpted buckets, but these make me concerned Ford is aiming the car at, well, a regular if decidedly well-heeled Ford buyer.

Fortunately I can't find much other evidence of pandering. The 11-litre boot is smaller than most gloveboxes. There isn't one of those. No cupholders either. Barely anywhere for a phone or wallet. But forget all that, because what matters is the way the cabin makes you feel, which aside from your comfy buttocks, is very, very eager to get going.

The Pacific Coast Highway is weird. It's Sunday afternoon, the views are stunning and we're set for a perfect peachy sunset. It's like I've entered dreamland, or maybe California is just one big film set and tonight it's been locked down for us. So I go for a drive. Not hard, just letting the car find its own pace.

The GT doesn't seek speed unless you demand it, doesn't run away with you or leave you clinging on. Instead it moves with you very naturally, seeming to concentrate on communicating all the sweeps and ducks of this magnificent road. Pedals and steering respond smoothly and evenly, it corners without effort, it feels lithe and athletic, unstressed, happy with whatever pace I choose. Sunset isn't a time for forcing the pace, or screeching about, is it? The GT tunes itself perfectly to the fading light.

One thing: it is very positive on the road. Very. It's like the suspension is rose-jointed, the engine rigidly mounted to the carbon chassis, as if all rubber was banished from its construction. It zizzes and chatters, so although it's content to move gently, I wouldn't call it relaxing. Comfortable? Hmm. The suspension is clearly beautifully damped, and has a lovely dexterity which speaks of long wishbones, but the movements are tiny and taut. This, and occasional jabs of the throttle to provoke the V6, serve to heighten anticipation for tomorrow – Laguna Seca day.

We eat dinner with Ford engineers at the Turn 12 diner. It's motorsport memorabilia central, inspired by the track nearby. We talk about rivals to the GT, and the chief engineer of Ford Performance Jamal Hameedi admits they started benchmarking against the 458 Speciale, but then got their hands on a McLaren 675LT. We talk about the work Multimatic has done on the long-wishbone suspension and active set-up. We don't talk downforce figures, because Ford won't – that might allow rival teams to calculate how much downforce the racing version produces…

A fitful night's sleep. Now we're in the pit lane at Laguna Seca. For the next seven hours, the track is ours, but at 2pm Ford insists we're gone. I suspect they'll be running lap times on the GT and 675LT. Right now, I'm more concerned about the GT's Track mode. It takes a McLaren P1 30 seconds to suck itself down and stick its wing up. You'll have seen footage of the GT doing it. It feels even more mad when you're sat in it – it's the heightened sense of anticipation. A suggestion that the good-natured GT you knew last night is no more.

We're now just 41.7 inches tall and the wheels have disappeared inside the arches. I'm not sure how it's actually able

to steer. The simplicity of the cockpit now makes more sense, the presence of cruise and sound controls on the wheel seems superfluous, somehow diluting your enjoyment of the slatted metal paddles and knurled thumb controls.

No matter, as I move up the pit lane I'm instantly aware of a condensed, focused energy. No slack, no slop, just this delicious sense of being strapped to a very honed, precisely engineered machine. Again, I call the seat into question. But my position in the car is faultless, X marking the spot drawn in diagonals between the four wheels. It may have two seats, but I feel almost perfectly central, shunted inwards, backside equidistant from front and rear axles and about four inches off the deck.

It's like being the conductor of an orchestra – you're not only perfectly positioned to feel what's happening, but also to give instruction. So, when you add in superb hydraulic steering, an ultra-low centre of gravity, tautly controlled movements, superb aero stability and stunning brake power, it comes together as a harmonious whole. It does your bidding.

What of the engine, though? Well, for a V6 it's certainly impressive. Noise is… well, there's more quantity than quality. Power is… plentiful. It's not as charismatic as a V8, lacks the ultra-visceral make-it-stop delivery of the 675LT, but blends very well with the chassis. And that's the thing. You very quickly become aware that the GT is a chassis car, not an engine car. The V6 is there to provide acceleration and to do that as effectively as it can, but you get your thrills, your value for money, from the handling, the cornering, the suspension.

Once in Track mode, lag is practically eradicated by an anti-lag system, but the power delivery itself is a bit one-dimensional. From both aural and acceleration perspectives there's not much point seeking out the 7,000rpm red line – the good work has been done by 5,500rpm and the gears are closely stacked enough that the next one in the chamber will force you onwards with plentiful urge. It punches very hard indeed, but it's nothing the chassis can't handle, so very quickly you feel confident using

a lot of the power, knowing the brakes, steering and suspension will do what you ask them to. This set-up is what impresses me most. Around Laguna Seca I can build a rhythm so quickly and easily: there's little weight transfer, so braking into corners doesn't destabilise the GT, there's a slight warning push of understeer at the apex, but that's neutralised by power and suspension geometry, so you exit flat, fast and fearless. It handles heroically well, because the lines of communication are so clear and the behaviour so predictable.

The Ford GT makes Laguna Seca glorious. The Corkscrew should be super nerve-racking, but the blind braking zone holds no fears, and it pitches in hard, flat and accurate, drives itself down the cliff, and carries a dizzying amount of speed onwards to Rainey Curve and the addictive camber at Turn 10. There's no downtime anywhere as 647bhp hits the straights hard and clean, no energy wasted thanks to the diff apportioning torque beautifully and the grip generated by 325-width tyres and aero pressure. Small mention here for the seats, which have better lateral support than I expected.

All those sensations: joyful, exuberant, the sort that make you want to whoop and sing round the circuit. And when we do some skids for the camera, it proves to be as delicately balanced beyond the limit as at the limit. It's the sign of a well set-up car when throttle, steering, rear axle and suspension are so biddable.

That the Ford GT is better balanced than a McLaren 675LT I have no doubt. I don't think its engine is as eye-popping as the McLaren's, but as a package it's right up there. It's a pure driver's car, a faithful representation of a road-going racing car and true to its origins. If it looked less radical, I think Ford would struggle to justify the £320,000 asking price, but that's the point. This is what it looks like, and it looks like this because aero said so.

Time to go. The temptation to lurk behind a tree while Ford battles McLaren is strong, but I've seen and experienced enough today. I'll let that particular mystery live on a little longer. Right now, I'm just happy the Ford GT is every bit as good as I hoped.

PRICE £420,000 **0-60** 3.0 SECONDS **TOP SPEED** 216MPH **POWER** 647BHP
DID YOU KNOW? IN TRACK MODE, THE GT IS JUST 41.7 INCHES TALL – STILL 1.7 MORE THAN THE ORIGINAL GT40…

FORD GT
MKII

Ford bids farewell to the GT in grand style

The GT Mk II is a track-only supercar "engineered independently of race series rules, regulations and limitations". Ford will build 45, and charge $1.2million for the privilege of owning one. Like the existing road and race cars, the Mk II was co-developed by Ford and Multimatic. And it answers one big question, as Multimatic's Chief Technical Officer Larry Holt explains: "The road car is obviously limited by the many global homologation requirements that it must comply with, and the race car suffers from the restriction of the dreaded Balance of Performance, resulting in it being 150bhp down to the road car. The Mk II answers the regularly asked question of how would the car perform with all the limitations lifted." Ford's Chief Product Development Officer Hau Thai-Tang says the Mk II is "the closest GT owners can get to the 2016 Le Mans-winning performance and exhilarating feeling of crossing the finish line in the Ford GT race car", from which the Mk II borrows some components and much know-how. This year's Le Mans was the GT's last – the official programme ends after the last round of the IMSA season in October, though amateur teams may run them further down the line. Aero changes – including a dual-element rear wing and massive diffuser, as well as new louvres and dive planes – mean the Mk II produces 400 per cent more downforce than the GT road car. Coupled with sticky Michelin Pilot Sport racing tyres, this means it can pull more than two lateral Gs quite comfortably. The road car's adjustable ride height and drive modes have been junked in favour of five-way adjustable shocks, while the 3.5-litre EcoBoost V6 engine has been turned up to 700bhp. It's as nature intended.

PRICE $1.2 MILLION **0-60** 3.0 SECONDS **TOP SPEED** 215MPH **POWER** 700BHP

DID YOU KNOW? EVER WANTED TO FEEL TWICE YOUR BODYWEIGHT PUSHING YOU SIDEWAYS?
THE GT MKII CAN GENERATE 2G IN THE CORNERS...

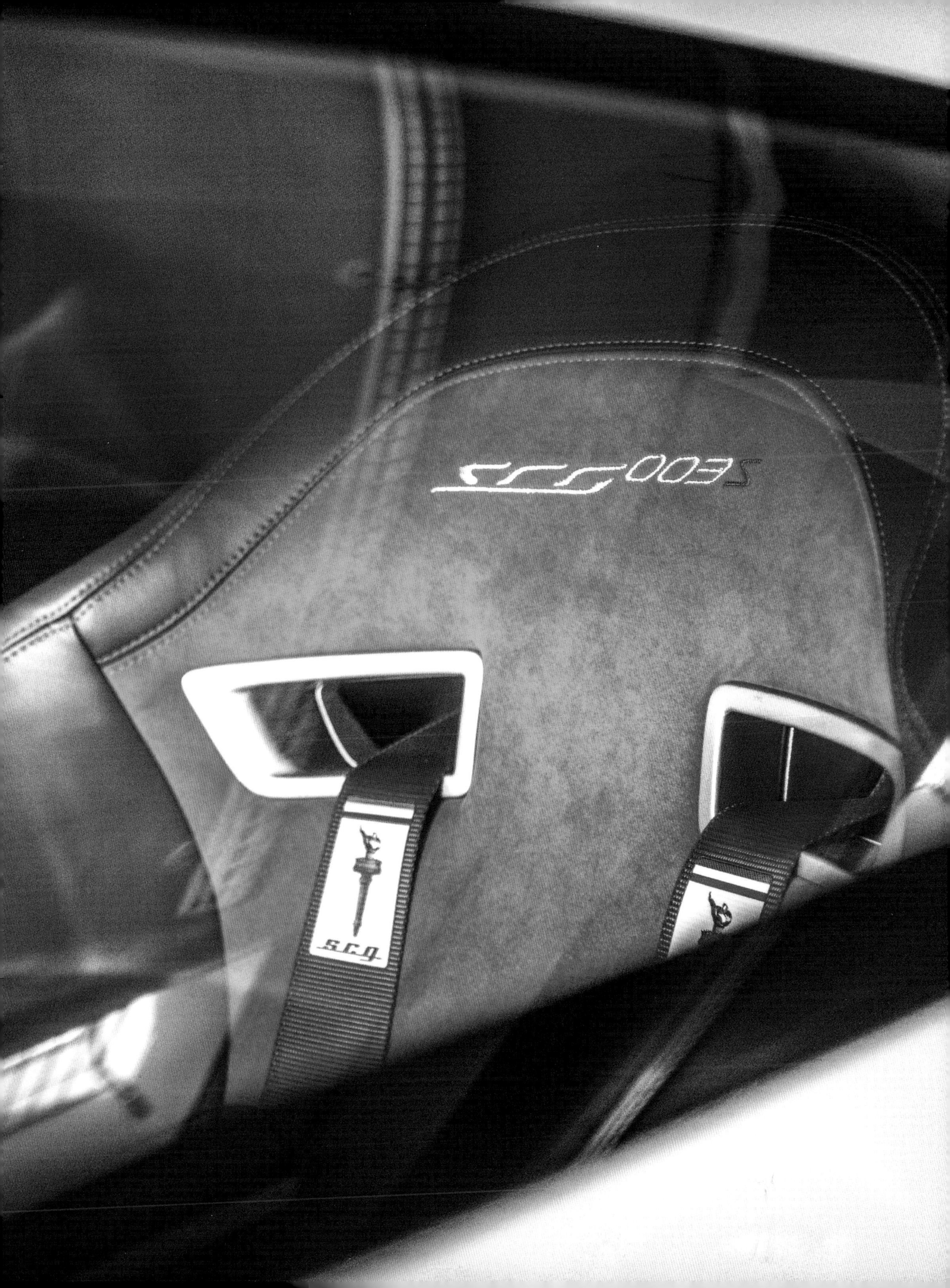
SCG003S
S.C.G.

GLICKENHAUS
SCG 003S

The SCG003S is a road-legal American hypercar that bears the DNA of a Nürburgring 24-hour endurance racer; a car that wants to play in the battlefield of the limited-run hypercar ateliers like Koenigsegg and Pagani, but demolish the big boys of McLaren and Ferrari via bludgeoning performance.

The man behind it is former film producer and ardent motorsport fanatic, Jim Glickenhaus. His car collection speaks volumes: the Ford GT40 Mk IV that finished fourth at Le Mans in 1967, a one-off yellow duckbilled 1967 Ferrari 206 Dino, an ex-Mark Donohue/Roger Penske Can-Am-winning Lola T70 with 65,000 road miles on it, the gorgeous Ferrari P3/4 and 412P, and the eye-popping 1970 Pininfarina Modulo. He also masterminded 2006's P4/5 – an epic one-off reimagining of the Ferrari Enzo – and its racing sibling, the P4/5 Competizione. The SCG003C was its successor – a ground-up racer using all the development knowledge from Jim's previous years competing at the 'Ring.

It worked, too: in 2015 it qualified in pole position and finished first in its class. This SCG003S (where the 'S' stands for

Stradale) shares a remarkable amount of DNA with its competition sibling. There's a carbon fibre chassis with carbon uprights and LMP2 levels of aerodynamic downforce. The engine comes via BMW: the company's 4.4-litre twin-turbo V8 from the M6 racer, producing 750bhp-plus and over 590lb ft of torque. Drive is sent to the rear wheels via a seven-speed single clutch gearbox (dual-clutch was too heavy), there are double wishbone pushrods all round with adjustable Bilstein damping, Brembo brakes.

And speed. It'll go from 0-60mph in less than 2.9secs, reach 217mph, generate more than 2G of mechanical grip, and 850kg of downforce at 155mph. It'll also lap the 'Ring somewhere in the range of 6m 30s, so it's a serious bit of kit in anyone's book.

The spine in the roof is there to meet minimum cockpit height requirements while keeping the roofline as low as possible. Same story for the ones on the arches. Amazingly, this is legal within the homologation under SCG's NHTSA status for low volume manufacturers (which exempts it from things like airbags and crash testing as long as they don't produce 325 cars

a year). All the important stuff is controlled off the wheel, while everything else is labelled in hi-vis to be as ergonomic as possible. It's not pretty but it doesn't half add to the occasion.

We drove a development car with 10,000 race miles on it. Things like the ABS, gearbox and traction control still need further calibration, but the most amazing thing is that the 003S feels like a road car. Which, given what it looks like, takes your mind a while to adjust to. It doesn't stutter or noisily galumph like an N24 racer. It's soft and manageable. Admittedly, there's 400kgs worth of sound deadening and softness added to make it more compliant compared to its racing sibling.

With rubber mountings where things are normally rose-jointed it's not jarring, and the three-way Bilstein dampers are amazing at ironing out New York's broken parkways. There's

even proper air conditioning and you can have a conversation at speed much more easily than in a McLaren Senna.

There are three driving modes, and lower in the rev range the car just floats on the torque, but if you commit it wakes up and comes in with a wave of fury. Yet that BMW engine feels more effective as opposed to characterful but runs up to the red line quicker than you'd expect, so you need to be quick with the paddles or you're bouncing off the limiter. On the road, the carbon ceramic brakes have top-end squidge and lack initial bite but are powerful and the hydraulic non-assisted rack offers

Yes, it's £1.7 million but you've now got people like Pagani charging £15m for a 20-year old chassis (the Zonda Barchetta). Plus, with only two or three being made a year, you'll have one of the rarest and capable road cars you can track in the world.

PRICE £1.7 MILLION **0-60** < 2.9 SECONDS **TOP SPEED** 217MPH **POWER** > 750BHP

DID YOU KNOW? GLICKENHAUS GOT THE FERRARI MODULO CONCEPT CAR OUT ON THE ROAD, UNTIL IT CAUGHT FIRE

HONDA NSX

A complex hybrid that channels the spirit of the ground-breaking original for a new era

IndyCar legend and NSX development driver Dario Franchitti is midway down the long straight at Thermal Raceway and, rather predictably, is disappearing into the distance. "If you want to catch him, try braking at the '3' board," offers my passenger. A few seconds later. "Actually maybe it's the '4' for this one," adds Jason Widmer, the NSX's performance development leader. The NSX sheds all the speed and gears it needs to, before the front-end torque vectoring works its automotive voodoo and pulls us out of the corner and onwards.

The back story here is as fascinating as the car's gestation was long. A V10 was initially investigated because it was congruent with F1 requirements. Since then Honda has left F1 – and then returned. We'll skate over that, but point out that the chosen V6 hybrid layout does once again have some F1 relevance. The NSX now has a 3.5-litre V6 twin-turbo generating 500bhp. Wedged between it and the nine-speed twin-clutch 'box lies a brushless electric motor developing 47bhp and 109lb ft of torque, which gap-fills the turbo lag at low revs. It also serves as the starter motor, which in turn saves weight. At the front end, two further motors, sharing a single clutch and producing 36bhp apiece, are mounted inboard, driving a front wheel each and allowing the NSX to indulge in the black art of torque vectoring. At the rear, a limited-slip differential divvies up the torque.

All three motors are powered by a lithium-ion battery pack running down the centre of the car and across behind the seats, forming a 'T'. This battery is charged by the V6 motor and regenerative braking. So what we're talking here is an AWD supercar with a combined output of 573bhp and enough computer processing power to make NASA blush. However, it's also led to a 1,725kg kerbweight – that's 100kg more than the Audi R8 V10, and a quarter of a tonne more than a Ferrari 488.

Styling is a fiercely personal thing, but despite being first created in Japan, then developed in Honda's LA studio, it channels a manga-meets-Tony-Stark vibe that has a sharp origami precision to it. The predominantly aluminium bodywork is stretched over the structure, manipulating the air, and cooling the battery cells and complex hybrid drivetrain. Not that it helped my laptop, which practically fried its circuits having spent an afternoon in the "trunk".

The NSX is a complex car to build. The chassis has a mixed materials construction, mainly aluminium, with special castings at the key suspension mounting points and carbon fibre for the floor. Honda claims the chassis is stiffer than anything the opposition has (it cites the R8, 911 Turbo and 458 Italia, which shows the length of the car's gestation), but won't be drawn on specific numbers. Nor will it talk aerodynamic efficiency or downforce, except to say the latter is "significant". That's commendable, given the NSX relies on clever aerodynamic channels rather than complex deployable spoilers, which in turn keeps the car looking uncluttered.

That dynamic mode selector has four modes: Quiet, Sport, Sport+ and Track. You can choose which the car starts in – based on how much you like your neighbours. Quiet allows you to leave in EV silence. It's good for about two miles if you're abstemious with the throttle. Sport blends V6 and e-motors together, but this is the NSX's least convincing mode: the V6 drones at low revs and you're more aware of the myriad complex systems' involvement in proceedings. Flick it to Sport+ and the car comes alive. The third-generation magnetorheological dampers stiffen, the steering and throttle response sharpen, and the whole car is more focused and purposeful. Push through the lower end of the rev range and the previously bland V6 comes alive and starts to sing. The combined thrust is mighty – every bit as forceful as an R8 V10 – the gearshifts are instantaneous, and with nine ratios to play with, there are plenty of opportunities to keep the V6 pushing to the 7,500rpm red line.

On the road, there's a suppleness to the ride that is reminiscent of a McLaren, and the NSX hides its mass well, too. There's initial understeer but once into the corner it hits a sweet balance point. It feels very together, deploying its considerable processing power to swallow tarmac at an alarming rate and with enough harmony to demonstrate how seamlessly integrated electricity and internal combustion are here. Like the Porsche 918, and even the BMW i8, this is a car where electrics add a dimension to the experience, broadening the appeal. And Honda describes the NSX as "not the finish line, just the start point". Cool.

PRICE £144,825 **0-60** < 3.0 SECONDS
TOP SPEED 191MPH **POWER** 573BHP
DID YOU KNOW? THE 'NEW' NSX WAS ANNOUNCED IN 2007, BUT TOOK UNTIL 2016 TO HIT THE MARKET

"THE NSX IS A CAR IN WHICH THE ELECTRICS ADD A SIGNIFICANT DIMENSION TO THE EXPERIENCE. HONDA ALSO SAYS THIS IS JUST THE START"

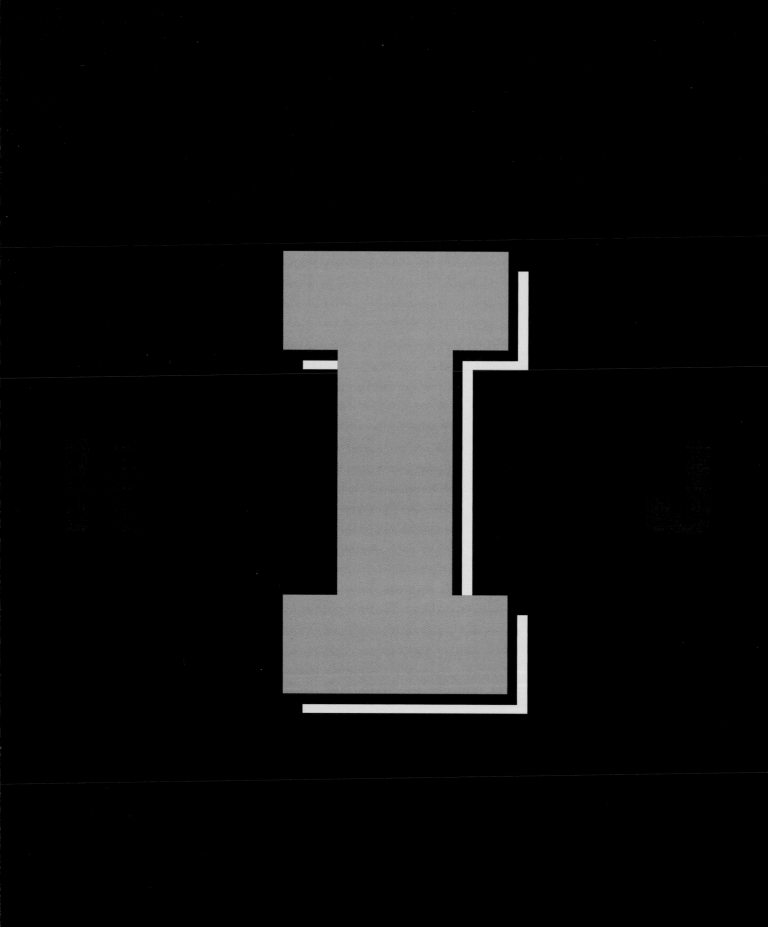

ITALDESIGN ZEROUNO

The famous design house turns its hand to car manufacture, with spectacular results

The Zerouno's rear end is fabulously over the top. It's also fully functional, conceived to hustle fast-moving air into suckering the car to the ground and cooling hot componentry, but as this is one of just five 'pieces', it's an abstract sculpture too. And the entire engine cover comes off, doubling as a superhero shield/portable wing. It really works, too. The road we've headed along takes us up above the clouds towards Moncenisio, about 50 miles west of Turin on the border with France. The SP212 is a corker, framed today by the most stunning palate of colours on the trees and wreathed in a sepulchral mist. It would be difficult to put a figure on this prototype Zerouno, but pretty soon its value and extraordinary rarity cease to matter; this is an easy car to drive quickly, and there's hardly anyone around so we can, um, take some liberties. It dives into corners with magnificent precision, and rockets up the straights with a familiar sounding bellow. Normally aspirated V10, you see. The Zerouno is a mobile manifesto for Italdesign, the company founded by the maestro Giugiaro but owned by the VW group since 2015. It's the first in a planned series of Italdesign-branded *automobili speciali*, conceived and realised in just 14 months. If it looks like a low-volume, ultra-expensive supercar, then that's because it is (€1.5m apiece, but all five are sold – the first off-plan when it was still just an idea). The development team have put 40,000km on prototypes at Nardo and elsewhere, stress-testing the concept and ensuring the wild race-car venturi at the rear actually works. (Audi LMP1 driver and Le Mans winner Dindo Capello is part of the development crew.) The nose's distinctive snout and 'Ypsilon' duct at the front aids airflow and promotes downforce. The rear end's artful aero origami includes an exposed section that reveals significant portions of 305/30 ZR Pirellis. The Zerouno is based on the modular aluminium chassis that helped transform the perception of Audi as a sports car maker. The engine is the same as the naturally aspirated 5.2-litre V10 found in the R8 and the Lamborghini Huracan, the all-wheel drive hardware is also identical, and the car is TUV-homologated. But as well as sitting 40mm lower than the R8, there's a more vigorous edge to its personality. The suspension and dampers have been reworked, so there's an extra layer of aggression, the seven-speed 'box changes gear with more snap, and the car turns in and changes direction beautifully. What a cool thing.

PRICE €1.5 MILLION **0-60** 3.2 SECONDS **TOP SPEED** 205MPH **POWER** 602BHP

DID YOU KNOW? ROGER DUBUIS HAS MADE A WATCH TO CELEBRATE THE ZEROUNO. WE'RE SURE IT'S SUBTLE, TOO

JAGUAR C-X75

Too good to be consigned to the dustbin of history, too complex to make production

What could have been… The C-X75 almost made it, but not quite – unless you count its dramatic appearance chasing 007 in *Spectre*. Jaguar and Williams started the project with the following simple but wildly contradictory goals: the looks of the original Paris motor show concept, the performance of a Bugatti (0–62mph in 3.0secs, 0–100mph in six), a pure-electric range of around 40 miles, the official-cycle CO2 of a Prius – 89g/km. So they ended up with a 500bhp, four-cylinder, 1.6-litre engine. It's a blank-sheet job, not derived from a road or race unit. Up to 5,500rpm, it's supercharged. After that, it switches to turbo, which keeps going to the limit of 10,200rpm. That is not a misprint. Meanwhile, there are two electric motors: one at the rear feeding through the seven-speed gearbox, and another at the front. They make almost 200bhp each. And 300lb ft of torque. Again, that's per motor. This is a six-seconds-to-60mph car, even before the engine has started. The chassis is terrific. Yes, at urban speeds, the stiffer springs make it pretty hard, but you can always feel the body is reassuringly rigid so, as you get some speed into the suspension movements and the inboard dampers begin to do their work, you notice the precision. It rounds off sharp impacts and breathes nicely over dips and crests. At speed, the aero pushes you into the track and reassures you by tightening everything up. It's a highly impressive machine. The decision to kill C-X75 production must have felt to Jaguar like strangling a puppy. There simply weren't likely to be enough buyers for this and the Porsche, McLaren. and the other rivals arriving in this sector. But the fast-track engineering it embodies lives on in hundreds of thousands of people's Jaguars and Land Rovers.

PRICE £750,000 **0-60** 3.0 SECONDS
TOP SPEED 220MPH **POWER** 900BHP
DID YOU KNOW? HAD A STARRING ROLE IN THE LATEST BOND FILM SPECTRE, AS DRIVEN BY BLOFELD'S HENCHMAN MR HINX

"WE KNOW THE REGULAR F-TYPE CAN SLIDE, BUT WITH THE PROJECT 7 THE SLIDE GOES ON FOR LONGER AND THE SMOKE SOMEHOW SEEMS TO FOLLOW YOU DOWN THE ROAD"

PRICE £135,000 **0-60** 3.8 SECONDS **TOP SPEED** > 186MPH **POWER** 567BHP

DID YOU KNOW? NO BAT IS TRULY BLIND – IN FACT, SOME HAVE BETTER SIGHT THAN HUMANS...

JAGUAR PROJECT 7

Lighter, faster, crazier, rarer, slidier, sillier, and altogether wonderful

Its name refers to the number of times Jag has won Le Mans. There are pictures of the old winners all down the corridors of the company HQ, a sort of Cool Wall to remind employees of the good old days. After walking past the framed images, designer Cesar Pieri felt inspired to get his pencil out. He showed the results to his boss, the now-departed Ian Callum, and eventually it was decided to make the thing. The project went from sketch pad to CAD renderings in a few weeks, and from CAD to clay in just 10 days. Then it was over to the team who'd make the real thing. But we're not just talking about some stickers and stripes here. Look at the windscreen – it's been turned into a thin sweep of Perspex like you get on the front of a speedboat. There's an entirely new face with stronger cheekbones, a pointy carbon chin and a bigger mouth lined with white lipstick. The side sills are dark blades of carbon that could probably slice your ankles. Then there's the fairing behind the driver's head, which is more of a hump than a fin, but still tapers like a neatly butchered chicken fillet. Back in the day, Jag's Le Mans racers were run by Ecurie Ecosse and painted the same colours as the team's native Scottish flag. The Project 7 gives all the right Celtic hints, and even has a man skirt, albeit a carbon-fibre job. The 7 also comes with a matching helmet, featuring a white stripe the same width as the one over the bonnet. Once the designers had finished, they handed over to the engineers. Their first job was to release more horsepower from the 5.0-litre V8, which was quickly achieved with laptop surgery. Goodbye 488bhp, hello to the 542. Then it was out with the fabric roof and its motors, saving 20kg. Down went the 0–62mph time from 4.3 seconds to 4.1. Next job: rear wing. With the front splitter poking out 15cm further than usual, and therefore pushing it harder into the ground, they needed a similar force to balance the tail. So on went an aggressive carbon wing set to a 14° angle of attack. Then it was over to Mike Cross, the quiet genius who makes all Jags behave properly. And let me warn you now, if you're considering going around any corners, you should hold your breath. We know the F-Type can slide… but with the 7, the slide goes on for longer and the smoke somehow clings to the car and follows you down the road. It's like being blown along on the breath of an especially grumpy dragon. Think of the Project 7 as a cartoon for grown-ups.

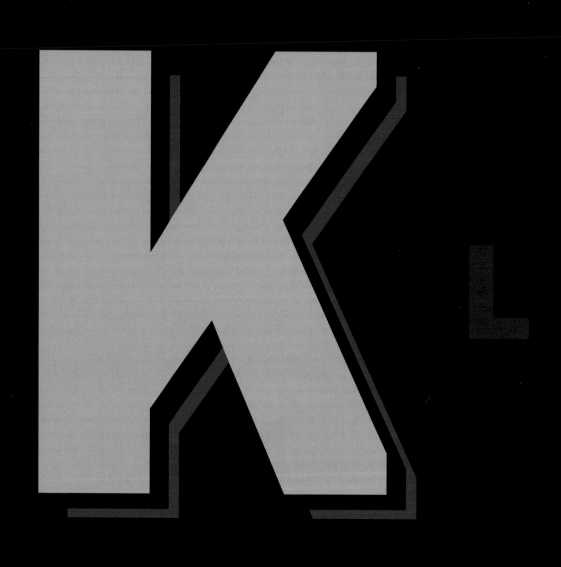

"I HAVE NEVER EXPERIENCED ANYTHING THAT BONFIRES ITS TYRES LIKE THE KOENIGSEGG REGERA. THIS IS WHAT A TWIN-TURBO V8 AND TRIPLET OF ELECTRIC MOTORS CAN DO TO A PAIR OF MICHELINS"

KOENIGSEGG
REGERA

The Swedish upstarts continue to rewrite and rewire the very concept of hypercar

Koenigsegg has a vision of the future. In it, 1,500bhp hypercars have cloaking devices. They're not only massively effective, rendering the car utterly invisible, but also activate almost instantaneously. Ingeniously, the system is linked to throttle position. So, say you're being pursued through a dystopian city by a rampaging gang of social-media supercar baggers, all you have to do is briskly take the throttle to ooh, about 30 per cent, a puffy white cloud appears and all they're showing on Periscope is the inside of that thick, choking cloud while, somewhere off in the distance, a plainly furious T Rex is bellowing in pursuit of a hapless triceratops.

I have never experienced anything that bonfires its tyres like the Koenigsegg Regera. Anything. Despite the best tractive efforts of the vast 345-width Michelins, they're as nothing in the 1,475lb ft torque deluge that descends on them from a twin-turbo V8 and triplet of electric motors. They act like they've hit ice, the revs spike and, a second or so later, Christian Koenigsegg and I can barely see each other across the cabin (although given what we must look like in here – a pair of naked fleshy orbs – perhaps it's best to keep the smoke screen deployed).

What do you know about Koenigsegg? It's a question worth asking, because it's often hard to look beyond the power figures and top speeds. They do tend to stop you in your tracks. So you might not know that Koenigsegg does almost all its own carbon-fibre work, was the first to equip a production car with carbon-fibre wheels, that it assembles its own ECU circuit boards, develops its own infotainment software, even. In the engine test cell sits a revolutionary 1.6-litre turbocharged engine that has no camshafts. And there's only 110 people working there. As Christian says: "If we can't find the right partner or solution for a problem, we basically bring it in house."

The confidence required to do this is immense – you've got to be prepared for a vast amount of trial and error and be sure you'll get the right solution at the end of it. But it does mean the solutions perfectly match the needs. Compromise, as anyone who has watched one man assemble 750 carbon pieces to create one "bio-hazard" wheel as used on the new Regera can attest (it takes a week), is not part of the equation.

So that, in brief, is the mentality at Koenigsegg. It's about

"AS WELL AS THE 1,160BHP INTERNAL COMBUSTION ENGINE, THE REGERA IS POWERED BY A PAIR OF REAR-WHEEL ELECTRIC MOTORS DEVELOPING 240BHP. A THIRD IS MOUNTED ON THE ENGINE"

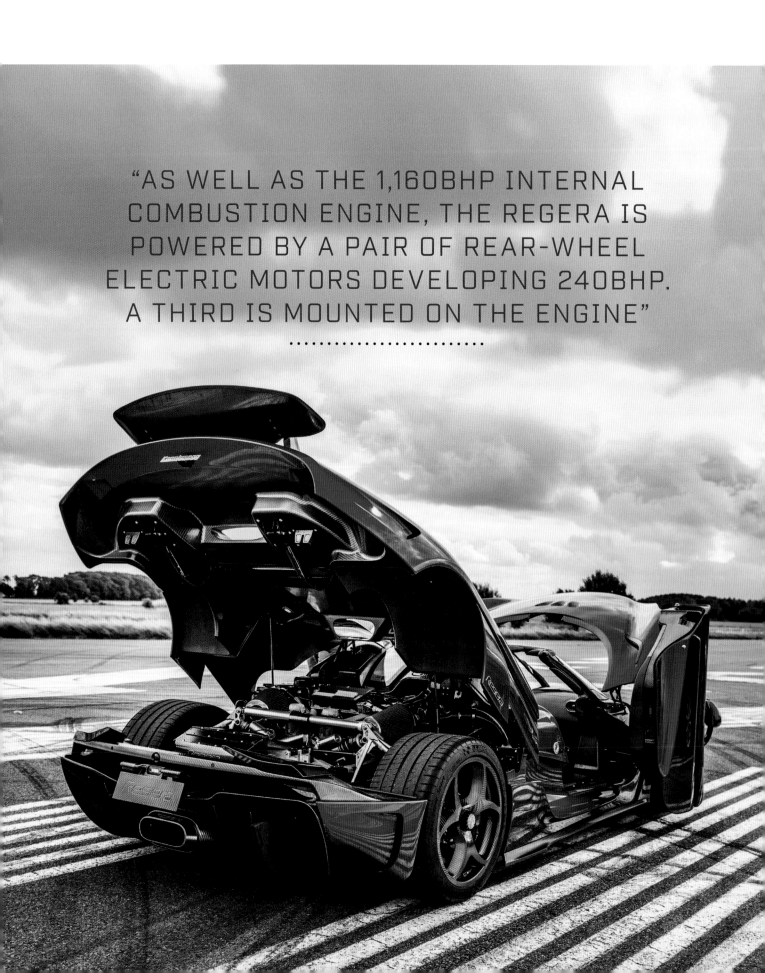

learning and investing and creating, and it's about one man's clarity of vision. Which brings us on to the Regera (pronounce it with a hard g, it means "to reign"). First, a quick recap: since the CC8S first appeared in 2002, Koenigsegg has only produced around 120 cars. There may have been around 15 different models, but on the whole each has been a development of the one before, the steps between them relatively small.

Broadly speaking the Regera is a development of the Agera RS. It uses a very similar carbon chassis, has the same 5.0-litre V8, except fed by slightly smaller, faster turbos, and the temptation is to believe this gives no more than a passing nod to hybrid power, a quest to prove that if Porsche, McLaren and Ferrari could, so could Koenigsegg.

But they don't think like that in Ängelholm. There are two key things to know about the Regera, one comparatively simple, the other ludicrously complicated. Let's deal with the easy stuff first: as well as the 1,160bhp internal combustion engine, the Regera is powered by a pair of rear-wheel electric motors. Designed and built by Yasa Motors in the UK, each weighs 32kg but develops 240bhp. There's a third one mounted on the engine that helps to recharge the battery, operates as a starter motor and generally smooths things out. All in, we're talking around 700bhp of electric force alone. Or, expressed another way, more than the electric power of the P1, 918 and LaFerrari combined.

But that's not the interesting bit – we need to talk about the gearbox. Because there isn't one. "I bought a Tesla Model S," Christian tells me, "and what interested me was how fun it was and how little I missed shifting. Even with a double-clutch, things have to happen before you overtake. So I was getting more and more pissed off – saying, 'Damn, this Tesla is good.' And conventional gearboxes are wasteful: you're only in one gear at any given point in time, the rest are laying around, adding weight, rattling maybe."

So wanting to do a hybrid, but not wanting it to be ludicrously heavy and complicated, they looked at obvious solutions: "CVT? No. Horrible. You have heat generation and it's continuously slipping, so it's inefficient where a gear is efficient. And the feel – I haven't driven one that feels good."

The answer, according to Koenigsegg, was to have no transmission at all, just direct drive from the engine through an open differential and out to the wheels, aided on either side by the torque-vectoring electric motors. However, as we all know, one gear has its limitations. It's why gearboxes were invented.

So they invented the Koenigsegg Direct Drive (KDD) system, which at its heart is essentially a torque-converter that allows clutch slip. "But a torque-converter sounds like something from 1922, so we call it HydraCoup, and what's different is that compared to its diameter it can convert much more torque than any other and weighs half as much."

So both electric and internal combustion powerplants are managed by one, slightly flexible gear with the whole lot, a combined 1,479bhp and 1,475lb ft, controlled by your right foot.

The figures are bananas – the one that truly blows my mind is the 3.2secs it takes to accelerate from 90mph to 155mph. Top speed? A little over 250mph, which it'll hopefully hit in around 20 seconds. "The thing we've realised is that chasing the ultimate top speed is starting to become a nonsense," Christian tells me, "so our philosophy is more like this: whoever gets to 250mph first wins." That's a philosophy I can get on board with.

The Regera intends to rain on the Chiron's parade, to make you question why Bugatti hasn't done something this radical for the Veyron's replacement. Of all the hypercar firms out there, Bugatti is the only one I can think of that might view a gearbox-less 1,500bhp hybrid as a good brand fit. In line with that, the Regera is intended to be a gentler experience than the Agera. The engine is rubber-bushed to lessen vibration, the rear wing whirrs up and down hydraulically, as do the doors and front and rear clams. The cabin is a work of art, the side sills massively wide, the carbon-shelled, memory foam seats built here from the ground up, the batteries contained in the transmission tunnel.

A quick word on the battery pack – it's the same spec as those used in F1 (a first for a production car), and weighs only 75kg, yet Christian expects it will deliver a 20-mile range. The power density is massive and running at 800 volts (another world first), the recharge and discharge rates are colossal.

Then there's the way it looks. This candy apple red Regera is sensational, there's real beauty in its long tail and taut curves and, like all Koenigseggs, the roof panel removes to store under the nose. Do so and the car's look changes totally, but sitting inside I prefer it with the roof on: it exaggerates the wrap-around widescreen view forward. The A-pillars are tucked right round the sides, and you sit so far back that I doubt the tips of my toes reach to the base of the screen. It's like looking out of a visor. And the materials, the look and feel of the cabin – I thought it was only Pagani that could do this artful stuff.

,

Driving this production prototype is simplicity itself. Pull the right paddle for Drive, left for Reverse, both together for Park. It's weird, initially: electric and internal combustion work together from the word go, when I'd expected it to creep around on e-power alone, after all, there's 700bhp of the stuff, so you might as well make the most of it. You can select electric drive, but at the moment Christian has it set up to run both simultaneously.

So, with both engaged and the clutch slipping, it feels like a lazy American V8 as we pull out of the factory onto public roads, the engine throbbing away, but drive takes a second to catch up. At 30mph, the torque-converter stops slipping and gives you direct drive, the V8 at about 1,000rpm. Then I start to love the Regera – the connection is natural and the low-rev thrust unearthly as electric motors add their bite.

"See, like a Tesla, but half a tonne lighter and with another 1,000bhp!" comes the voice from the other seat.

It's about then that Christian reminds me that this development car "has no traction control, none whatsoever". I back off and concentrate on how it's behaving. The steering is heavy, but delicious to use. It's hydraulic, with no slack, but real meat and reward. If anything, the ride is even better. Long wishbones, in-board dampers and reduced unsprung mass thanks in part to the carbon wheels, mean the Regera rides beautifully, precise and polished. How does it manage that? Look at the wheelarch clearance – where do the wheels go?

I'd expected a car that felt compromised by its vast vmax, that failed to come to life until well into three figures, but the Regera is instantly alert, corners flat and tenaciously, actually feels like it wants to attack a good road. Lord knows how you approach full throttle on a windy road with this much twist on tap, but the car is keen, even if this particular driver feels… apprehensive.

We head to the Koenigsegg's runway where there's room to play. The force… oh my God. As we discovered at the start, the Regera is viciously traction-limited, so full throttle – well,

Christian believes it might wheelspin up to 150mph, so actually getting a picture of what full chat feels like is rather tricky.

The revs spike as the torque-converter opens, the noise crashes in, guttural and savage through the fabulous upright flattened pipes. You're aware of some initial electric assistance, but that's then lost in the torque torrent as the pressure wave builds, a relentless, urgent push onwards. I think I was on top of it, could just about keep pace with my eyes and mind – but then I looked down, tore my bewildered eyes away and saw how fast we were actually going. I thought 150, the speedo said 180. Shock and awe, that is all. I'd driven a P1 a few days before. This was vastly faster.

There's still development work to be done. I think the electric motors need to do more work from the word go, to hit harder and faster, and there needs to be more of a handover to the internal combustion engine as they tail off. That was the single thing I loved most about the Porsche 918 Spyder. At the moment, it feels too much like a CVT – the response isn't quite quick enough and the drive not direct enough, so revs and speed don't quite correspond. Although it defaults to direct drive, a pull of the paddle or simple press of the throttle opens the HydraCoup and gives the system control. It often chooses to slip the clutch a little, which feels CVT-ish and it's that disconnect between noise and speed that disguises the rate of progress. Which, when you have 1,479bhp at work, is alarming.

But the basics are there, and during the day laptops were occasionally plugged in and settings altered so I could try it with more electric influence low down, different throttle response. For a day I got to play at being a Koenigsegg development driver, and days don't get much cooler than that, do they?

So some tuning is needed, but the mechanical package is complete. That's an achievement in itself, leaving aside the fact it's refined and comfortable enough to drive every day. The concept works, the detail will be made to work. Because this is Koenigsegg, and they do hypercars their own way here.

PRICE $1.9 MILLION (APPROX) **0-60** 2.8 SECONDS **TOP SPEED** > 250MPH **POWER** 1,479BHP
DID YOU KNOW? THE 'G' IN REGERA IS A HARD G, SO IT'S 'RE-GERA', NOT 'RE-JERA'

K

KOENIGSEGG JESKO

Is there no limit to what these dudes can do? This could be the car that cracks 300mph...

Just when you thought the Hennessey Venom F5 or Bugatti Chiron was on course to top 300mph first, Koenigsegg once again reminds us that nobody does speed like the Swedes. OK, they haven't cracked it yet, but according to Christian his all-new Jesko hypercar is capable of over 300mph in simulations (the current production record-holder, the Agera RS, hit an average of 277mph in 2017), albeit in a lower downforce set-up than you see here. They would still need to find somewhere to do it, someone mad enough to drive it and a tyre manufacturer to back an attempt but the science says it's possible.

Before the details, the name. Jesko is Christian's father, the man who helped him set up a supercar company when he was a skint 22-year old with a dream, and has supported him every step of the way. Now 80 years old, this is Christian's way of thanking him. It certainly beats chocolates and a card. Better still, the name was kept a secret from Jesko until the car's unveil at the Geneva show. Christian even had his PR team work up a fake press release to placate his dad, who was desperate to know all the details. Sounds like our kind of guy.

Let's start with the engine, a heavily modified version of the Agera's 5.0-litre twin-turbo V8, now with a flat-plane crank shaft that's 5kg lighter than the old 90 degree one, which allows it to rev to 8,500rpm and "changes the exhaust note quite a bit," says Christian, modestly. Active rubber engine mounts from the Regera (the Agera RS engine was solid mounted) mean the extra vibrations from the flat crank are absorbed, while the two equally large turbos are supplemented by a 20-litre carbon tank (topped up by a small electric compressor) that fires jets of air into the turbos at 20 bar, to help them spool up and reduce lag.

The result is 1,262bhp running on 95 octane unleaded, and 1,578bhp and 1106lb ft of torque if you fill it with E85 biofuel. You see, going green has its advantages.

Problem is, you need a mighty gearbox to cope with that sort of twist, and you can't buy Bugatti's DSG off the shelf. So Koenigsegg just shrugged and built its own, from scratch, except it's even smarter, smaller and, at 90kg, a lot lighter than the Chiron's. Dubbed the Light Speed Gearbox, it's a 9-speed multi-clutch transmission. A bit like a bike that has three big cogs at the front and seven at the back to make 21 possible ratios, here there's two sets of three, with six clutches that can select any

"EACH WHEEL IS HAND-MADE, IN-HOUSE, AND TAKES 40 HOURS TO FINISH. IT PROBABLY ALSO EXPLAINS WHY THEY COST $65,000 FOR A SET"

combination at any time. As a result you can jump from one gear to any other without going through the ratios between.

Pull the two-stage paddle half way and you'll swap down one gear (shifts take 20 to 30 millseconds), pull it all the way and it'll jump to the gear that offers the best acceleration at that time. Because, y'know, when you're driving a Koenigsegg you need all the help you can get with overtakes. Koenigsegg's evocative name for the system is UPOD – Ultimate Power on Demand.

Unlike the Agera, which only had one at the back, the Jesko also gets a Triplex damper at the front (a socking great horizontal damper to prevent the car squatting under acceleration at the rear, and to keep it level under extreme downforce at the front) to complement the more traditional Ohlins dampers. The carbon tub is now 40mm longer and 22mm higher than the Agera to create a bit more space inside, rear-wheel steering has been added and it wears Koenisegg's lightest ever carbon fibre wheels – 21-inch and 7.7kg at the rear, 20-inch and 5.9kg at the front – fitted with Michelin Pilot Sport Cup 2s as standard and optional Cup 2 Rs. Each wheel is hand-made, in-house, and takes 40 hours to finish… probably why they cost $65,000 for a set.

What next? Oh yes, downforce. It has some. Quite a lot actually. Thanks to that enormous front splitter and boomerang shaped, tilting rear wing, around 800kg of it at 155mph, 1,000kg at 171mph and 1,400kg at its undisclosed top speed. That's around 30 per cent more than the One:1, previously Koenigsegg's highest downforce model. The whole car weighs a little over 1,400kg so no, it can't drive on the ceiling - if it could you know Koenigsegg would give it a good go. The lower downforce version, that's the one with 300mph potential, will still produce up to 500kg of downforce, we're told.

And a Jesko driver won't be wanting for luxury. For maximum peacock mode the front bonnet, doors and rear clamshell can all be opened on hydraulic struts at the touch of a button, there's climate control, an infotainment system with Apple CarPlay, USB sockets and wireless charging for your phone. New for the Jesko is a screen attached to the wheel that displays all relevant information, but when rotated the digital dial stays upright – much like the wheel centre caps on a Rolls Royce. That's not the only Koenigsegg quirk, either, an optional analogue G-Force meter perches on top of the dash, behind the wheel.

Only 125 Jeskos will be built, at a rate of around 40 to 50 a year, so compared to the 25 Agera RS and 80 Regeras sold, that's progress. But with prices starting at just under $3m plus local taxes, it's up there with the McLaren Speedtail and Aston Valkyrie for inaccessibility. And yet, this is a company expanding its horizons… There will be a new car next year: a joint venture with electric car specialists NEVS. A hybrid built in larger numbers (think 100s) at a lower price (around $1m). What form that car will take we'll have to wait and see, but we're told to expect something entirely different. We can't wait to find out.

PRICE £2.5 MILLION **0-60** NOT LONG **TOP SPEED** 300MPH (EST) **POWER** 1,578BHP
DID YOU KNOW? EACH CARBON WHEEL TAKES 40 HOURS TO PRODUCE. JUST DON'T KERB IT

"THE LAMBORGHINI AVENTADOR IS NOT A CAR IN NEED OF EXTRA DRAMA, BUT IN THE SVJ SANT'AGATA HAS SOMEHOW FOUND SOME"

LAMBORGHINI
AVENTADOR SVJ

More aero and even more power turn this into one of the most extrovert Lambos ever made

The request from the *TopGear* mothership was to go north. We're on the SS36, heading towards the Swiss border and the Passo dello Spluga – or Splügen Pass, if you prefer – an Alpine road that unfurls itself in spectacular fashion at an elevation of almost 7000ft and whose Google SEO takes you direct to a dangerous roads website.

Danger? I'll give you danger. Danger is listening to the differential whine on a £360,000 Lamborghini on full lock in first gear on a road so twisty it seems to be eating itself while the fog and rain battle each other for supremacy in the 'who's more elemental?' weather stakes. And, yes, that's definitely snow out there so we'd better factor that in as well, and crank the demisting up to 11 while we're at it. The SVJ's A-pillars, meanwhile, are so thick they almost go to Z.

There's so little forward visibility (rear visibility on the Aventador is a meaningless concept regardless of the weather) that my passenger, Mr Charlie Turner, has resorted to giving me pace notes. It would be easier to thread the Lamborghini through the eye of a needle than drive it up here. Meanwhile *TG's* indefatigable Rowan Horncastle follows behind in our Fiat 500L hire car, maintaining a Loeb-like pace compared to mine. Whatever. The murkiness means that we have no idea how steep the drops are. Be grateful for small mercies.

The Lamborghini Aventador is not a car in need of extra drama, but in the SVJ Sant'Agata has somehow found some (maybe there's an *estroverso dipartimento* tucked round the back). Despite having driven and conquered a few over the years – including on a PCOTY around Clermont Ferrand in 2012 – the moment you first climb aboard an Aventador sends every childhood memory you have of a big, hirsute, mid-engined Italian supercar galloping straight into your cerebral cortex. Isn't this exactly how it should be? Scary, stupid, sensational. The doors scythe up. The sills are wide and awkward. The driving position, although much better than it used to be, still takes some getting used to. The transmission makes its way past your elbows in a tunnel that's about as wide as the one that burrows under the River Thames in Rotherhithe. The windscreen is vast, and sweeps down towards a nose whose extremities you can't see. As for the view behind… well, at least there's a reversing camera now, although if you're like me you still won't trust what you can't see with your own eyes.

Similarly, your first few miles in the SVJ will be as faltering as Bambi's first steps. There is so much to take in, and you don't uncork 759bhp until you know how much and what sort of fizz there is. From past experience, I'm not certain there's a road in Europe long enough to let the Aventador properly pop its cork, never mind that the SVJ now redlines at 8700rpm and is torquier at the top end. Test drives were conducted on the circuit at Estoril, where the car was reportedly doing 170mph at the end of the pit straight. Sheesh. Not to mention the new production car lap record set at some track in Germany everyone's always banging on about (6.44.97). Yes, Lamborghini has thrown everything at the SVJ. And some more besides.

Which makes the edict from the office to go north to the Alpine snow line adventurous to say the least. That route also involves a lot of significant tunnel action, which is a great way to explore the full bandwidth of the SVJ's 7.1 surround sound. Bring the noise, as Public Enemy once instructed us.

But first, the rush hour. That might sound like hell on earth, but even this elastic ebb and flow is somehow special in a car like this. It's deliberately overcooked inside, much like the exterior, but mostly works surprisingly well despite some notable idiosyncrasies. The graphics on the main instrument display – including a graphic for the active aero – are too bright, and the MMI is ancient Audi. There's nowhere to stash your phone, so you rest it on the central screen where it heats up nicely and obscures the display. But at least it's next to the electric window switches, because that's the obvious place to put them. And you push to lower the windows rather than pull. The single-shell carbon fibre seats are surprisingly comfortable, though.

What is SVJ? Super Veloce Jota, which basically means really f**king fast. Apparently Jota also references appendix J of the FIA rule book, back when the Miura was being homologated for racing, but imagine using a rule book for inspiration…

So to the engine. It is part of a blood-line back to the Miura, but now has titanium inlet valves, its innards operate with reduced friction, and there's a lighter flywheel for even sharper throttle response. The SVJ's ultimate torque figure, 531lb ft, is reached at 6700rpm, 1250rpm higher than on the lazy old SV. The torque curve is flatter, too. It hardly needs pointing out that this engine is normally aspirated Lamborghini pretty much now casting itself as King Canute in an effort to hold back the hybrid tide. Though for how much longer who knows.

The SVJ's aero package is the bigger deal, and more relevant to the car's repurposing as the apogee of track-going Aventador (although by Lambo's calculations only 45 of the 900 lucky sods who'll end up owning one will ever venture on a track). Better to think of this as a tech showcase. Second generation 'ALA' – Aerodinamica Lamborghini Attiva – gives the SVJ 40 per cent more downforce than the Aventador S, pushing turbulent air beneath that huge rear wing, stalling it to reduce downforce and drag, but also separating the airflow left to right. In other words, the SVJ has more downforce on the inside of a corner, which helps sharpen turn-in and means you need less lock in the entry phase, which in turn will also enhance your exit speed. There's an active rear axle, too, which is less intrusive than the one on Ferrari's 812 Superfast. Giant carbon ceramic brakes brilliantly erase all that momentum when you're in that phase.

I drove a prototype SV around the Nürburgring a few years ago, and had zero quibbles with its steering or turn-in. Can't imagine what the J must feel like there, especially if it's wearing the newly available Pirelli P Zero Trofeo rubber. I know how it sounds, though. Italy has approximately 560 miles of tunnels, and introducing the SVJ to them is to broker a meeting between one engineering masterpiece and another. Giving a Lamborghini V12 the berries in a long Italian tunnel is bucket list stuff, and you don't even need to go particularly fast to unleash a noise few road cars in history can match. From 3000rpm, the sound intensifies and swells through a baritone whose dynamics are perfectly attuned to the movement of your right foot.

Then the note hardens and sharpens in frequency, the linearity of response just untouchable. Even the car's weak link – the single-clutch ISR (independent shifting rods) gearbox – doesn't seem so bad, although whatever finesse you've acquired after a hundred miles or so goes out the window on a quick, sustained blat through the gears. There's more head-banging than the front row of a Slipknot gig. Lambo says the parameters on the four drive modes on the Anima set-up have been tweaked for greater engagement and precision. The SVJ's exhaust also emits a lick of blue flame, and up- and downshifts are accompanied by a variety of pops, crackles and bangs; they just can't help themselves. And neither can the driver.

The SVJ weighs 50kg less than the SV, for a dry weight of 1525kg. It'll hit 62mph in 2.8 seconds, 124mph in 8.6, and its top speed is 217mph. These are the facts. But as the Aventador heads into its twilight years, this is a car that's so much bigger than all the numbers that surround it. It's the greatest, the loudest, the baddest, the archetypal supercar. Nothing else generates the monumental sense of occasion that the Aventador SVJ does.

PRICE £356,000 0-60 2.8 SECONDS TOP SPEED > 217MPH POWER 759BHP

DID YOU KNOW? THE SVJ IS STILL THE FASTEST PRODUCTION CAR AROUND THE NORDSCHLEIFE, IF THAT MATTERS

"THE SVJ'S EXHAUST EMITS A LICK OF
BLUE FLAME, AND UP- AND DOWNSHIFTS
ARE ACCOMPANIED BY A VARIETY OF POPS,
CRACKLES AND BANGS"

LAMBORGHINI ASTERION

Lost in the mists of the recent past, this hybrid GT is an intriguing concept car

Two things immediately strike you about the Asterion. Firstly, it's a world away from the wilfully mad conceptual eye candy that Lamborghini has thrilled us with in the past. Secondly, it's a plug-in hybrid. This is either sacrilege or the only way forward, depending on your view. A mid-engined two-seater coupe measuring 4.7m long, it uses an adapted Aventador carbon fibre monocoque, mostly in the lower section, with a different roof structure, and its wheelbase has been stretched to create more interior space. It borrows the Huracan's stunning 5.2-litre V10, which is hooked up to a blistering dual-clutch seven-speed rear transaxle auto 'box. But it's also a parallel hybrid, with an electric motor bolted onto the transaxle that incorporates a starter motor and generator. Two other electric motors are located on the front axle. Between them, they contribute an additional chunk of energy worth 220kW, equivalent to almost 300bhp. Like the Porsche 918, the Asterion uses the motors on the front axle to deliver four-wheel drive, as well as torque vectoring. There's no mechanical connection between the front and rear axles. The batteries live in the central tunnel where you'd normally find a propshaft. This benefits both safety and the car's centre of gravity, Lamborghini claims. Electric power can also be used to fill in gaps in the engine's torque curve. All this techy cleverness results in an unavoidable porkiness. In all, the electrification process adds 280kg to the Asterion's overall weight. That's a lot of battery cells, cooling gubbins, and control electronics. The Asterion's total power output is a thumping 907bhp. It'll do 185mph all-out, and accelerate to 62mph in just over three seconds, while coughing out 98g/km of CO2s. A real-world range of 30 miles on pure electric power is a hell of a party trick. Finally, a claimed overall combined average of 282mpg sounds like silly talk. "You can imagine the discussions we had,' Lamborghini's R&D boss Maurizio Reggiani says. 'We are Lamborghini, we must be the best in terms of performance and handling…" In the end, we decided this concept was the right solution for a technological demonstrator. This is a car you can drive in cities in pure-electric mode, but also a car whose thermodynamic engine delivers the same emotion as a pure Lamborghini."

PRICE N/A **0-60** 3.0 SECONDS **TOP SPEED** > 185MPH **POWER** 910BHP

DID YOU KNOW? ASTERION WAS THE NAME OF A MINOTAUR. SO, THAT'S ALMOST A BULL. NAMING CONVENTION UPHELD!

"THE ASTERION IS A PLUG-IN HYBRID, WHICH IS EITHER SACRILEGE OR THE ONLY WAY FORWARD DEPENDING ON YOUR POINT OF VIEW"

· ·

LAMBORGHINI
TERZO
MILLENNIO

Nano-technology and self-healing body panels
vault the idea of the hypercar into the future

In an automotive landscape littered with radical concept cars and vapourware that'll never see the light of day, it would be easy to dismiss the Lamborghini Terzo Millennio as an irrelevant flight of fancy. The fact that the specification includes a yet-to-be-invented supercapacitor, energy storage in the carbon fibre through the use of nanotechnology, self-healing bodywork and propulsion by in-wheel motors doesn't help make it feel any more realistic. But dig below the headlines and there's method in the madness.

Lamborghini has a problem. The future, whichever way you look at it, is going to be electrified, and, for a supercar manufacturer whose heritage lies in vocal V12s, there's work to do to preserve the brand for the next generation. While the arrival of the Urus has helped give the V10 and V12 a stay of execution (it's been confirmed that both will live on in hybrid form in the Huracán and Aventador replacements), the future vision for Lamborghini needs to be defined for the brand to remain relevant in an EV world.

Seeking this definition, TG headed to Lambo HQ for exclusive access to the Terzo Millennio and the team who commissioned it. While the project is being driven out of Lamborghini's home in Sant'Agata, the crew has enlisted the help of some people with seriously large foreheads to help think beyond the current understanding of automotive performance. Rather than take centre stage at a motor show, the car was revealed at MIT (Massachusetts Institute of Technology) on 6th November 2017, and the relationship with MIT's department of oversized crania is at the core of some of the more radical thinking.

We head deep into the bowels of Centro Stile, Lamborghini's Area 51. The first thing that strikes as you approach the Terzo is its proportions. The super-aggressive cab-forward stance, which tapers towards the rear, has a pugnacity that would give a Ford GT an inferiority complex. Then it's the height, or lack of it, that intrigues. Clearly, the ridiculous track-focused ride height and arch-cramming tyres help the Terzo's stance, but it looks barely possible to fit two full-sized people in there.

As you continue to circle it, trying to absorb those hypercar design staples – flying buttresses, the tapered keel, a clever use of negative space – you notice there's also some familiarity in certain areas that make it a realistic vision of a future generation of Lamborghini. If a key part of the brief was to create a car to occupy the bedroom walls of hypercar fans, as the Countach

and Aventador did before, then it's job done. You'll find evidence of this on Mitja Borkert's [Lambo's head of design] Instagram account: in images of it being deposited outside a local Bologna school and being mobbed by enthusiastic kids.

"I brought the car back here and asked if we could do a lap around Sant'Agata. I wanted to photograph it in front of cool places," says Borkert. "One of the most enjoyable moments ever in my career was when we brought it out in front of the school. All the kids were freaking out… it was super."

But this car's role is about more than shock and awe, it's a statement of intent to be a tech leader. Given we're about to deep dive into nanotechnology, we need an articulate guide. Fortunately, Lamborghini chief technical officer Maurizio Reggiani is on hand. "The project started from a discussion about electrification in Lamborghini, if Lamborghini could have an electric car. The specification was clear: we needed to be able to reach 300km/h, but also complete three laps of the Nordschleife. That means that you need not only a peak of power, but also an extensive range of high power. Why three laps? Because if you really made three hot laps of the Nordschleife, you'd need to replace the tyres anyway," he says.

"We started to look at what's available on the market in terms of batteries, in terms of single cells, in terms of electric engines… and we discovered there was nothing able to fulfil our wishes.

"So we started to discuss internally, if we had a project starting from scratch, a totally clean sheet of paper, was it possible to have a huge quantity of batteries without penalising the weight or packaging of the car? To restart our way of thinking, we decided to head back to the laboratory, because in the laboratory you are not contaminated by the normal development process."

Current trends see a new EV hypercar arriving every few months that promises to propel its millionaire occupant from 0-60mph faster than the internet eye candy of the previous creation. Look into the spec, and they're all based around the same basic "skateboard" layout, a development of the technology as we understand it today, deployed in everything from the Tesla Model 3 to the Aspark Owl. Technology that Reggiani describes as "evolutionary, not revolutionary". The Terzo is designed to leapfrog the current thinking in all aspects. So, with no traditional battery pack, how and where do you store the energy?

The somewhat technically challenging answer is to use the

bodywork. By working with MIT, Lamborghini is exploring ways of using nanotechnology to thread millions of copper anodes and cathodes into the carbon weave, turning every single body panel into part of the battery system. The three-year project with MIT is focused on developing this radical new technology. According to Reggiani, MIT has already tested it successfully, so the task over the remaining 18 months of the deal is to deliver a solution to put it into production. "The lab at MIT already proved it can work on a small scale," Reggiani claims. "The big job now is in what way we can industrialise it. In research, you have to be flexible, to alter the scope of the goal. It's research and innovation, not development."

While it sounds fanciful, if MIT can deliver it, the technology would be transformational. And the wizardry doesn't stop there. The panels will also have self-healing properties – an idea in development in the aerospace industry, where a combination of nanotechnology and polymer chemistry actively repairs any small structural damage. Harnessing the body-panel energy and delivering the target performance will require another huge leap forward in technology. Again, Reggiani's team is working with MIT to develop a supercapacitor fit for purpose. The main advantages of supercapacitors compared with standard batteries is their ability to store up to 100 times more energy, their capacity to accept and deliver charge much faster and to tolerate many more charge and discharge cycles. In short, they're lighter, more energy-dense and would meet the criteria set out for the Terzo Millennio's three-lap max-attack assault on the 'Ring. But use of the technology at this scale is in its infancy in the automotive world, something Reggiani is keen to solve.

"We have this guy that has a brain 10 times bigger than my brain. He's looking into what exists today in the market and has discovered something exceptional. To give an impression, what we have found with MIT is an element that is able to deliver 4.5V, this means you can have three times more peak energy [than current options] that you can use in every condition," says Reggiani with a glint in his eye. "I'm confident that this will be possible by the end of this project."

If you're tackling battery technology and weight distribution issues with nanotechnology circuitry, current drivetrain technology must look positively arcane. The Terzo team's

solution was to allow each of the wheels to be driven by an in-wheel motor, allowing for individual torque-vectoring and fly-by-wire steering, braking and acceleration. And there's an autonomy play too... but with a unique Lamborghini flavour.

Reggiani: "You buy a Lamborghini for yourself. I cannot imagine somebody that buys a Lamborghini leaves a computer to drive the car. What we want to do in a car like this is to create a kind of human or virtual interface that is able to talk with you, to give to you feedback about what you can achieve with the car, how far you are from best performance, and what you need to do in order to improve – a kind of autonomous supporter. This is our idea of autonomous driving."

So while others are concentrating on autonomy to get you home from the pub after a night out, Lambo's virtual assistant will be able to overlay your pitiful efforts around a track with the absolutely optimal lap, then dial up the correct level of assistance to help you find your inner driving god.

While this future-gazing technology pushes every element of our current understanding, possibly the biggest challenge for any current supercar manufacturer grappling with the EV future is how to deliver a soundtrack worthy of the brand with precisely zero cylinders and no exhaust. The Terzo Millennio tackles this head-on. Not content with working on finessing the shaping of the e-motor's drive gears to deliver a soundtrack, the team is currently in the process of signing another soon-to-be announced deal to examine how to harness the airflow across the bodywork, using the form of the Terzo like a musical instrument. To heighten the sound and optimise the aerodynamics, the two air-separator planes on the side of the fuselage move subject to requirements.

As with most of the Terzo Millennio, the ideas challenge conventional thinking so dramatically it's easy to deride them as fiction. But every giant leap in automotive technology has come from radical thinking. As Reggiani says, "The credibility of Lamborghini is to look forward, not backward."

The Terzo Millennio looks a very long way down the road and, by doing so, and by challenging every aspect of current EV thinking, Lamborghini is providing a fascinating insight into the future extremes of EV performance. If these guys can deliver it, the future of the supercar is in safe hands.

PRICE N/A 0-60 N/A TOP SPEED N/A POWER N/A
DID YOU KNOW? APPARENTLY, THE TERZO MILLENNIO HAS 'SELF-HEALING BODYWORK'. WOLVERINE? IS THAT YOU?

LAMBORGHINI HURACAN PERFORMANTE

This track-focused model is also insanely clever

This is the harder, faster, stickier and more track-focused version of Lambo's baby supercar designed to monster race tracks, but retain a whiff of usability on public roads. The engine is still a naturally-aspirated 5.2-litre V10 screamer, but with power and torque topped up by 30bhp and 30lb ft for 631bhp and 443lb ft – making this Lambo's most powerful V10 to date. Changes include titanium valves and a freer-flowing exhaust with higher-mounted pipes. Let the V10 and quicker shifting seven-speed dual-clutch 'box do their party piece and 0-62mph takes 2.9 seconds, 0-124mph takes 8.9 seconds and despite the extra downforce, top speed is still north of 200mph. Significantly, the Performante also debuts the Aerodinamica Lamborghini Attiva (ALA) system – active aero. Jutting front spoiler and peacocking rear wing are present and correct, but both feature high and low downforce modes and, at the rear, the ability to vector downforce from one side to the other, according to your cornering requirements. How? A motor implanted in the front spoiler actuates two flaps. With ALA off they remain closed, delivering maximum downforce at the front axle. With ALA active they can open, reducing drag and underbody pressure. Meanwhile, the forged carbon fibre wing and two upright supports are actually hollow. Airboxes at the base of these uprights, also with motorised flaps, are fed by air rushing over the engine cover. Flaps closed and the rear wing acts as you'd expect, producing maximum downforce (750 per cent more than a normal Huracán at the rear axle). Flaps open and air rushes into the spoiler and out through a narrow channel on its lower surface, stalling the airflow and dramatically reducing drag and therefore downforce. One side can be open while the other is shut, increasing downforce only on the inside rear wheel during cornering and helping to rotate the car in. Under hard braking you can have maximum downforce, while on the straights the wing effectively disappears. By tuning the spring rates and anti-roll bars, vertical stiffness is up 10 per cent, while roll stiffness is up by 15 per cent. The Performante is louder and lairier, in the great Lambo tradition, but also easier to use.

PRICE £215,000 **0-60** 2.9 SECONDS
TOP SPEED 207MPH **POWER** 631BHP

LAMBORGHINI HURACAN EVO

In becoming the Evo, Sant'Agata's smallest car imports some radical technology

Rarely has a fast car been so easy to drive while keeping the driver front and centre of the action. The Evo overhaul has its foundations in four key areas: vehicle dynamics, engine, design (and aerodynamics), and interior HMI. So that nat asp V10 now produces 631bhp at 8000rpm, 442lb ft of torque at 6500rpm, for a power-to-weight ratio of 451bhp per tonne, good for a top speed of 201mph, and zero to 62mph in 2.9 seconds. Lamborghini claims seven times the aero efficiency of the outgoing car, thanks to a new front spoiler, diffuser and air curtain, new rear diffuser, cleaner underbody, repositioned exhaust (now with titanium intake valves), and ducktail spoiler. It's practically a Performante, minus the active aero. More significantly, the Huracán Evo represents a philosophical step-change by introducing Lamborghini Dinamica Veicolo Integrata (LDVI), a central super computer that corrals everything the Evo's chassis and powertrain has got while adding a predictive element. A set of accelerators and gyroscope sensors positioned at the heart of the car's centre of gravity provide real-time monitoring of lateral, longitudinal and vertical loads, as well as body roll, pitch and yaw. The suspension's magnetic damping is also part of the equation, as is the traction control, the Evo's all-wheel drive, torque vectoring, Lamborghini's dynamic steering, and the active rear axle. Three driving modes are available: Strada, shoutier Sport, and sharper track-day Pirelli-shredding Corsa. Sport also contains what to all intents and purposes is a drift mode, and the Huracán Evo lets you exit corners like a pro, before riding out the kerbs and maximising traction. There's almost zero understeer, incredibly exact turn-in, and in fast, sweeping corners the algorithmic interventions are mercifully unobtrusive. The combination of slick electronics and the car's enhanced aero properties combine to substantially broaden the Huracán's spectrum of possibilities (a nod here to Pirelli's super sticky P Zero Corsa rubber). The V10 is still cool, the old-school heartbeat of an increasingly technofied Lamborghini experience.

PRICE £206,000 0-60 2.9 SECONDS TOP SPEED 201MPH POWER 631BHP
DID YOU KNOW? THE EVO WAS NAMED IN HONOUR OF THE MITSUBISHI RALLY-SPEC FOUR-DOOR. THIS MIGHT BE A LIE

LAMBORGHINI CENTENARIO

Our kind of birthday present... created to commemorate the company's founder

It's 6am, and the mercury is already heading rapidly north at Nardò, VW Group's top-secret test facility on the heel of Italy. After multiple security checks of increasing ferocity, we're finally into the inner sanctum and staring at the reason for all the secrecy: the Lamborghini Centenario. Hunkered down on the tarmac, it's a monument to carbon-fibre precision that would rival any modernist sculpture on its visual merits. Except, in this case, your appreciation of its stunning lines are disturbed by thoughts of its brutish potential.

The Centenario is Lamborghini's posthumous birthday present to its legendary founder Ferruccio Lamborghini. But it represents more than a nod to the old man – it's the most recent in a chain of jaw-dropping motor-show unicorns that started with the Reventón, then punctuated the last decade with highlights including the Aventador J, Sesto Elemento, Estoque and Veneno. More poignantly, it was the last car presented by Stephan Winkelmann at the Geneva show, following the announcement of his sudden departure to quattro GmbH (and then on to Bugatti) and the appointment of former Ferrari F1 team principal Stefano Domenicali in his place. Sticking to the brief of its forebears, the Centenario is strictly limited production, and only 40 will be made: 20 coupes and 20 roadsters.

Nardò is where the VW Group comes when it wants to develop something anti-socially, intergalactically fast. It's where the team comes to cruise up to and through the 200mph zone, and with the Centenario's vmax in excess of 217mph, today will not be a slow day. Best concentrate, then, and avoid erasing five per cent of the model from existence.

The Centenario is powered by a mighty 6.5-litre V12, which idles at 850rpm and red-lines at 8,600rpm; it produces 760bhp (20bhp more than the Aventador SV, not a car you would ever accuse of lacking punch) and 507 torques. It'll smash to 62mph in 2.8 seconds and, if you're brave enough (and have enough air left in your lungs after the shouting) will rocket to 186mph in 23.5 seconds. Harnessing all the madness and applying it to the road are bespoke Pirelli P Zero Corsas: 255/30 ZR20 on the front and 355/25 ZR21 on the rear, poor things. At the front, the more aggressive twin-deck splitter generates massive downforce and channels the air flow over the car and down the sides via the sideblades, but it's at the rear where the dark art of air flow is let

"THE CENTENARIO IS LAMBORGHINI'S POSTHUMOUS BIRTHDAY PRESENT TO THE COMPANY'S FOUNDER, FERRUCCIO. IT'S A STRICTLY LIMITED SERIES UNICORN"

off the leash. The Centenario features one of the largest diffusers this side of a Le Mans racer; combine that with the removal of much of the bodywork behind the rear wheels and an active rear wing which extends 150mm, and you get 227kg of downforce at 174mph.

The biggest hardware news is that the Centenario is the first Lamborghini to employ rear-wheel steering, a system that provides increased manoeuvrability at speeds below 45mph and increased stability at higher speeds, in effect shortening and lengthening the wheelbase by 1,200mm depending on attack speed. Despite all this added technology, the Centenario weighs in at 1,520kg, 55kg lighter than an Aventador. While the carbon-fibre obsession runs deep, it's the materials science in conjunction with the aerodynamic and tech developments that deliver the numbers. I'm part of an exceedingly small group that's been invited by Lamborghini's head of R&D, Maurizio Reggiani, to experience and give feedback on the whole package. "Today you work for Lamborghini," I'm told.

After a safety briefing on the four-mile ribbon of tarmac that forms the handling circuit in the centre of Nardò, we're led out to four Aventadors of various potency. At the back of the queue lies the standard white Aventador coupe, next in line is an Aventador SV which is fitted with the first iteration of the rear-wheel-steer system and is the car that persuaded the board that the tech was worth pursuing. In front of that is the Centenario and then the lead car, another SV driven by Lamborghini test driver Mario Fasanetto.

I opt to build up my tolerance to the insanity and start with the Aventador, immediately regretting my decision as the others disappear up the road while I'm left doing all I can to keep them in sight. After the first four-lap stint, I'm still struggling to process the track layout, the fact that the other three cars made the Aventador look relatively ordinary, and seriously questioning my ability. It is clearly coffee time.

Recaffeinated, I grab the SV with the prototype rear-wheel steering and am relieved to find myself keeping pace with the Centenario. The difference isn't just the additional 49bhp but the stability and responsiveness of the car. Where the Aventador felt large and brutal, the SV feels predictable and nimble. It's a genuinely eye-opening comparison, and the laps pass with addictive repetition.

After more coffee, I finally lower myself into the familiar, yet subtly different surroundings of the Centenario's cockpit. With only 40 being made, the lucky owners are able to be more demanding regarding the personalisation of their slice of Lamborghini history, and the carbon-fibre-clad interior of our

car (no. 0) is exquisitely executed. It's hard to know what a £1.7m interior should be like, but this feels close, helped in no small part by the bespoke 10.1-inch portrait screen which occupies the centre console and features an all-new infotainment system Lamborghini describes as its take on the connected car. It comes with suitably angular graphics and features the usual suspects (media, nav, car set-up) plus telemetry that logs your lap times, gear selection, throttle inputs and braking points – all of which will be reviewed by the development team and its boss, Maurizio Reggiani, following the laps. No pressure, then.

I lift the fighter-jet safety flap (something I never grow tired of) to reveal the start/stop button, turn the engine, and the familiar V12 barks into life. But this one has a far harsher, deeper bass tone which suggests its potency and builds as I head down the straight after Mario.

Where the SV was a leap forward over the "standard" Aventador, the Centenario moves the needle a lot further and represents a more complete package. In full-fat Corsa mode, on the first flying lap of the session I'm seeing 172mph at the 100m braking point for Turn 1. BRAKE, drop a gear and let the aero work its magic through the long left-hander, which tightens to a super-late apex. After which you need to shed a lot of speed and another three gears. The Centenario remains wonderfully stable throughout the high-speed transition as the balance of the front and rear aero weaves its magic, while the rear wing and magnetorheological dampers constantly adjust to optimise the car's attitude. It's hugely confidence-inspiring and totally addictive. As the Centenario devours the 6.2km course it's constantly communicating: dive too deep into one of the tighter corners, and it will understeer, but let it flow, and the way it batters entry, apex and exit makes you grin… broadly.

In Sport, the Centenario becomes a lot less focused on obliterating lap records and a LOT more amusing. Want to slide your £1.7m hypercar? This is the mode for you. As the laps accumulate, you learn to trust the Centenario in a way that feels unnatural in such a rare and precious thing. You delve deeper into its aero, and it rewards each committed approach with scintillating speed. Where the Aventador was mildly dismissive of your efforts, the Centenario keeps pushing you to go deeper, work harder and help it bully physics. Changes from the remapped gearbox are rifle-bolt fast but come without the SV's ferocity, which keeps the car more stable as it hunts down its next target. The brakes are spectacular, but I'd have liked a firmer pedal with more feel. Lamborghini makes cars that exist at the furthest margins of acceptability and are all the better for it. Cars like the Centenario demand respect, and then reward it.

PRICE £1.7 MILLION **0-60** 2.8 SECONDS **TOP SPEED** > 217MPH **POWER** 760BHP

DID YOU KNOW? TOPGEAR DELIVERED THE CENTENARIO TO THE STAND AT THE GENEVA MOTOR SHOW. WELL DONE US.

LAMBORGHINI STERRATO

A jacked-up Huracan designed to monster dirt tracks might be the coolest car in years

The gun-slit-narrow rear view frames a huge Lamborghini-manufactured explosion of road detritus. The noise is a combination of dust, stones and rocks being thrown up by all four driven wheels and their impact in, around and under the car. The road hits a rise which we crest and the car goes light, we touch down and I hit the brakes, turn in and the car starts to rotate. Get back on the throttle and aim in one long sideways spray of dust and noise around the long left-hand turn.

While for most supercars this would be the wincingly embarrassing paragraph describing the moment when it all went badly wrong, I ran out of talent and ended up talking to our insurers… this is actually what the Lamborghini Sterrato was made for. So, rather than my co-pilot bracing for impact, he continues to offer encouragement: "This is nice. Gas, gas, gas."

Let's rewind a bit. We're in Nardò with Lamborghini's head of R&D, Maurizio Reggiani, to test drive this skunkworks project: the Huracán Sterrato. While there's no direct translation of 'sterrato' in English, the best approximation is 'dirt'. Yes, this is the Lamborghini Huracán Dirt. Like all the best projects, this one has been developed by a highly enthusiastic team in their own time, alongside other projects. While on first acquaintance your reaction may well be that they must have spent too much time in the sun, dig a little deeper and these guys could well be on to something. Just look at it. If, like me, you grew up on a diet of Tamiya and Kyosho catalogues and building/racing/jumping RC cars around your neighbourhood, the Sterrato is the full-size realisation of those days.

In a world all too often stymied by analysis and user clinics, it's refreshing that Lamborghini still has the passion to create something it thinks people will simply like. If we're honest, Lambo is the only carmaker provocative enough to develop a project like this and show it, just to see how its audience reacts. The technical recipe for the Sterrato is as follows. Take one Huracán Evo with naturally aspirated 5.2-litre V10 delivering 631bhp to the all-wheel-drive, rear-wheel steering drivetrain. Next, raise the ride height by 47mm (handily improving ground clearance, plus approach and departure angles) and retune the standard dampers. Increase the track by 30mm. Leave the wheel size the same at 20in, but fit special high-profile balloon tyres developed with Pirelli to work on-road and off. Move the front axle 30mm forward by redesigning the suspension geometry, ensuring the wheels clear the arches on compression, and revise the front wings to accommodate the 30mm shift.

Add a new steel front splitter, cladding around the wheelarches and side sills, and a reinforced undertray. To help the engine breathe and prevent the V10 from swallowing much dust, add aero flicks in front of the air intakes and fit a revised air filter. Finally, add roof rails, a light bar and two front spotlights and you have a Huracán Sterrato. Inside, it's familiar Huracán, but a titanium rollcage, new adjustable sports seats (comfy), four-point harnesses (fiddly) and aluminium flooring differentiate it.

What does the Sterrato feel like on the 3.8-mile tarmac handling track? The short answer is: comfy, rear-biased and amusing to drift. The more detailed analysis is that, thanks to the Sterrato's increased ride height and tyre sidewalls, the car pitches and squats on braking and acceleration, which is unnerving at first and feels slightly foreign in a modern Lambo. But the R&D team has spent a lot of time modifying the Lamborghini Dinamica Veicolo Integrata (LDVI) system to make the Sterrato more rear-biased. After a couple of laps, you begin to enjoy this new supple Lamborghini, turning in on the brakes to get the car sliding, and then powering out on oversteer. It's clearly not going to threaten the regular Evo's lap times, but its accessibility and the enjoyment you get from a completely different kind of Lambo experience is addictive. Moreover, it's far less compromised on track than you would have thought looking at it sat in the pitlane.

The Sterrato breaks the stereotype the supercar has backed itself into, and offers a broader capability and appeal. What Lamborghini has created here is a diverse, enjoyable and usable supercar for the battleground of the world we find ourselves in today. It looks crazy, but the Huracán Dirt really is something.

PRICE N/A **0-60** 3.0 SECONDS (APPROX) **TOP SPEED** 200MPH (APPROX) **POWER** 631BHP

DID YOU KNOW? LAMBO TEST DRIVER BOB WALLACE MADE A RALLY-READY LAMBO OUT OF THE JARAMA IN THE SEVENTIES

LOTUS EVIJA

Flush with cash courtesy of a new owner, the latest Lotus comeback is the craziest yet

The name. Before we get to the looks of Lotus's first hypercar, the power of Lotus's first hypercar, or why indeed Lotus thinks it can blindside Bugatti & Co., we really do have to deal with the name. What four-wheeled piece of unobtanium would dare show its angular face in Casino Square or a climate-controlled Abu Dhabi garage without a *Countdown* wordjumble branded on its backside?

You've deciphered Huayra, Rimac, and Koenigsegg. Now, limber up your jowls and stretch your lips around this: Evija. No, not "Ee-vee, yahh", like some *Made In Chelsea* mannequin guffawing over a Nissan Leaf. It's "Evv-eye-ah." Could have sworn she was one of the minor Stark children from *Game of Thrones*, but apparently it means 'the first in existence'. Roughly, it translates from Hebrew as 'living, to breathe'. And it begins with the letter E, which ought to keep the Lotus purists happy. Little else about the Evija will.

Welcome to the age of the electric hypercar, and Britain's first entrant. Whether this will be a long chapter in the history of very fast cars, or a curious cul-de-sac on the way to future forms of power and performance remains to be seen. But Lotus isn't waiting to see which way the tech wind blows and then cash in its Chinese-funded chips.

The latest corporate giant to tee up a Lotus moonshot and propel it into exotica's premier league is Geely, China's third-largest carmaker and backer of a resurgent Volvo, start-up carsharers Lynk & Co and the new London black cab company. And what does the portfolio have in common? A dive into electrification. From Polestar to hybrid cabs and now to rural Norfolk – where all 130 Evijas will be built – Geely wants to conquer the world with its belief in batteries. And it's fallen on Lotus to wade into battle against the upstart likes of Rimac, Pininfarina and, dare we say it, Tesla.

While you're still digesting the looks, I'll divulge what we possibly can about the Not-Oily-Bits. When word first filtered onto the internet about Lotus's mystical 'Type-130' project, the power figure being mooted was a nice, round 1,000bhp-plus. Four- figure horsepower has quickly gone from being the preserve of Bugatti and Koenigsegg to the minimum requirement for a newbie to be taken seriously.

And when it comes to electric hypercars, the numbers really

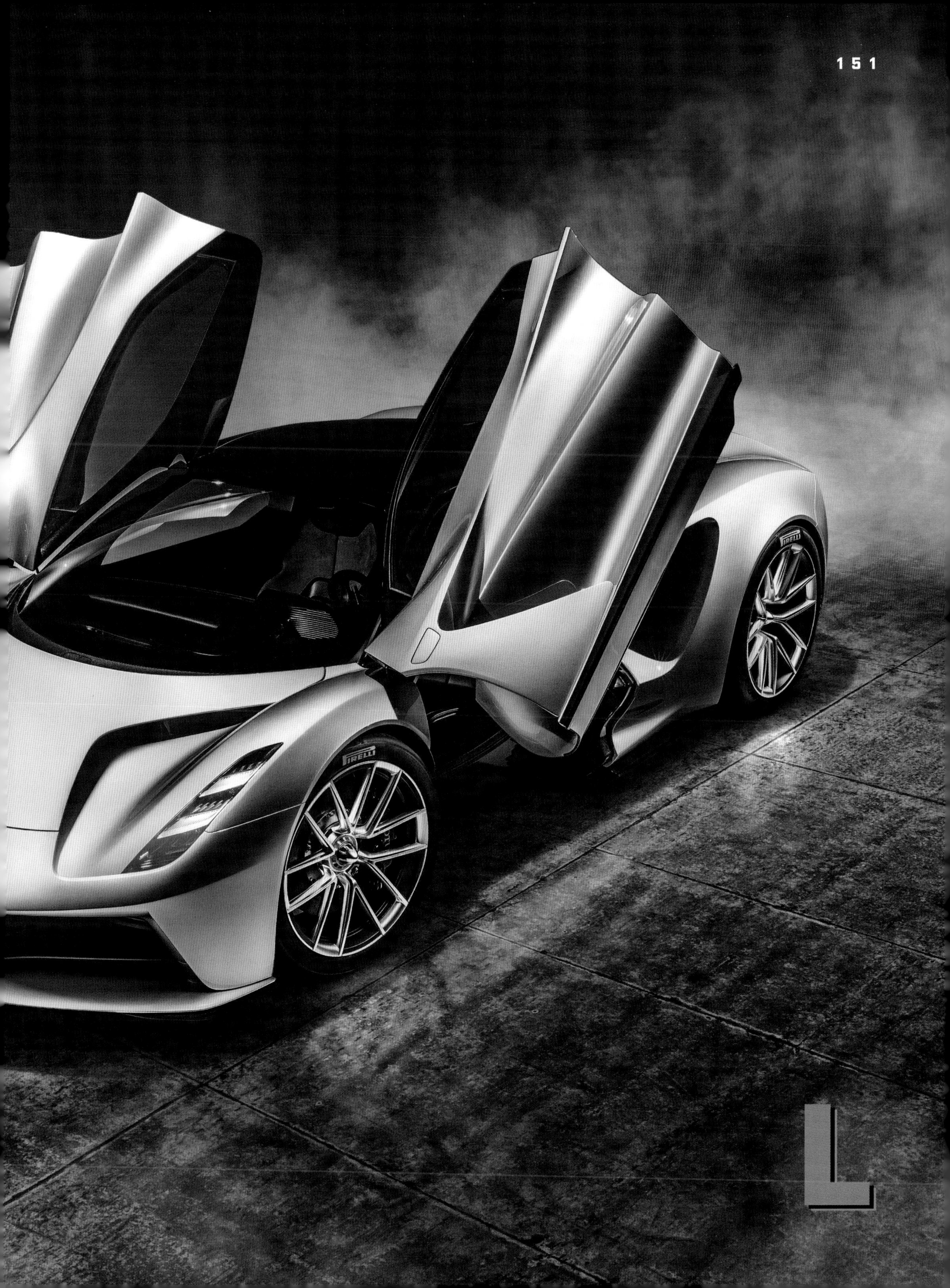

L

"WELCOME TO THE AGE OF THE ELECTRIC HYPERCAR AND BRITAIN'S FIRST ENTRANT. WHETHER THIS WILL BE A LONG CHAPTER IN THE HISTORY OF FAST CARS OR A CURIOUS CUL DE SAC REMAINS TO BE SEEN"

"LOTUS SAYS ITS TARGET IS TO BE THE WORLD'S MOST POWERFUL PRODUCTION CAR – 1972BHP. THE EVIJA ALSO PRODUCES DOUBLE THE AMOUNT OF TORQUE GENERATED BY THE MCLAREN SENNA" are bananas. The Rimac C_Two promises 1,888bhp. Pininfarina's Battista rounds that up to 1,900bhp. It's the end of car tuning as we know it. So long as all those microprocessors can handle the maths, you can pretty much name your power output. And to hell with what the tyres can manage.

Lotus says its target is to be the world's most powerful production car, with 2,000PS, or 1,972bhp. Torque, totalling some 1,700Nm (1,253lb ft – over double what a McLaren Senna churns out) will be vectored between all four wheels, because yep, it's four-wheel drive. Turns out that Lotus's first road-legal 4x4 isn't the long-mooted SUV after all.

These power boasts are nigh-on impossible to get your head around. And that's unusual for a Lotus, because instead of asking "How have you made it so light?", we're left wondering "Why is it so powerful?" It's a big philosophical switch. But Louis Kerr, the chief Evija platform engineer, insists Lotus isn't switching focus from weight-saving to power-craving. "Light weight and efficient, elegant engineering have always been at the heart of the Lotus DNA. That will not change," he promises.

So, the weight. Again, we're only being fed preliminary figures, but the target spec is 1,680kg "in lightest specification". Hypercar buyers will pay through the nose and back again to cut kilos, as evidenced by the unpainted, trim-shorn Porsche 918 Spyder mit Weissach Pack. Still, with a driver on board, no amount of carbon trim is going to get the Evija under 1.7 tonnes. Hefty for a Lotus. And massive – it's Aventador-big. Two metres wide. Is this really the right direction for supercars to plunge in?

The good news is it's a quarter of a tonne lighter than the 1,950kg Rimac, so while it's not a feather per se, it's the least leaden of the new e-hypercar breed. And the balance, despite the batteries being heaped up under the Not-Engine-Bay window, is spread 50:50 between the axles.

The performance claims sound coy for something that weighs the same as a 5 Series diesel but has more power than three M5s. Right now the targets are 0–62mph in sub-3.0secs, 0–186mph in sub-9.0secs (a Chiron takes 13.6secs) and a top speed north of 200mph. Once it's off the line and the torque-vectoring is doing its thing, acceleration should be savage. And silent. Kerr makes no mention at all of any attempt to give the Evija a soundtrack, beyond the "digitally created sound required by regulations to alert pedestrians to its presence".

Surely the looks will have alerted folk to the spaceship whispering past their navel? You've never seen a vehicle like this. Norfolk residents who spot one undergoing shakedown will feel like those old Navy pilots who caught glimpses of the secret SR-71 Blackbird. What the heck was tha- oh, it's gone.

All 130 individuals who spend £1.5m–£2m on an Evija (plus taxes) are getting a whole lot of nothing for their money. Or as designers prefer to call it, 'negative space'. Lotus's design boss Russell Carr explains that EVs give a whole new toybox to unlock. "The packaging of the battery pack and rear motors offers some flexibility when designing the rear bodywork and diffuser. This has helped us create the distinctive Venturi tunnels. Cooling requirements are less aggressive than on a 1,000bhp-plus combustion powertrain, and this has allowed us this 'porous' quality, with air going through the car."

Lotus's design boss is adamant that a deliberately retro-inspired-design, like the latest Ford GT, was never on the table. Neither, says engineering, was a hybrid drivetrain. The Evija is a virtuous circle. No engine means less cooling, means neater packaging, means slicker aerodynamics. Those rear tunnels are outrageous, aren't they? What's fascinating is how the car seems to shapeshift as you walk around it, like a piece of perspective art hung in a gallery.

From the front-three quarter, it's a solid object, of punchy stance and brooding haunches. Take a broad step to your left or right. Suddenly, voids open before your very eyes. Light pours through gaping chasms in the car's shoulders. Shadows are cast beneath the twin-skinned bonnet. The tyres peek through Le Mans racer-like vents ahead of the doors. Supercars always aim to look fast when they're standing still. This thing looks like it's almost coming apart at the seams.

We're confidently told that the look won't change from what you see before you here. From the pop-out cameras for door mirrors to the inboard suspension visible at the nape of the rear window, it's all approved. Hopefully the Huracán-esque interior, with its driver-selfish digi-screen and birthday card-sized steering wheel will be left untouched, too. Because believe me you've never sat in a better assembled Lotus than this one. It doesn't even smell of fibreglass and panic.

Maximum cruising range is said to be 250 miles – about what you'd get from a big V12 Lambo or Pagani, if you're careful. Which you won't be. Not with this much insta-poke. And it'll fully recharge in 18 minutes. If you've got access to a 350kW charger. Great news, if you live in Kent. Because Kent's home to the UK's sole 350kW charger.

There's a strange-yet-wonderfully true story that on 16th November 1990, the British Parliament debated the morality of Lotus selling its 377bhp take on the Vauxhall Carlton: a family saloon with a top speed of 177mph. Thirty years on, Lotus is going to mic drop a two thousand horsepower road car on the world. Good job all our MPs are otherwise occupied.

PRICE £1.5MILLION + **0-60** < 3.0 SECONDS **TOP SPEED** > 200MPH **POWER** 1,972BHP
DID YOU KNOW? LOTUS IS AIMING FOR THE EVIJA TO BE THE LIGHTEST EV HYPERCAR. STILL ON BRAND, THEN

MERCEDES AMG ONE

The dominant force of F1's hybrid era takes all that tech and puts it on the road

As we reported live from the Frankfurt show on the unveiling of the Project One, topgear.com's comments threads lit up with the inevitable hue and cry: you guys must get this thing into a comparison test with the Aston Martin Valkyrie. Or the Koenigsegg, or the Bugatti, or the 918 or whatever. And of course we will. But really, we're well beyond the realm of consumer advice with these cars. Every one of the 275 production examples of this AMG that will ever be built has already been sold. No doubt each of those buyers will already own every other hypercar that ever took his or her fancy. There is a pool of global purchasers on whose shoulders the burden of selection simply does not weigh. They don't choose just one. They get one of each. It's like when I as a 99-percenter arrive at the buffet table. I don't regard chicken and salmon as a matter of choice, I get a helping of both.

So what really counts for a hypercar isn't to be better than the others, but to be different from the others. And having a genuine Formula One power unit is a point of difference. When it's the very same engine and hybrid system employed by Lewis Hamilton to win the 2015 World Championship, that's a proper conversation- stopping point of difference.

While unwrapping the car at Frankfurt, AMG stayed coy about many things. Even the final name, which won't be Project One. This was an inverted-commas nod-and-wink "concept car". It had to be called a concept because there are no offcial fuel consumption figures or crash tests yet. But AMG boss Tobias Moers says it really is the final thing, bar a few differences we wouldn't even notice.

The overall system power, from the engine and four electric motors, is "more than" 1,000bhp. The combustion section is a little 1.6-litre V6 that revs to 11,000rpm, given the wind-up by a honking great turbo. It's the best turbo you can get, because it's hooked to a Formula One-style MGU-H (motor generator unit – heat). Then there's a further hybrid motor/generator attached to the crankshaft – in F1-speak, the MGU-K (motor generator unit – kinetic). This complex bundle of tarmac-melting power is pretty much the assembly that ran in F1 in 2015, and, with little change continued to dominate F1 for the era since.

The only published performance numbers are these: a top speed of "over 350kph" – which is 217mph. A high number,

"THE POWER OUTPUT IS MORE THAN 1000BHP. THE COMBUSTION PART IS A 1.6-LITRE V6 THAT REVS TO 11,000RPM, GIVEN THE WIND-UP BY A HONKING GREAT TURBO. THEN THERE ARE THE F1 EXTRAS…"

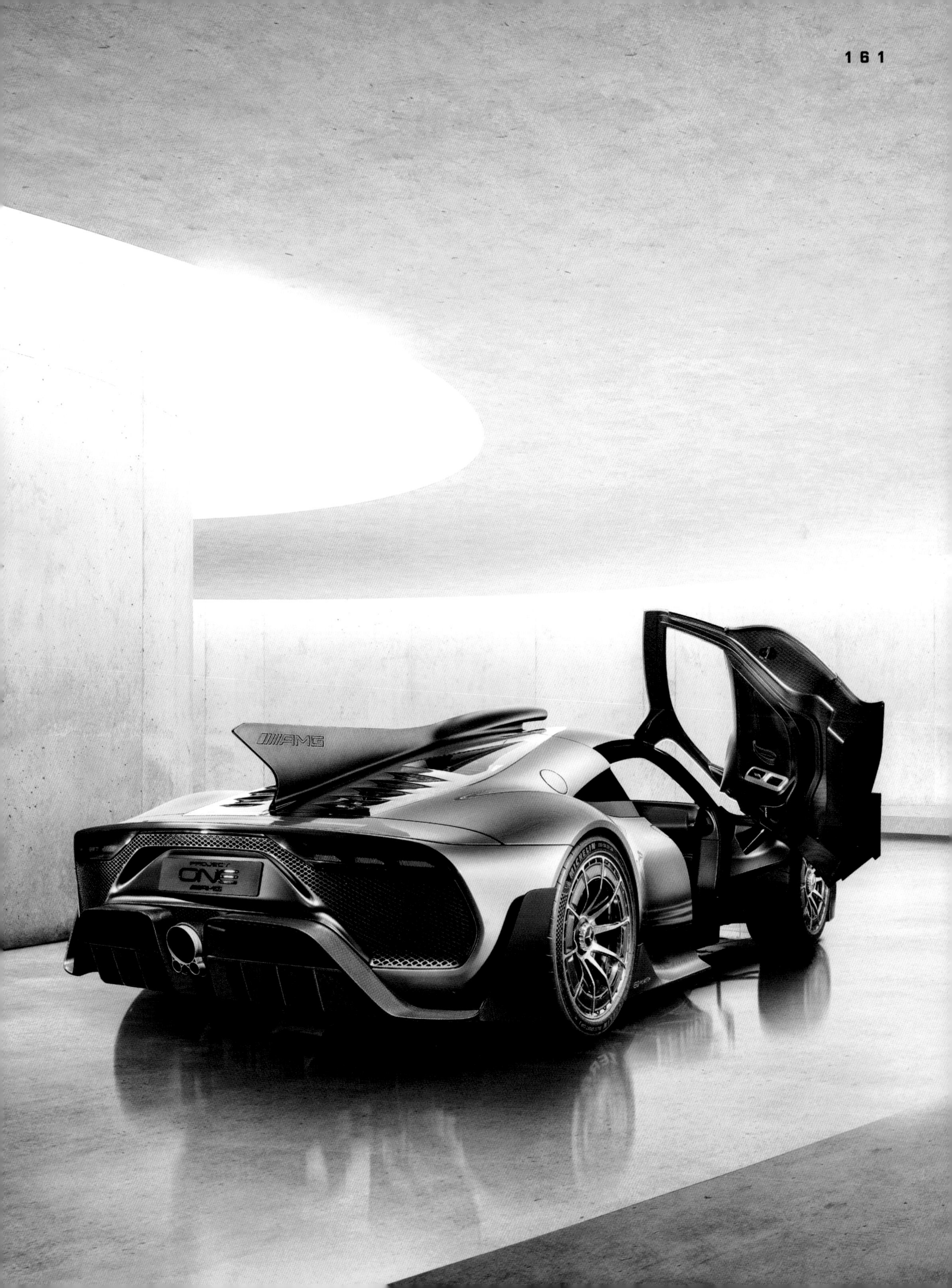
AMG
PROJECT
ONE
MICHELIN

however, a small number of cars – one of them decades old – go higher. But excuse it because there's much downforce, and because the electric front motors, with their single gear ratio, will be beyond their useful rpm range by then. Focus your incredulity instead on this: the zero to 125mph time is "less than six seconds". A Bugatti Chiron is in the upper sixes, while the Porsche 918 is in the low sevens.

I suggest to Moers that the acceleration off the line might be equal to the racing car. Sure, the Project One is heavier, but it's got all that instant 4WD stomp. His reply starts evasively. "Zero to 100kph [0–62mph] is not a serious figure anymore. Many EVs are quick: they have traction and no lag." Then he arrives at the actual answer, and it's astounding. "But yes, the Project One will match a Formula One car."

Moers reckons the Project One is an idea whose time has come. Since he took it over, the AMG division has leapt ahead. Sales have tripled, largely thanks to the more accessible AMG 43 family. Stature has risen through the standalone GT series two-seater. AMG owners had been asking him to build something more drastic. Lewis Hamilton says he had been, too.

So Moers was ready to mount an ascent on the very pinnacle of the hypercar mountain. "Electrification is key to future success. Having a hypercar with a V8 or V12 wasn't the right approach for AMG," he tells *TopGear*. "We have to move forward. We are no longer a small player in sports cars. Besides, 2017 was the 50th anniversary of AMG and therefore we knew we should do something really special.

"So, in October 2015, I called Andy Cowell [MD of the Formula One powertrain division] and asked whether the F1 engine would be capable of road use and meeting emissions. I gave him a month. A month later he called back and said yes." Moers won't say exactly how long after that he got the nod from Daimler CEO Dieter Zetsche, but it was soon.

Moers says the broad layout of the car all but designed itself. That's mid-engined, with a low-mounted battery, and front motors to allow both torque vectoring and plug-in pure-electric-drive capability. As with a racecar, the main tub is carbon fibre, and the engine and transmission take the rear suspension and aerodynamic loads. Though in this case there's a supplementary titanium support frame for the suspension.

Downforce at speed is equal to a GT3 car's, Moers claims. But the whole thing is riven with flaps and spoilers and intakes and exits, many of which are adaptive. This should take care of different cooling needs at low and high speeds, and variable drag/downforce ratios. Even the moving tail wing has another moving wing within it. The front splitter extends at speed for downforce, in concert with opening louvres above the front wheelarches. The nose is shaped to force air into the roof intake. Behind the roof is the stabiliser fin. When the car's still, it looks gawkily hacked off at the back edge, but that's to allow the rear wing to rise and nestle against it. NACA ducts feed into the rear-mounted oil coolers for the engine and gearbox.

With all this downforce, grip from the specially designed 335/30 R20 Michelin tyres is going to be beyond the skill, experience or even the descriptive powers of us mortals. The suspension is horizontally arranged coilover units. Adaptive damping is aimed at coping with the car's extraordinarily wide range of speeds, aerodynamic loadings and use cases.

The car's palpitating heart is the racing hybrid power unit. Sure, they've had to make small changes – mostly for low-speed running, not at screaming peak. Moers and indeed Hamilton claim that once it's hit its mighty stride, the driver really is getting close to an experience previously reserved for a very, very few epically skilled men in Nomex. Why the differences? It has to run on pump fuel, not the doped race liquor. It has to meet all worldwide emissions regs. It idles at 1,000rpm vs 3,500rpm. So compression is slightly lower, and the management is recalibrated. But those things weren't hard, claims Moers. "The biggest issue is noise. Not vibration: you expect vibration at 10,000rpm. But structure-borne and airborne noise is really high, partly because the engine is bolted directly to the carbon-fibre tub with no cushioning mounts. They never gave a thought to that when they designed the race engine." Why would they? But he reckons his people are on top of the issue.

I raise the drearily obvious point that race engines aren't exactly long-lived. What about durability and reliability? "It's not

"THERE'S A STUPENDOUS DATABASE ON THE ENGINE, THANKS TO ALL THE F1 TELEMETRY THAT'S BEEN ACCUMULATED"

hard. The racers drive at full power and full braking." The mortals who buy these cars won't, he adds. Making the engine reliable when driving slowly is actually the issue. "We have to make it idle in traffic, make it cold-start, ensure it doesn't coke the valves and has low-rpm lubrication."

There's a stupendous database on the engine, thanks to Formula One telemetry, and AMG has just installed a four-wheel dyno at the Mercedes F1 engine division's base at Brixworth in Northamptonshire. There are also two full-size aero models under test in a moving-floor tunnel at Stuttgart University. One more surprise. The power units, it's already announced, will be built alongside the F1 ones at Brixworth. But Moers says it's likely the whole car will be assembled somewhere in Britain too, though he refuses so far to be more specific.

The visual design definitely split opinion. From lukewarm to hostile, really, as is always the way. Thing is, Mercedes design director Gorden Wagener is currently honing a theme he calls sensual purity, across the Mercedes range. It means removing almost all the creases and letting the surfaces do the work. It can look very classy when he has absolute control of those surfaces, but clearly here he didn't. So we end up with brutally edgy aero devices hacking across the oily-smooth coachwork.

But it's a clear contrast to the way Ferrari and McLaren always aim to cohere the aero and the style. It's also very different from the Aston Martin Valkyrie, which draws knee-trembling drama from the voids that flow under its suspension, engine and cabin. Moers says he was never going to build a car the shape of the Valkyrie: an AMG needs a bigger, roomier cockpit that doesn't lift your feet to chest height. "It's a proper car. It's usable. The two of you don't sit too close."

We know it isn't terminally off-putting, because potential buyers were shown a full-size model in March, and by September, claims Moers, the car's production run was four times oversubscribed. They have an agonising wait until 2019. And Lewis Hamilton reckons they're behind him in the queue.

PRICE £143,245 **0-60** < 3.6 SECONDS **TOP SPEED** 198MPH **POWER** 577BHP

DID YOU KNOW? THE GT3 VERSION USES THE PHENOMENAL, NATURALLY ASPIRATED 6.2 V8 FROM THE SLS

MERCEDES AMG GTR

Regular AMG GT 4-door a bit too lily-livered for you? Then you'll be needing one of these

This is a car of wonderful detail. For example, the GT R's power unit is set so far back it's effectively mid-engined. It uses the same 4.0-litre twin-turbo V8 as the standard GT, but the turbochargers nestled in the engine's vee are new, boost has been increased from 1.2 bar to 1.35 bar, and they can spin up to 186,000rpm – that's 3100rpm per second. Peak power is 577bhp and there's 516lb ft of torque, enough to hustle the 1,630kg GT from 0 to 62mph in 3.6 seconds, and on to a 198mph top speed. The GT-R features a new nose, inspired by the old 300 SL Gullwing racer that won the Panamericana road race in Mexico in 1952, and largely carried over from the GT3 racer. Wider wheels and special Michelin Pilot Sport Cup 2 tyres are held further away from the body by double wishbone, forged aluminium suspension and controlled by new coilover adjustable spring/damper units. Unseen under the engine, an electrically operated carbon panel pushes 40mm down into the airflow at speed, decreasing the amount of air passing under the car, and lowering air pressure. This hidden feature delivers as much downforce as the rear wing itself – about 40kg at 155mph. Along with the pumped-up arches and vertically slatted grille, the rear wing is one of the GT R's signature features. Its angle of attack can be manually adjusted. Built around a carbon core, the standard finish is black plastic, but a £3,265 carbon-weave finish can be specified. There's also a carbon-fibre torque tube (40 per cent lighter than the GT S's aluminium item), carbon roof and extra carbon bracing underneath the exhaust (itself now titanium and 6kg lighter) which improves torsional rigidity by 7.5 per cent. At the rear you'll find the transmission (contributing to a rear-biased 47:53 weight distribution) and a whole new back axle. Now 57mm wider, it features a rear-wheel-steering system run by two electromechanical actuators (there's no mechanical link to the steering wheel), and can alter the toe angle by 1.5°. at lower speeds and improve high-speed stability. Despite all the mods and the chunky rear wing, all-up the GT R is 15kg lighter than the GT S. Other highlights? How about traction control that comes with *nine* modes, switchable via a racecar-like toggle slap bang in the middle of the dashboard. As to the Nordschleife lap time, the GT R did it in 7.10 – faster than the Viper ACR, Lexus LFA Nürburgring, and Ferrari 488 GTB. As we say, detail.

MERCEDES AMG GTR 4-DOOR

What happens when AMG makes a family car

This is only the third model developed entirely by AMG (following the SLS and GT), but the sharky nose, bonnet 'powerdomes' and, in the parlance of exterior designer Vitalis Enns, 'fantastic ass', give the GT four-door a sharper street presence than the Porsche Panamera or BMW M5. The GT four-door uses the MRA platform that underpins the C-, E-, CLS and various other Mercedes, and therefore isn't a GT four-door at all. But at least that allows it to run the 4Matic all-wheel-drive hardware, promoting daily usability in shabby weather over arrant hedonism. Good job, given it weighs 2,045kg. The 63S 4Matic+ is powered by AMG's magnificent 4.0-litre V8 bi-turbo, which delivers 630bhp and 627lb ft from 2,500 to 4,500rpm. If Ferrari's 3.9-litre twin-turbo leads the way, this AMG unit is close in terms of zero-lag exibility and charisma and performance is blistering, with 62mph blazing past in just 3.2 seconds and a top speed of 195mph, all overlaid by full-fat, non-turbo-ish old-school sonics. That said, the four-door 63S is certainly easier to deal with than the GT coupe, swatting away surface noise and riding compliantly despite its hefty rubber. It's an able, amiable cruiser, but its darker side is liberated by a veritable tech arsenal. The nine-speed 'box uses a wet clutch to cut weight and improve response; the gear changes are finger-snap fast and crackle emotively. The steering, suspension, engine and transmission parameters are all governed by the Dynamic Select drive system, which spans six set-ups, from Slippery through to Race. Within that, there's a further Dynamics Plus palette, encompassing Basic, Advanced, Pro, and Master. There's also a Drift mode, if you have money and rubber to burn. It's sublimely controlled into corners and on the brakes (390mm discs at the front, ceramics are a £6,995 option), able to find incredible traction on the exits, happy to play fast and loose if you want it, but progressive on the limit. The GT four-door's cabin is dominated by Merc's widescreen cockpit, with all the principal multimedia functionality displayed on the central screen. A revised central 'bridge' now uses recessed TFT displays rather than buttons.

PRICE £135,550 **0-60** 3.2 SECONDS **TOP SPEED** 196MPH **POWER** 631BHP

DID YOU KNOW? MERC WANTED TO APE MASERATI QUATTROPORTE AND CALL IT GTR VIERTÜRIG. THIS MAY BE A LIE

PRICE £230,000 **0-60** 3.6 SECONDS (EST)
TOP SPEED > 196MPH **POWER** 622BHP
DID YOU KNOW? ENGINE REVISIONS MEAN
THAT WHILE THE BLACK IS MORE POWERFUL THAN
THE 'STANDARD' SLS, IT HAS LESS TORQUE

PRICE €812,000 (AUCTION RESULT) **0-60** N/A
TOP SPEED > 155MPH **POWER** 380BHP
DID YOU KNOW? THE ORIGINAL GULLWING HAD
A SPACEFRAME CHASSIS AND FULLY INDEPENDENT
SUSPENSION. NOT BAD FOR A 1950S ROAD CAR

MERCEDES SLS BLACK VS AMG GULLWING

Modern-day AMG Black Series meets a specially fettled 300 SL Gullwing

The Rumpler Tropfenwagen was the first car to use a swing rear axle. That was in 1921, which was pretty good going for what was effectively an independent suspension set-up. The Mercedes 300SL 'Gullwing' is better known than the Rumpler – as are most things, to be fair – a lot faster, and also has a swing rear axle. Anyone who's ever driven one quickly on an undulating road will, once they've had a long sit down and a warm drink, tell you that high speeds and sudden camber changes can make the Gullwing officially 'interesting'. Even Stirling Moss says so, and he knew what he was doing. The 300SL you see here gets round this problem by junking the original suspension and replacing it with the rear set-up from its late-'80s SL successor. It also has AMG's 6.0-litre 'M119' V8, good for around 380bhp and previously best enjoyed in the über-rare mid-'90s AMG SL60, a four-speed automatic transmission, adjustable Bilstein dampers, and proper brakes. You no longer need to imagine what a 300SL Gullwing fettled by AMG might be like, because this is it. How does it compare to the thundering SLS Black Series? On a dry road, and with its Michelin Cup tyres on song, the SLS Black manages to be eye-poppingly exciting and a reminder that not all contemporary supercars make life easy. This is an old-school handful, partly because it's so wide and low, partly because it has 622bhp and is perfectly prepared to introduce you to each of them personally. But get into the zone with it, and it's one of those increasingly rare cars that really does give you the driving equivalent of an out-of-body experience. The SLS Black Series cost £230k new, but a quick scout around suggests that these cars are now worth up to £500k, with even the regular SLS now rapidly appreciating. Must be something to do with those gullwing doors…

BRABUS G WAGEN 6X6

Not technically a supercar, but are you planning to argue with it?

The car it's based on has a 5.5-litre 536bhp twin-turbo V8, with 560lb ft of torque. This, plainly, was not enough, so Brabus fitted two bigger turbochargers, upgraded the ECU, wrapped gold around the intakes to keep them cool, and popped on a new, rumblier exhaust. This boosts output by 154bhp and 130lb ft to 690bhp, and 708lb ft. So roughly a 1.2-litre Golf's worth. That means the three-and-a-bit tonne 6x6 now gets to 62mph in 4.4 seconds, but the tyres limit its top speed to 99.4mph. This makes it faster than a previous-gen Porsche 911 Carrera, Maserati MC Stradale, Lotus Evora, Jaguar F-Type and Bentley Continental GT V8. Around London – or rather several feet above it (it's 2.21 metres tall) – it's smooth as an escort's compliment. Really, you don't notice that it's 3775kg, and 5.9 metres long (70cm longer than an extended wheelbase Range Rover), nor do you notice that it has 50 per cent more wheels than everything else on the road. The interior definitely helps. Like everything else that comes out of Brabus' Bottrop workshop, it's a bit kinky. There's diamond stitching and leather and carbon fibre everywhere, but it still feels factory-Mercedes. Prod the throttle, there's a big rumble, and you're off with no great disturbances in the force. It's a con trick par excellence. Of course, it's also 2.11 metres wide. Which several roads around London aren't. But remember, this has five locking differentials, with power split 30-40-30 across the axles, and 37-inch tyres that can self-inflate and deflate. So mounting a kerb doesn't really trouble it. Corners, on the other hand, do. If you can find a road wide enough to pitch it into a bend, there's plenty of lean. That said, the unique spring and Ohlins damper setup makes it a lot more obliging and controlled than you'd suspect. As for that monumental acceleration, well, if you floor it, it vibrates like you've driven into a ball of static electricity. Then, once the power's filled up every inch of the drivetrain, the wheels join in and it takes a great bite out of the horizon. It tends to make people look at you like they're being told two very important things at the same time. That or mouth a word we *think* is anchor.

PRICE 3.5 SECOND **0-60** 3.5 SECOND **TOP SPEED** 3.5 SECOND **POWER** 690BHP
NUMBER BUILT 100

McLAREN P1 GTR

More power, more aero, more of everything that really matters for maximum McLaren

We're going to send someone down to show you the ropes, tell you what's what, give it a bit of a demo run for you". McLaren is on the phone, and understandably they want someone to make sure I don't sling £2 million worth of race-bred, track-ready hypercar into the wall at Turn 1 on the Red Bull Ring. "Anyway," the voice continued – and I could tell he was building up to something here, "Bruno Senna will be flying into…"

Now Bruno is imparting tips. I'm trying to listen, but I'm feeling slightly overwhelmed. I mean, just look at the GTR. More specifically, look at that rear wing. That's 400kg of downforce right there. It's nuts. Earlier I watched it being backed off the truck, the star of the show. The big kahuna. The main event.

How much fast do you want? How fast can a road car, or even an extreme track car, actually be? How far can they be taken? There are no lines drawn, the only limits are those provided by physics. So we start with 1,000bhp, and to that we add racing slicks to help transfer that to the tarmac, and to make doubly sure it doesn't come unstuck we plonk on 660kg of total downforce at 150mph. The GTR hits 150mph three times on each lap, a lap that takes under 93 seconds at an average of over 105mph. Nothing else here would get within 12 seconds of it.

The P1 GTR is being built on the production line at Woking alongside the 'regular' P1. It does a stint at MSO (McLaren Special Operations) a few miles away late on in the build process, but for the most part the underpinnings are common: carbon tub, front and rear aluminium subframes, a twin-turbo 3.8-litre V8 and an electric motor nestled under the left flank of the vee, drawing power from a battery pack behind the seats and adding its torque to the driveshaft before the gearbox.

There's now 197bhp from the e-motor (up 21bhp) and a heftily unnecessary 789bhp from the fossil-fuel-fed one (plus 62bhp), yielding a pretty heady 1,000PS (986bhp). Oh, and weight has been stripped out almost everywhere – the fixed rear wing means there's no need for heavy hydraulic struts, polycarbonate replaces glass all round, including the windscreen and there's extra carbon. In total, about 150kg has been shaved out. Plus the suspension components and geometry have been heavily revised – although that's all adjustable anyway.

This is a track car after all. McLaren isn't as prescriptive as Ferrari is with its XX cars: it will let you take your car home (and rumour has it Lanzante has McLaren's tacit approval to convert customer GTRs to road use), but this is meant to be the ultimate track- day weapon. And we're at a track, where an ex-F1 driver is attempting to bolster my confidence...

"Really, you have nothing to worry about," says Bruno (he's a genuinely lovely bloke), "I think you'll find it friendly to drive." You won't find 'friendly' among the many adjectives I'd use to describe the standard P1. We look at the steering wheel (it's based on the design of Lewis's 2008 F1 rim), talk about the controls, the IPAS and DRS, get comfortable in the car, pull the straps down tight. Bruno is going to take me out in it to start with. The wheels, freshly removed from tyre-warmers, go on with a fierce screech from the airguns, the internal jacks are retracted and, when instructed, Bruno fires the GTR into life and we're waved out.

Let's cut to the chase. It's PREPOSTEROUS.

I have no idea how I'm going to get close to it. Bruno may be laid back and endearing in real life, but he's the last of the late-brakers. Twice, slowing from 170mph, he overshoots the braking point for the Remus hairpin. Thank the god of all track marshals for tarmac run-off. It appears the addition of 75kg of extra passenger has upset the weight distribution, so in the bumpier braking zones, the ABS is getting confused, grabbing one side, then the other, the end result being we're not only braking stupidly late, but the back end is jinking left and right like a sped-up Scandi flick. It's... discomforting.

Bruno muscles it into corners under brakes, sorting out oversteer and understeer with faster steering inputs than I've ever witnessed, lightning jabs at the wheel that leave me astonished and daunted in equal measure. He's a driving mongoose. If the car needs inputs like that to stay on top of...

Eventually it's over, and I'm allowed to flop out of the GTR. Bruno apologises for the extra-curricular excursions, blames it on the ABS and has a word with the engineers. I'm left to contemplate what I'm up against. I will say one thing for the GTR – it seems uncannily stable on the straights, and the traction out of corners is utterly astonishing. My neck hurts. Five laps of 2.4g side loadings is enough.

My turn. I resolve to take it steady, to spend 2–3 laps getting familiar with the power, the grip, the brakes. But here's the thing: the snatchiness, the dartiness I experienced with Bruno – that's all down to driving style. Because you know what? The P1 GTR is an outrageously magnanimous car to drive. Far more so than the road car. The problem with the road car is you have this light, accurate front end, and then a 903bhp sledgehammer arriving at the back, easily capable of spiking the tyres. It's exciting alright, but not easily managed.

The GTR gives the P1 the grip it needs to cope with the power. I'm tentative for about two straights and three corners, but that's about as long as it takes to feel confident in it. Then you can start to push, to be blown away by just how much front-end grip and turn-in strength there is and how clearly it communicates. And now you don't have to be scared of the throttle pedal, you can use more of it, earlier in a corner, than I'd have believed possible.

On my second lap, I think I'm getting fuel starvation through the downhill section. I'm not – it's the traction control cutting in. How has McLaren managed to make a 986bhp car this approachable, this drivable? The set-up is astonishing. There's so much feel through the chassis, the steering is so beautiful to use, you always know precisely where you are with it. You can take it to the limit – how ridiculous is that in a car with a Nomad's worth of downforce working on it? The speeds are outrageous, just bananas, but the GTR is so talkative and engaging you can use everything it's got, rely on the whiff of understeer to let you know the car is working hard.

I can only assume the e-motor is doing its stuff – there is too much noise, excitement, accessibility and power higher up the rev range for me to bother sampling the lower end. The only indication is that there's no turbo lag. None. Just instant, perfectly metered response. The only thing I struggle to get my head around is the brakes. I just can't bring myself to brake as late as Bruno, nor push the corner entry quite as hard.

I ought to be so intimidated by this car, but instead I'm just dazzled by it, blown away. It makes me laugh out loud, this £2 million track weapon – it's actually fun to drive, wonderfully unintimidating. On my third flying lap I'm within a second of Bruno. He probably wasn't trying, but that made me feel good.

PRICE £2 MILLION **0-60** < 2.8 SECS **TOP SPEED** 217MPH **POWER** 986BHP
DID YOU KNOW? THE ORIGINAL MCLAREN GTR WAS A RACING VERSION OF THE EPOCHAL F1

McLAREN SENNA

Only a truly special car deserves to wear a name like that. And this one is

The McLaren Senna has 789bhp, but 789bhp is the least impressive aspect of the whole car. The brakes, oh my God, the brakes. I still can't get my head around them. The Senna is the next product in McLaren's Ultimate Series line-up. It isn't a direct replacement for the P1, but instead answers a different question. I'm not quite sure what that is, but it involves aerodynamics. The Senna ain't pretty, but if you only see it in terms of beauty, you're looking at it wrong. Forget aesthetics;

think function. Now, isn't what you're looking at one of the most fascinating things you've ever seen? The rear wing's underside develops more downforce than its top side. Really. Best stat? Not 0-124mph in 6.8secs or the 211mph top speed, not even a dry weight of just 1,198kg (call it 1,300kg with fluids), but 800kg of downforce at 155mph. Above that speed, McLaren actually reduces downforce by bleeding off the rear wing – apparently they think 800kg is adequate. Well, since it's 300kg more than the latest GT3 RS produces at 193mph, they might have a point. Best quote came from Andy Palmer, director of the Ultimate Series line when I asked him how they'd made it road-legal, "Well, we have a very good relationship with Pete at the VCA" came the reply. That's right, he's on first-name terms with the chap at the Vehicle Certification Agency, the people that ensure cars comply with road regulations. Pete had initially told him there was no chance the wing could be made road-legal, but there it is, towering and globally homologated. First things: you're aware of how light the door is (just 9kg, about half the

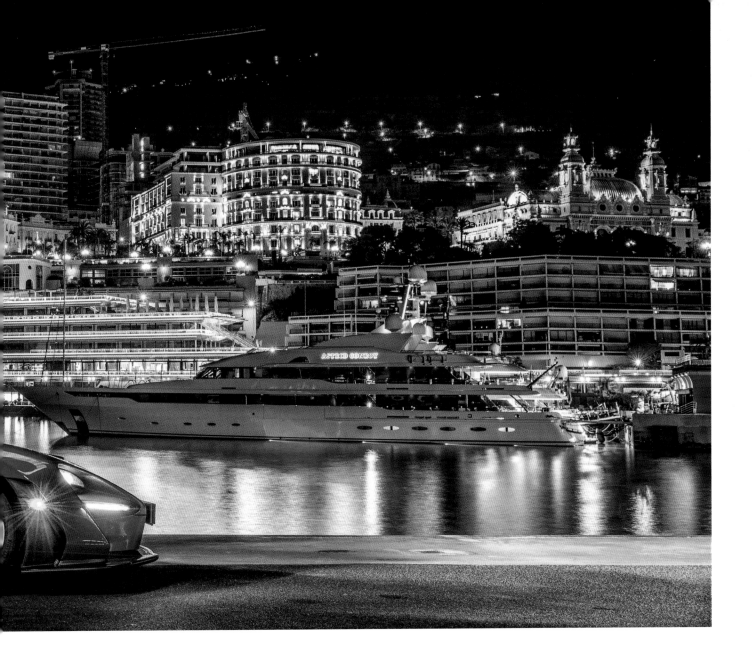

weight of a P1 door), how snug the fixed carbon seat feels and how bare the carbon trim. Those glass panels in the roof and door? You don't notice them once you're rolling. The ambience is business-like, a road car, but with all the trim scraped off. No sense of aggression, just a commanding authority, alert, ready. Different from a P1 GTR: less blood, guts and thunder. It's not much faster than a 720S (but then not a lot is), but it's the stability and usability of that power that's so surprising. No skittishness from the back end, just this huge – and hugely secure – thrust. It becomes sort of... unremarkable. But not the brakes. Palmer won't tell me who they've been developed with, but the production process is new, the carbon composite laid up as solid and then drilled afterwards: "They run at much lower temperatures, which means we can size them smaller, get them

lighter and still get the performance." It may sound weird, but I have more fun smacking the brakes than the throttle pedal. I'm used to acceleration of this magnitude, but not braking – 124–0mph in 100m. And all the time, utter, ruthless stability. That's the aero for you. Internal winglets at the front, plus a rear wing that can swing through almost 90 degrees. Combine this with the adaptive dampers, and the car is able to keep itself planted and on line in almost any situation. The steering is a delight, all inputs reflected instantaneously through a chassis whose responses are clean, pure and immediate. McLaren says the Senna pulls around 0.2–0.3g more through a medium-speed corner than the P1 or 720S. It's in a different league, a league beyond what is comprehensible to a road car driver, no matter how exotic that road car is. The Senna is plain faster than you.

PRICE £750,000 **0-60** 2.8 SECONDS **TOP SPEED** 211MPH **POWER** 789BHP

DID YOU KNOW? THE SENNA'S EXHAUST HAS BEEN ENGINEERED TO BUILD BY 10DB EVERY 2,000RPM

McLAREN 720S

This second generation McLaren goes searching for soul. Does it find it?

The 720S's performance pretty much hits it out of the park. Full-noise away from an Italian motorway toll booth or slip road, it's quite the rocketship. The gears shift so fast they kind of merge, but once you're into fourth it's possessed of the goods to resist the usual decline in acceleration.

As with Ferrari's turbo V8, the 720S's engine delivers more as you climb the gears. There's a different boost map for each gear, so that in the low ones the mid-range torque is moderated. That keeps wheel-spin under control, and also makes it feel more naturally aspirated; with reduced boost there's less lag, which means it's worth going to 8,200rpm to collect the full 710bhp.

So it doesn't feel too turbocharged. That isn't the only reason of course. It's now 4.0 litres instead of 3.8 and is heavily reworked in other ways. It answers the pedal sharpish at mid revs, and if you keep it planted then the red line exerts a black-hole gravitational pull on the rev needle.

Its noise begins soft and smooth, and as you climb it progressively strengthens its tenor. But that's it. Progressive and well-mannered. From 6,000rpm upwards there's real excitement there. It'll hum through a town with a soft throttle, gently greased take-up of its clutches and very little noisy disturbance of the streetscape beyond this one's loud orange paint. The doors open diagonally, so they don't need much space alongside the car and they present a huge aperture through which you drop to your seat. Once there, your outward vision is panoramic. The door-hanging and the vision are intrinsic advantages of the new structure, which uses carbon fibre for the pillars. It's so strong they can be made uncommonly thin, and the ones behind you are split into two fine spars with glazing between.

Looking backward is all very well, but this is a supercar and we need to see ahead. For that we have deep windscreen pillars far back, and LED active headlamps. Even the instrument panel does its bit. The readout doesn't just alter its graphics depending on need and situation. That's so last-year. It also physically moves. Go to track mode and it drops towards you to show only the vital info, via a second shallow screen. Clever.

Every other carmaker claims that electric steering is needed to save the odd gramme of CO2. But its endless march is also being perpetuated by the fact it enables lane-keeping and self-parking and other stuff that has little place on a sports car. Whatever the truth, McLaren has dug its heels in and stuck with the hydraulic sort. It's even improved the system, via front-end geometry changes. The result is magical. This is no mere command-and-control apparatus from you to the tyre treads. It talks back, engaging you with endless messages yet it has discretion too: despite all the feedback on grip, it never blurts too much about potholes or cambers. The weight and gearing are spot-on too. And it avoids the fashion for gearing that's so high it's nervy. No, this system remains calm and collected, even as you ask it to do hectic works.

The coolness of the chassis' reactions stems in part from McLaren's cross-linked adaptive – proactive – suspension. It was present on the 650S and 12C, but for the new car it gets more sensors and operates with even more complexity and lightning speed. Fluid pipes link across the car, giving roll control. And conventional electronic damping control adds to the mix. The moment the need presents itself, it can stiffen itself in roll as well as damping, so the Comfort mode is actually all you need for most road driving. In too many cars you're ceaselessly fidgeting the knob between different chassis modes. In the McLaren, Comfort or Sport modes are both perfectly OK.

So many cars with huge grip are pretty much mute until you're about to exhaust it. That's boring, because on the road you seldom will. If you want to have a good time all the time, the 720S is your supercar. Because it's almost all peak and no trough, it doesn't lend itself to caricature. Does it have a character? The first new-generation McLaren, the 12C, was also a dramatically competent car for its time, but called soulless. This 720S is a car with immense speed but a surprisingly subtle nature. It's brilliant, but it brings you along.

PRICE £208,600 **0-60** 2.9 SECONDS **TOP SPEED** 212MPH **POWER BUILT** 710BHP

DID YOU KNOW? WONDERING WHERE THE DOOR HANDLE IS? IT'S A BUTTON HIDDEN IN THE DOOR'S AERO CHANNEL

"TOO MANY CARS WITH HUGE GRIP ARE PRETTY MUCH MUTE UNTIL YOU'RE ABOUT TO EXHAUST IT. IF YOU WANT TO HAVE A GOOD TIME ALL THE TIME, THE 720S IS YOUR CAR"

McLAREN 600LT

With its roots in endurance racing, the LT is a masterpiece of agility and poise

Strictly speaking this is the fourth in McLaren's 'Longtail' range after coupe and Spider versions of the 675, and the car that kick-started it all back in 1997, the F1 GTR Longtail. Only nine of those were made. More of these will be made, although McLaren hasn't put a limit on exact numbers. In order to maintain the separation between Sport Series (570S et al) and Super Series (720S) models, the 600LT does without movable aero devices and hydraulic cross-linked dampers – those features are still reserved for the (even) more expensive models. Aside from that, just about everything has been seen to. The engine gains new camshafts and a retuned ECU for an extra 30bhp, over 30kg has been removed from the wheels, tyres, brakes and forged aluminium suspension (all important rotational and unsprung weight), the dampers have been recalibrated, the uprights are from the 720S, the track is wider, the ride height lower. It's 74mm longer overall as the front

splitter and rear diffuser have both been extended to enhance downforce. Together with the new rear wing, the 600LT develops 100kg of downforce at 155mph. Given the Senna develops 800kg at the same speed, that's not particularly significant. But the 600LT isn't about downforce, it's about handling involvement and crispness. And speed, obviously. The headline figures are 62mph in 2.9secs, 124mph in 8.2secs (0.1secs faster than a 911 GT2 RS, 0.6secs slower than a 488 Pista), a 204mph top end and the standing quarter done and dusted in 10.4secs. All this, and top exit exhausts? Yes, please. Even at £185,500. It's how the 600LT gets itself into the corner that most impresses. And that starts the moment you hit the brakes. The pedal is reassuringly firm, the bite is huge and the ABS barely intrudes, so it feels like the car has basically snagged an aircraft carrier's arrester wire. There's barely any dive and no differential to get twisted up once you start to turn, so the LT is clean and flat into the corner. It changes direction in a way that defies belief for anything running on modest 225-width tyres. They might be Pirelli Trofeo track day tyres, but the grip is still immense. So, you can turn and brake at the same time and know exactly where you are with grip at both ends. If you push it very hard you will get the front end to nudge into understeer, but the McLaren responds so fast you can get that nullified, adjust the balance, correct your line and carry on before you've reached the apex. The most agile supercar on sale today? The 600LT is right up there.

PRICE £185,500 **0-60** 2.9 SECONDS **TOP SPEED** 204MPH **POWER** 591BHP

DID YOU KNOW? HENNESSEY IS CURRENTLY PLANNING POWER UPGRADES FOR THE 600LT THAT'LL YIELD 1,000BHP

McLAREN 675LT

It may no longer be the hot new thing, but the 675LT remains mind-blowing

The McLaren 675 LT, Woking born-and-bred, hurls you down the road with such staggering force it's what you imagine bungee-jumping off the back of the Space Shuttle as it breaches the mesosphere must feel like. And 'feel' is the word. The 675 LT throws so much information at you – fabulously analogue information – that it's difficult to process it in real time. One thought takes hold, though: this might be the best McLaren road car since the original F1 25 years ago. The official McLaren line is different, of course, but still illuminating. It says the 675LT represents a bigger jump from the 650S than that car was over the 12C. CEO Mike Flewitt sums it up thusly: 'The 675LT is the closest thing there is to a McLaren P1. Alongside [that car] it's the most extreme expression yet of McLaren road car engineering.' Suddenly, £260k doesn't seem quite so steep… To be reductive about it, the 675 LT – it stands for Long Tail, a tribute to McLaren's elongated 1997 endurance racer – is the company's answer to the Ferrari 488 Pista a lightweight, more powerful, track-focused

limited series car, absolutely dripping with aerodynamic know-how and aimed at the unrepentant hedonist. It'll rip to 62mph in 2.9 seconds, 124mph in a barely believable 7.9 seconds, and thunder on until it's all done at 205mph. It weighs 1320kg – 100 less than the 650S – which translates into a 542bhp-per-tonne power-to-weight ratio. Approximately one-third of the car is new, the aero detail really is immense for a road car. The LT's front and rear track have been widened to 20mm, to improve grip, turn-in, and overall agility, and the ride height at the front has been reduced by the same amount, so that it cleaves the air at a more rakish angle. The centre of pressure has moved forwards, resulting in superior downforce – 40 per cent more overall than the 650 generates. The engine now produces 666bhp (at 7100rpm) and/or 516 torques (between 5500rpm and 6500rpm). In fact, 50 per cent of the engine's components are new. The result is a monumentally fast car. Fortunately, speed is only part of the McLaren's matrix. A faster rack means that the steering is sublime and the linearity of its major control responses – primarily the throttle – utterly superb. The brakes are unchanged, but have perfect feel. Like the 650S, the LT uses McLaren's ProActive Chassis Control (hydraulically interconnected dampers) and Brake Steer, but the Normal, Sport and Track settings have all been reworked to deliver edgier responses. The result is a car that attacks corners with an insatiable hunger, relaying every morsel of information into the palms of your hands, while remaining astonishingly composed.

PRICE £260,500 **0-60** 2.9 SECONDS **TOP SPEED** 205MPH **POWER** 666BHP
DID YOU KNOW? GIRAFFES HAVE THE LONGEST TAIL OF ANY LAND MAMMAL, AT UP TO 2.4 METRES. C'MON, AT LEAST THIS ONE LINKS BACK TO THE CAR…

McLAREN SPEEDTAIL

Successor to the epochal F1, this car proves that McLaren is idiosyncratic

Sleek, isn't it? Long and low and lean and, well, sleek. A streamliner. This is it, the McLaren Speedtail, the car formerly known as BP23 and likely forever known as the spiritual successor to the F1. Three seats, stratospheric top speed and a price tag that's similarly out of this world.

Facts, though, have been in short supply. And when we're starved of facts, we feed off myths. The rumour mill spooled up with tales of a 300mph target, of Chiron-beating power, and, to be fair, all we did was fan the flames. Let's rein in hyperbole and exaggeration right now, because here's what we do know. The McLaren Speedtail will, when deliveries start in early 2020, have cost each of its 106 owners north of £2.1m for a car that boasts 1,036bhp and a 250mph maximum speed. When they do strap themselves into the centre seat, line up on a runway, press the Velocity button above their head and nail the throttle, they'll feel what it's like to accelerate from zero to 186mph in the same time it takes a diesel supermini to hit 60mph.

How is it powered? That still hasn't been fully revealed, but let's start by looking at a broader picture. McLaren likes its Ultimate Series cars to answer questions. Take the Senna, which answers "is it possible to road- legalise racing levels of downforce?". Turns out it is, and nothing else comes close to the 800kg of downward pressure the Senna is able to produce at 150mph. Now we're in the realm of "What if we forgot about downforce and went low-drag instead? Say grand touring was still a thing, what would the ultimate 21st-century GT car look like? What would it be able to do?"

McLaren's leap of faith is that grand touring is still a thing, and that people will want to do it as a threesome. Hyper GT is the pitch; Bugatti Chiron, even if McLaren isn't admitting as much, the target. The Speedtail is about luxury as much as speed. Well, heading that way. We'll come on to talk about the clean lines of the cabin, the tactility of the materials, but first just look at it: the length of the tail, the elegance of those rear lines. It's plain stunning, a shape that treats the air passing over and around it with respect. What air it needs is subtly taken, used as appropriate for combustion or cooling and then calmly reintroduced, before being precisely and delicately detached by the samurai blade tail. At 5.13 metres long, it's 60cm longer than a Chiron, the sweeping carbon cape carrying with it a suggestion

"McLAREN'S LEAP OF FAITH IS THAT GRAND TOURING IS STILL A THING, AND THAT PEOPLE WILL STILL WANT TO DO IT AS A THREESOME"

of art deco/steampunk Thirties cool. The kind of car the Rocketeer would have driven. That's the back, at least. The front is more challenging. What initially springs to my mind are mid-Eighties concept cars, stuff such as the MG EX-E and Lotus Etna. Think it's something to do with the wheelspats and low, low nose. The more I look, the better it gets, though, and I really admire how the intakes and air channels have been hidden away. Still at this end of the car engineering is more important than aesthetics. Design chief Rob Melville describes it as a "comet, with the mass at the front, then this long tail".

He's also interesting about the wheelspats: "Without them, the car would not have been able to deliver on its top speed and acceleration parameters." The spats (which remain static as the wheel rotates) reduce turbulence almost entirely, the air allowed to escape from the wheelarch through a single notch, smoothing air flow. They can be removed, but McLaren suggests you don't. Notice also the absence of exterior mirrors. Instead, there are pop-out cameras with screens at the base of the A-pillars.

I don't think I've seen a smoother transition from window into roofline – there's no header rail, nothing to delay the air's passage. And how about the cuts at the back of the rear deck? Flexible carbon fibre, moved by hydraulic actuators to adjust the centre of pressure or aid braking stability. We must assume that somewhere in Woking that vast one-piece clamshell is undergoing not just air-proofing, but child-proofing, being continuously flexed, bent and pressurised so that the Speedtail can resist the challenges of Casino Square.

Which, let's face it, is a likely destination. Let's just hope it's been able to use a decent proportion of that 1,036bhp on the way there. No word yet on how that's balanced between combustion engine and e-motor(s), but let's guess 750bhp from the familiar 4.0-litre twin turbo V8 and approaching 300bhp of electric. There's a conventional battery pack, but no plug-in socket. Instead, inductive charging.

Rumour is it won't run on electric alone. Shame. If true, this hybrid will have regressed from the P1. Will electricity still be helping out at high speed? Is there a clever gearing system to allow that? We just don't know, beyond realising that the 1,430kg dry weight means the battery pack can't be that big.

There are a couple of elephants in the room. Anyone else slightly underwhelmed by the stats? Only 7mph faster than the 25-year old F1, no more e-power than the Porsche 918 Spyder probably, a mere 1,036bhp total when Koenigsegg's Agera RS has a full megawatt (1,341bhp), and the Chiron has 1,479bhp. And 1,650bhp seems the entry point if you want to talk 300mph.

The only stat available so far is 0-186mph in 12.8secs. Bugatti's time is 13.1secs (the Bug might have a hefty power advantage, but it's also getting on for 600kg heavier – the two have near-identical power-to-weight ratios of around 740bhp per tonne). Nothing in it really, but McLaren has confirmed the Speedtail is rear-drive only. It'll be doing well to match the Bug's 2.4-sec 0–62mph time, but might just have caught up by 100mph (4.7secs). Mad enough, however you measure. For reference the F1 took 22.0secs to reach 186mph, the P1 16.5secs. So it's deeply, deeply fast, but not as rapid as the Koenigsegg Agera RS (11.9secs). Bragability is good, but not F1-level at launch.

But maybe that's the point. McLaren isn't talking 300mph, because the faster you want to go, the more you have to compromise – stiffer tyre sidewalls are just the beginning. Going back to first principles, McLaren wants the Speedtail to answer the hyper-GT question, not simply battle for bigger numbers. Seen from that point of view, it's hard to conclude that 250mph isn't ludicrously adequate. So 250mph it is, reached very quickly.

We can also assume McLaren is focusing on high-speed stability as a core facet, to make distance relaxing and undemanding. Wind and tyre noise will need to be minimised – in that respect, it's encouraging that the front tyres are modest 235-section, that there's nothing to snag the air passing over the canopy. I suspect it'll have a massive fuel tank ("more than 60 litres" is all Ultimate Series line director Andy Palmer would admit). Even so, it ought to be an efficient car.

The Speedtail's USP isn't speed, but seating. That central driving position is superb, as is the fact that McLaren has incorporated recessed handles in the headlining, and engineered "directional leather" that aids sliding in, then "subtly holds the occupant in place while they drive". This was necessary because the central seat couldn't have high bolsters. You do miss them. The centre seat makes the Speedtail egocentric. The symmetry is emphasised by how much it's been decluttered. No sun visors; instead, the Speedtail is fitted with electrochromic glass which darkens at the press of a button. The LED interior lights have been incorporated into the glass, too. The steering wheel is finished in glorious wood-like machined carbon. That material, super-tactile, carved from billet carbon where each layer is just 30 microns thick, is used for the paddles too. That's where you find the car controls, buttons for gearlever, start/stop and switchable dynamic modes. The most interesting one is Velocity.

This prepares the Speedtail for high speeds. "No extra key or anything," Palmer tells me, "this will do 250mph straight out of the box." It lowers, the active aero is optimised and the wing cameras fold away. Whether this makes it an illegal mode on the road, like the P1's track mode, McLaren has yet to admit.

PRICE £2.1 MILLION   **0-60** 2.5 SECONDS (EST)   **TOP SPEED** 250MPH   **POWER** 1,036BHP

DID YOU KNOW? IT HAS ELECTROCHROMIC GLASS, WHICH DARKENS WHEN ELECTRIC CURRENT RUNS THROUGH IT

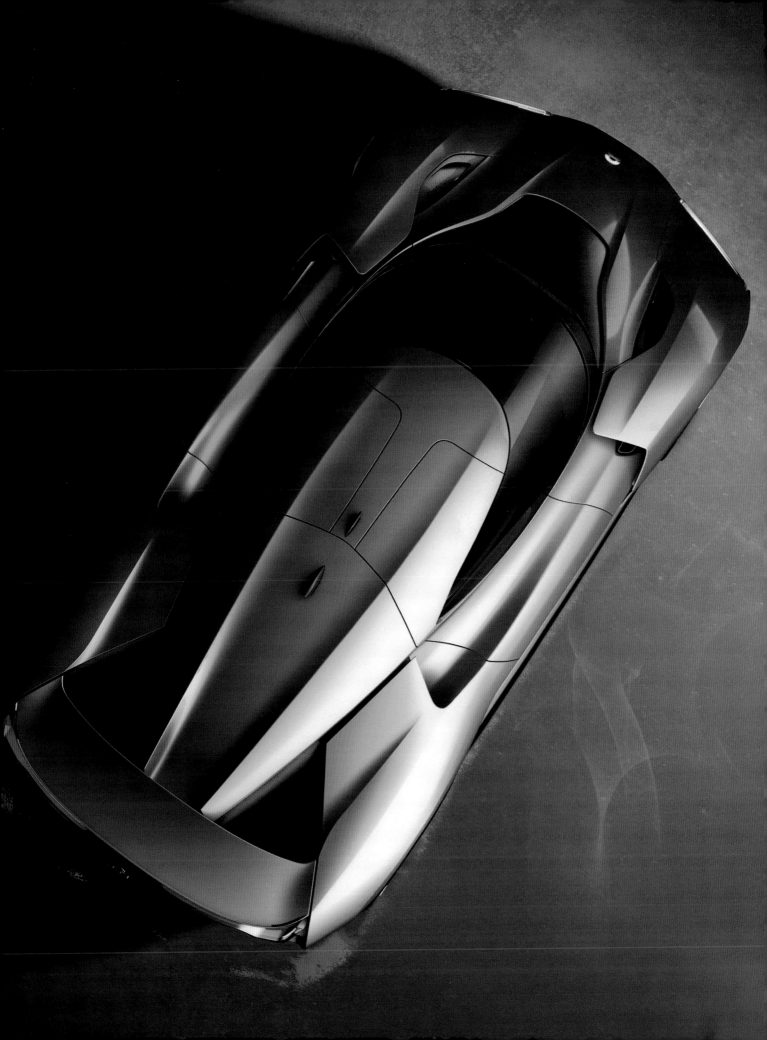

NIO EP9

A Chinese EV company is leading the
charge for a Nürburgring lap record

Like the Koenigsegg One:1, the Nio EP9 comes with one whole megawatt of power, which translates into 1,341bhp. That's enough for 0-124mph in 7.1 seconds – quicker than a Mazda MX-5 will complete 0-62mph – while its top speed is 195mph, unusually high for an EV. Perhaps more pertinently, it will apparently charge up in a mere 45 minutes, endowing it with a 265-mile range figure before you need to plug it back in again. It's got race car tech, trick aerodynamics and battery stacks hidden in enormous side sills so the weight is kept neatly within the wheelbase but allowing for vast Venturi tunnels which, apparently, reward 2.53g in lateral cornering and 3.3g longitudinal under braking. The EP9 is also trading blows with the likes of Lamborghini and McLaren on the modern-day battlefield that is the Nürburgring. Having set a lap time of 7min 5 seconds, a renewed attempt shaved an amazing 20 seconds off that, in the hands of endurance racing legend Peter Dumbreck. Over to the man himself. "The motors are the same [as the ones used when the Nio EP9 did a 7min 5sec lap], but I wasn't getting one megawatt of power (1,340bhp) for the full lap. We have to think about how long the lap is, how long the battery will last,

and what my top speed will be. A combustion engine burns a lot of fuel at top speed, likewise, it 'burns' a lot of batteries pushing a car through the air. So they can't let me have full power, because it'd burn the batteries out so quickly. They optimise the power I get for the full lap, and how quickly the batteries will heat up. Once we reach a certain temperature, we're doing damage to the batteries. I was getting somewhere around 700bhp. We're on specific NextEV tyres to withstand the weight and G-force, but aerodynamically, the car is the same as it was before. I also had more time in the car. When you've got an electric car and that kind of power, we do one lap on one charge. You can't run lap after lap after lap getting quicker and quicker. I start around the corner, having gone the wrong way down the track, line the car up, then say, 'get ready here I come'. I have to push right from the start. I've still only done eight laps of the Nürburgring in this car, across three separate days. And the second day I only got one lap because it was soaking wet. If you look at the Porsche 918 [6min 57sec], they ran day after day after day, whittling the time down, but we had to get it right [straight away]. The homework was done at the factory, we did

two days testing in good weather, and the pressure was on. I was thinking 'I'll do what I can', but it quickly became apparent that the outright record was on. On lap one I took four seconds off my previous record, after lap two I took another seven seconds off it, and then I took nine seconds off it, and that was me giving it everything, throwing caution to the wind. You can never drive the Nordschleife at 100 per cent because if you make one small mistake, you're in the barrier. The car's very stiff – that's why there's so much steering wheel movement in the on-board – so you've got to push it beyond comfort-level to get the lap time. And I'm really happy and proud that I got the time after all the team were relying on me… The basics are the same – racing line and what have you, but I have to adapt my style. In some places it's way faster than a GT3 car, but in others it's so stiff I can't carry the same sort of speed out of corners. The strangest thing is having no engine braking or downshifting –

it's all done with my right foot. I hammer into corners, slam on the brakes, and it locks up a little bit – we're not running ABS and traction control – so I'm basically driving as you would a bog-standard racecar. As of the latest update we do have regen on the brakes. It was a bit abrupt and strange, but by the end of the session it wasn't an issue for me. The car will be optimised more. It isn't even running full power. If they could optimise the batteries to give me 1,300bhp all the way around the 'Ring, imagine that! I can keep pushing on in the corners, but on the straights, you win free time if you've got more power. That's the next step – another 400 horsepower. I actually don't want to think about it – I'm still recovering from the last lap! If you watch the on-board closely you can see me give a long blink as I come onto the final straight, and that's me thinking 'bloody hell that was intense, but keep going, you've got one more section to make it through.'"

PRICE $1.2 MILLION **0-60** < 2.7 SECCONDS **TOP SPEED** 195MPH **POWER** 1,341BHP
DID YOU KNOW? THE BATTERIES WEIGH 317KG EACH, AND CAN BE SWAPPED FOR FRESH ONES. IF YOU'RE QUITE BURLY

MONSTER MILE

PRICE £1 MILLION **0-60** < 2.7 SECONDS **TOP SPEED** > 196MPH **POWER** 710BHP

DID YOU KNOW? ITALDESIGN STYLED JAPANESE CARS BEFORE: ISUZU PIAZZA, SUBARU SVX AND... MITSUBISHI NESSIE

NISSAN GTR 50

An £800k, 712bhp NISMO-spec limited run GTR in a very special set of clothes

Italdesign is the design powerhouse that gave us the VW Golf, Fiat Panda and Fiat Uno, amongst countless other far-reaching cars and concepts. The Nissan GT-R needs little introduction. Now they meet, and how, in the shape of the GT-R50 by Italdesign. Nissan's senior vice president for global design, Alfonso Albaisa, takes up the story. "We were approached by Italdesign just before the Geneva Motor show in 2017 with a proposal to make 'something special'. They showed us their creation Zerouno and walked us through the business of making a limited series. The idea to make 50 limited vehicles celebrating the 50 years of both the GT-R and Italdesign came from that meeting." While Italdesign developed, engineered and built the car, the GT-R50's extraordinary visuals are the work of Nissan's London Paddington and San Diego design outposts. Gold is definitely a thing on the GT-R50. There's an expanse of it on the car's nose, executed in such a way that it looks as though it belongs to another car altogether that's trying to push its way through. It's there in the 'samurai blade' cooling outlets behind the front wheels, and again in the rear of the car, to such an extent, says Nissan, that it appears as a separate modular element in the structure. "Not only is it a 50th anniversary colour, gold is used in Formula One and other performance machines due to its heat deflecting characteristics," Albaisa says. "We played with this and used it to represent the inner structure of the car. It is a kind of car within a car". The effect is set off in dramatic fashion by twin rear lights that really do look like they're floating free. A huge rear wing and diffuser anchor the GT-R50 in aerodynamic reality, but in every other sense this is a genius mash-up of European sensibilities and Japanese anti-design. It's still a GT-R, though. Pretty much the ultimate one, as you'd hope for a car whose starting price, if (when) it goes into limited production is approximately £800k. This is a full-blown NISMO machine, with a hand-made 3.8-litre V6 making 712bhp and 575 torques, featuring high flow, large diameter GT3 comp-spec twin turbos, enlarged intercoolers, heavy duty crankshaft, pistons, connecting rods, reworked intake and exhaust, beefed up dual-clutch 'box, and reinforced diff. The rear suspension uses Bilstein continuously variable dampers, there are huge Brembo brakes, and Michelin Pilot Super Sport rubber wrapped around 21in carbon fibre wheels. The GT-R50 may not be 'pretty', but it's pretty magnificent.

NOBLE M600

Ultra-low volume British car maker flies the flag for old-school dynamics

On paper, the Noble M600 is mildly rather than defiantly anti-establishment. The engine is Yamaha's surprisingly characterful 4.4-litre V8, ramped up to 650bhp with the help of a pair of turbochargers and bespoke pistons, conrods and crankshafts. It's mounted in the middle, longitudinally, and the transmission is a Graziano six-speed transaxle number. There are some interesting touches, including three power modes, 'road', 'track' and 'race', accessed via a switch that alters the boost pressure from 0.6 bar through to 1.0 bar, equating to 450bhp, 550bhp or 650bhp, and there's traction control.

Weighing just 1250kg, the M600 is unlikely to be found wanting whichever mode you're in, and with ZR-rated 255/30 Michelin Pilot Sport rubber on the front and enormous 335/30 tyres at the rear we should be talking electrifying turn-in, mid-corner neutrality, and an ocean of grip with a side order of sideways if that's your thing. Personally, I don't like prodding the laws of physics quite as hard in a mid-engined car as I would if the engine was upfront. The margin for error is that bit smaller, the slip angles harder to manage. We shall see.

It packs a far bigger visual punch in the flesh than it does in pictures. The chassis is a tubular steel spaceframe clothed in carbon composite panels, which lends its shape a fairly generic quality. Its nose, in particular, is a bit featureless, but it gets better as the eye travels along, and the rear end is stunning. It has the uncomplicated aesthetic appeal of a '90s Ferrari.

The real eye-opener, however, is inside. Not since the steampunk swoop of the TVR Cerbera's cabin has a low-volume Brit car looked or smelt as good as the M600. The flat-bottomed wheel is lovely, the instruments are simple and clear but have a nice typographic twist, and the mix of carbon fibre, leather, Alcantara and aluminium is expertly done. Less impressive is the driving position: the pedals are annoyingly off-set to the left, and if you have feet bigger than, say, size nine and aren't wearing your finest suede Alpine Stars, you will struggle. You may even find your left leg goes to sleep, which is unhelpful given its key role in the gear-changing process.

The Noble is generally a doddle and delight to drive. Very little acclimatisation is needed here; you get in, you get comfortable, you fire the V8 up, paddle for a bit in its endless sea of torque (604lb ft at 3800rpm), and surf along at five-tenths extremely gracefully indeed. The M600's steering is light and linear, the other major controls have a delicacy and engineered feel that feels expensively resolved, and though the gearchange isn't quite as consistent and doesn't like to be rushed, it's still lovely to use. Only the brakes belie the car's fundamentally aggressive remit: there's barely any servo assistance, and feel at the top of the pedal is lacking. But with 380mm ventilated discs at the front and 350mm at the rear, ultimate stopping power is not in question.

In 450bhp 'road' mode, this is no more taxing an experience than, say, an M3. With a similar breadth of ability. But the M600 is a car that will light up its rear wheels in race mode in fourth gear at 120mph, so this isn't exactly a beginner's experience. Once you've dialled into it, its chassis and steering are a revelation; you might run out of talent eventually, but you'd have to be going some. It's an amazingly polished effort from such a tiny company. Jump out of a McLaren or Ferrari and into this, and the credibility gap is much slimmer than you'd imagine.

PRICE £250,000 **0-60** 3.0 SECONDS **TOP SPEED** 225MPH **POWER** 641BHP

DID YOU KNOW? NOBLE HAS BEEN IN BUSINESS SINCE 1999, MAKING IT YOUNGER THAN PAGANI AND KOENIGSEGG

"THE M600'S STEERING IS LIGHT AND LINEAR AND THE OTHER MAJOR CONTROLS HAVE A DELICACY AND ENGINEERED FEEL THAT FEELS EXPENSIVELY RESOLVED "

*is for ODDBALLS

ODDBALLS

Aspark, Vanda and Hispano Suiza: an optimistic trio of supercar wannabes

The Aspark Owl is a Japanese EV hypercar that looks like a 1990s Le Mans prototype, costs a reputed $3.6m (£2.8m) and does 0-62mph in a verified 1.9 seconds. Not often, thanks to a 93-mile range, but once is probably enough to make Elon Musk's humanoid suit twitch.

It'll never be built, right? Vapourware. Well, you might think that, but Aspark has other ideas. Aspark has signed a contract with Manifattura Automobili Torino (MAT) "for the final development and build of the Owl," and "is sure to have found the right place and the right partner to develop the fastest accelerating EV." Why so confident? Well, MAT has become the go-to place for blank cheque clients with a hypercar itch to scratch. Currently on the books is the reborn New Stratos and the '5,000bhp' Devel Sixteen. MAT was also the outfit bringing the Apollo Intensa Emozione to life, before development was curiously handed over to German racing team HWA AG.

With the first of the 50 Owls set to be delivered in 2020, the clock is ticking for Aspark. The company says: "M.A.T. will support Aspark in the vehicle development and in reaching the very aggressive targets that Aspark has set for this full electric hypercar. The Owl will be manufactured in a bespoke facility that will take full advantage of MAT experience in hypercars manufacturing. "The Owl project will allow MAT to continue the company growth and to expand into a new sector: the full electric hypercars. MAT strengths and experience are well known internationally and have been recognised during the selection process."

The Vanda Dendrobium is a nature-inspired two-seat EV is being co-developed with Williams Advanced Engineering. The radical two-seat all-electric concept wants to sniff out other hypercars with a top speed in excess of 200mph and 0-60mph in 2.7 seconds. That first stat is impressive – and difficult to achieve – for an EV, while the second isn't exactly hypercarish given a seven-seat EV family can already better it. Supercar, yes. Hypercar, no. Possible? Err, maybe.

Like the upcoming AMG One and Aston Martin Valkyrie – both utilising the expertise of F1 firms to make barely-believable performance believable – Vanda, a small (as in 20 employees small) electrics firm has done the same by roping in Williams (another firm with F1-nous) to co-develop the car and get its

head round the drive-y bits but also give this ambitious project a sliver of credibility by proxy.

However, unlike Aston Martin and AMG, Vanda does not have decades of road car experience and a proven portfolio of rip-snorting road cars to build from. Instead, it has a small electric truck with a 62-mile range called the Ant, and a 37-mile all EV monkey bike called the Motochimp. Combined top speed of both? Less than 30mph. We have a feeling there could be some late nights ahead in Camp Vanda.

Now meet the Hispano Suiza Carmen, named after the current president's mother, Carmen Mateu – who's also the Hispano Suiza founder's granddaughter – and uniquely styled. It uses Formula E developed battery tech to send 1,005bhp to the rear wheels only, and with its top speed curtailed at 155mph. "I don't want to compete with the performance of a Koenigsegg or a Rimac," says technical directior Lluc Marti. "We limit the top speed because we don't think there's sense in any more." It's a bold statement when Marti's CV includes three years at Koenigsegg itself, working on the One:1. While there's a carbon tub at its core, this isn't a honed hypercar that's aiming to out-handle its contemporaries. "No, not at all! We are closer to visiting Pebble Beach than the Nürburgring."

PAGANI ZONDA LM

A day out in a one-off, £3.5m Zonda is a day to savour. And prepare for

Coachbuilding. Doesn't sound right, does it? It has the whiff of stiff-shirted Victorian artisans polishing walnut until they can see the reflections of their handlebar moustaches. Now try *carrozzeria*. In their pre-or post WWII pomp, these guys weren't just panel-beaters, they were alchemists. Princes, playboys and industrialists patronised them like Vienna's barons kept Beethoven afloat 130 years earlier.

Rarity is the ultimate calling card, and nothing is rarer or more desirable than a one-off, especially if it's Italian. Or, best of all, a Pagani. Horacio Pagani, of course, is actually Argentinian, and his wonderful little company isn't strictly speaking a *carrozzeria* at all. But nor is it a conventional car company. Not since Enzo Ferrari has an individual followed their vision with such singular passion. Pagani's cars have more in common with Fabergé eggs, or Stradivarius violins, or maybe even an 18th century symphony. Pagani himself has a well-documented fascination with the Italian Renaissance, and named one of his sons Leonardo (Da Vinci-inspired rather than Di Caprio).

There have been 300 or so Paganis since 1999, including many Zondas, none of which are identical. Despite their hand-made construction and 20th century motive force – or possibly because of it – they have a fanatical following among some of Silicon Valley's most significant powerbrokers. I also know of one Pagani owner who overcooked it badly while driving his car in the Alps somewhere. Such is the integrity of the Zonda's chassis, both driver and passenger were completely unscathed; the owner phoned the factory to inform them of the incident, and simply ordered a new car with his next breath.

Pagani will build you whatever you want, not because the company is riding the bespoke bandwagon for all it's worth, but because it helped resurrect the bandwagon in the first place, then gave it some carbon fibre clothes.

Today we're in Gran Sasso, a vast tract of impossibly beautiful national park inland and not far from L'Aquila – still recovering from 2009's terrible earthquake – on Italy's eastern seaboard. There will be no limit-baiting up here. Not only does the road unfurl in a sinuous ribbon through serrated mountain peaks, it's virtually deserted. Better still, the full-lock hairpins at the lower end give way to long, fast, possibly even full-bore fifth gear sweepers and straights. The thought of fifth gear up here in the

Zonda LM makes my throat constrict a little.

Many, many things bounce around your brain as you grapple with a Pagani for the first time. As befits Horacio's enlightened remit, this is as close as any car comes to being a piece of art or sculpture. Just sitting in it seems enough to defile it, never mind driving the thing. On the other hand, the Zonda is the perfect vehicle for anyone who reckons that the contemporary supercar isn't as scary as it should be. The quality and uniqueness of the experience is what characterises truly memorable cars these days, which is why a Rolls Phantom or Bentley Mulsanne is worth the price of entry. But in a world where a Honda Civic has 300bhp, fast cars need to be extra special.

The Zonda delivers fear, and demands respect. Alongside the knurled aluminium switches, the atmosphere inside is loaded with the unusual and distinctive emotion that only comes when you're driving someone else's £3.5m, 700bhp-plus, carbon-fibre bodied one-off masterpiece up an Italian mountain. A mountain that still has fingers of ice and snow clinging to the toppermost part of the road. In June. And do you know what, this really a scary car. It has that wonderful fighter jet cockpit feel, and the LM's nose features tumescent new front wings that give it a son-of-LMP1/Group C racer throwback look, enabling you to place it on the road accurately. It has electrifying turn-in, which helps too. But it has curvy hips, over-your-shoulder visibility is negligible, and it's oh-so-very fast. It doesn't like to trundle or tootle, and the non-airbagged wheel wriggles constantly in your hands. It makes a Bugatti Veyron feel like a Polo.

It's a very special place in which to sit and be slightly scared, though. Engineering is one thing, but you've got to love a car created by a man who clearly knows his Michelangelo from his Michael Schumacher. For something designed to plonk you directly onto the expressway to visceral fun, the Zonda is impressively pretentious. I've never used my iPhone's camera to take pictures of a throttle pedal before, and the indicator stalks are like RKO-era *Flash Gordon* rocketships.

The LM is owned by an Argentinian, but registered in Andorra. I'd like us to remain friends. When I ask the man from Pagani what sort of business he's in, he smiles and says, "Lots of businesses." He worked with Horacio for two years on this car, and the result is 'one of one', as it says on the engine bay.

It's also deliberately bipolar. An Italian tricolore runs the length of the driver's side, with the German national colours on the other (the owner has German roots). They meet in the prow of the Zonda's bonnet, and even appear on the brake calipers and in the headrests. The highly personal nature of Pagani's products puts this beyond objective debate. Um…

There's no doubting the rest of it, though. The reworked nose also contains a new headlight design. If you can get past that, the exposed carbon-fibre remains a stunning Pagani USP, but even that is outpointed by the LM's roof-mounted air intake and fin and rear-wing party trick. The Cinque summons 750kg of downforce at 186mph – the McLaren P1 GTR has a weedy 660kg at 150mph – so Lord knows what the LM is generating.

Supplies of AMG's 7.3-litre engine are dwindling, and although the LM's has never been on a dyno, Pagani reckons its power output is now well north of 700bhp. Consider this car a testimonial. Its red line has been raised to 7500rpm, and the exhaust system features an inconel ceramic-coated manifold and titanium muffler. It's blue, and extremely expensive looking. It would win plaudits from berks in polo necks if it were mounted on Charles Saatchi's wall, Gatling gun exit set-up and all.

The LM explodes into life with the expected ferocity, but settles into a cultured idle, which is unexpected. Its ride is amazingly supple, courtesy of a suspension set-up whose magnesium uprights, titanium springs and Ohlins dampers mimic the same competition cars the LM's styling draws from. As the LM's core is made of Pagani's patented carbon-titanium über-material, its sense of structural integrity, the immediacy of its movements, and its body control will be unlike anything you know unless you're a top-flight racing driver. No wonder Lewis Hamilton keeps one in Monaco.

Probably a proper manual, though. The LM uses a six-speed robotised sequential 'box made by Cima, and it's kinda old school. experiences that takes all the stuff you thought you knew about 'fast' and rearranges it. Never mind trees and hedges blurring past, the Zonda LM can make entire mountains disappear. Brake hard and they all rush back into view again. It's surreal and unreal. It's emotional. The other big challenge comes from simply holding on when you open the taps. The road to the top of Gran Sasso unspools into a spectacular – and welcome – straight, giving you some idea of this crazy landscape. It even looks lunar. The Zonda beams its way across the plain, part-Batmobile, part-spaceship, and I can see it shed tiny nuggets of rubber from those vast 335/30 Pirellis on what is a pretty abrasive surface. If it started to hover above the surface or take off altogether, it wouldn't be that surprising.

It's also truly personal. That is the essence of Pagani's success. The engineering and execution is superb, but it also channels the spirit of an earlier, artisanal age. Money can buy most things, but this sort of experience is priceless. These days, the wealthy are pouring cash into tangible assets, like art or cars. Pagani has figured out how to combine them better than anyone.

PRICE £3.5 MILLION **0-60** < 3.4 SECONDS **TOP SPEED** 217MPH (EST) **POWER** 750BHP

DID YOU KNOW? AUSTRALIAN SOFT-ROCK SINGER JOHN FARNHAM FIRST RETIRED IN 2003... AND, AS FAR AS WE CAN TELL, HASN'T MANAGED TO MAKE IT STICK YET.

PAGANI HUAYRA BC

A special edition Pagani in honour of the man who helped grease the wheels

It's time to concentrate. Exiting the final turn, I pin the throttle and feel my neck muscles strain. And strain some more, my head not so gently forced backwards as 811lb ft pours through the rear 355/25 Pirelli P-Zeros. The Sicilian countryside peels back at the edges and fires out of the rear-view mirror through the letterbox between the BC's rear wing and the tail-mounted mobile ailerons as they dance and adjust to optimise the downforce.

It doesn't take long to figure out that this is a seriously fast car, a brutal assault on the senses, and I quickly form the opinion that small and perfectly formed Sicily might not be quite big enough for the BC. The initial assault plateaus slightly as we pass 5,500rpm, but as we hit 6,000, it's time for another gear and after a brief interlude, another sizeable volume of Sicilian atmosphere is sucked up by the V12's huge turbos and detonated rearwards. This island is definitely not ready for fifth, unless I want to bury BC no.2 into the side of Mt Etna, so it's time to jump on the bespoke carbon ceramics, which bite and slow Sicily down... sometime later, I remember to breathe.

Rewind. Let me explain what I'm in and why I'm here. The Huayra BC is Horacio Pagani's latest hypercar. In a lineage peppered with some of the most unique automotive creations on the planet, the BC is a rolling tribute to someone without whom the Pagani brand would have remained a few scribbles on a sketch pad: Benny Caiola. Caiola – who passed away in 2010 – happened to be Pagani's first-ever customer and a man who was so taken with Horacio's passion to create automotive works of art that he became a lifelong Pagani fan and mentor. Over breakfast, Horacio talks passionately about Caiola and the pressure of creating a car that needed to do justice to the memory of the man. It's a tribute and a requiem. For Horacio Pagani, only the best would therefore do.

Horacio is keen to walk me around the BC and explain the detail – as you may have guessed, Pagani is all about the detail. And this is a fairly hefty transformation of the type. For a start, the purity of the Huayra's original form has been modified somewhat in the pursuit of downforce. Pagani spent months working with Dallara on the aero, resulting in the modi cation of every panel of the original car, with the exception of the roof. The final shape is striking, complex and aggressive, and probably

better shown off without this two-tone paint job. Pretty? I'll leave that decision to you. But it looks... purposeful. The complexity of the aesthetic reworking is a visual touchpoint to the fanatical massaging of minutiae and general technomancy that lies beneath. As the front and rear bodywork are hoisted and the guts of the thing exposed, Horacio gets animated.

We start at the front, where the external aero work is complemented by plenty of internal fettling (mainly to reduce drag and optimise the ow of cooling air across mechanical components) and work through from there. There are channels and intakes galore. The new bespoke Brembo carbon- ceramic brakes come equipped with six-piston calipers (four-pot rears), are generously sized at 380mm and also happen to be six per cent lighter than those fitted to the standard Huayra. The forged APP wheels – 20 inches at the front, 21 on the rear and delivering a further 9kg weight saving – are wrapped in Pirelli P Zero Corsa rubber, developed in conjunction with the manufacturer.

You know I mentioned attention to detail? Each tyre uses 12 different compounds across the section to maximise performance. And there's more. The suspension uprights and wishbones are made from Avional, a lightweight aluminium alloy usually used in aeronautical applications, reducing the weight by 25 per cent. The dampers are, again, bespoke Öhlins creations, and the BC sees the first use of a new and as yet unnamed type of carbon fibre which is claimed to be 50 per cent lighter and 20 per cent stronger than 'regular' weave.

At the heart of the BC sits the now familiar 6.0-litre AMG V12 bi-turbo, uprated to deliver 789bhp and 811 torques to the wheels through all-new tripod drive shafts – a technology and design derived from Le Mans prototypes. Most significantly, the mighty V12 meets CARB (California Air Resources Board) and EU6 emissions legislations – no mean feat for such a big motor – and Pagani has a commitment from AMG that it will continue to supply engines (and engineer them to pass for emissions testing) until 2023, something that guarantees a V12 Pagani at least a handful of years into the future.

Transmitting all that power and turbo torque to the wheels is an all-new seven-speed automated manual transmission developed from the ground up with Xtrac, and mounted transversely to focus the mass towards the centre of the car. After all, better c-of-g means better turn-in and stability. It's still a single-clutch 'box, but features new electro hydraulic actuation and carbon- fibre synchronisers (Horacio likes carbon fibre), halving shift times from 150ms in the standard Huayra to 75ms. No zeitgeisty double-clutch? Pagani argues that the combined weight of 'box and sympathetic electronic diff is 40 per cent

lighter than a current generation DSG. And the BC is all about staying nippy. More? The V12 exhales through an exhaust system that could sit in a sculpture park. Made from titanium, it weighs 2.9kg, a staggering 7.1kg lighter than the standard exhaust. All this fastidious and unrelenting attention to development delivers a total weight saving of 132kg... or the weight of a new-born elephant. Actual fact.

Inside, the BC is a predictably special place to occupy, in this case the combination of deep red leather, anthracite suede and matt carbon fibre contrasting with inky gloss-black highlights demonstrating Pagani at its best. If you're in any doubt, the naked gear linkage remains a stunning creation.

Briefing over, we leave Horacio to his morning constitutional, twist the BC's key and head up to Sicily's mountain pass with Etna looming in the distance. Time to find out if it feels any different. The first thing that strikes you is how supple the BC feels: there's a compliance in the chassis that allows it to isolate where other hypercars would crash. There's also a refreshing simplicity in its operation. Simply press the somewhat unassuming button on the steering wheel and dial through the settings, Comfort, Sport and Race... and beyond that your options boil down to whether to change gear via the stick or paddles.

Despite the complexity of its design, the simplicity and usability is something Horacio is particularly proud of, as is his focus on the safety of his customers: you can turn everything off in the BC, but it has a fail-safe, which reactivates traction control if it senses the temperature drop below nine degrees. Icy road embarrassment foiled.

As for the driving, it's obvious the steering is sharper than in the original Huayra, the brakes are comfortingly mighty, the power delivery immense. But having experienced the aural insanity of the unboosted V12 in the Zonda F, I can't help but miss its nerve-shredding soundtrack and epic rev range. The bi-turbo V12 is hugely potent at the bottom end, but, by 5,500, its initial bite tails off and, by 6, it's pretty much done. That's not to say that it's not startlingly fast, but that it makes power in a different way to the older naturally aspirated cars. The same can be said of the noise – immense but a different flavour when equipped with chittering blowers.

The reality is that for Pagani to survive it had to go turbo, but managing emissions also opened the door for what is now Pagani's biggest customer base, and Benny Caiola's home market, the USA. With AMG promising a continuous supply until 2023, the bi-turbo V12 allows the story to continue, and with all 20 €2.3m BCs sold and orders being placed for a Huayra BC Roadster, it's clear the Pagani journey has a way to go yet.

PRICE £2.1 MILLION **0-60** 2.8 SECONDS **TOP SPEED** > 230MPH **POWER** 789BHP

DID YOU KNOW? MERCEDES DOESN'T MAKE V12S FOR ITS OWN CARS ANY MORE – BUT IT DOES FOR PAGANI

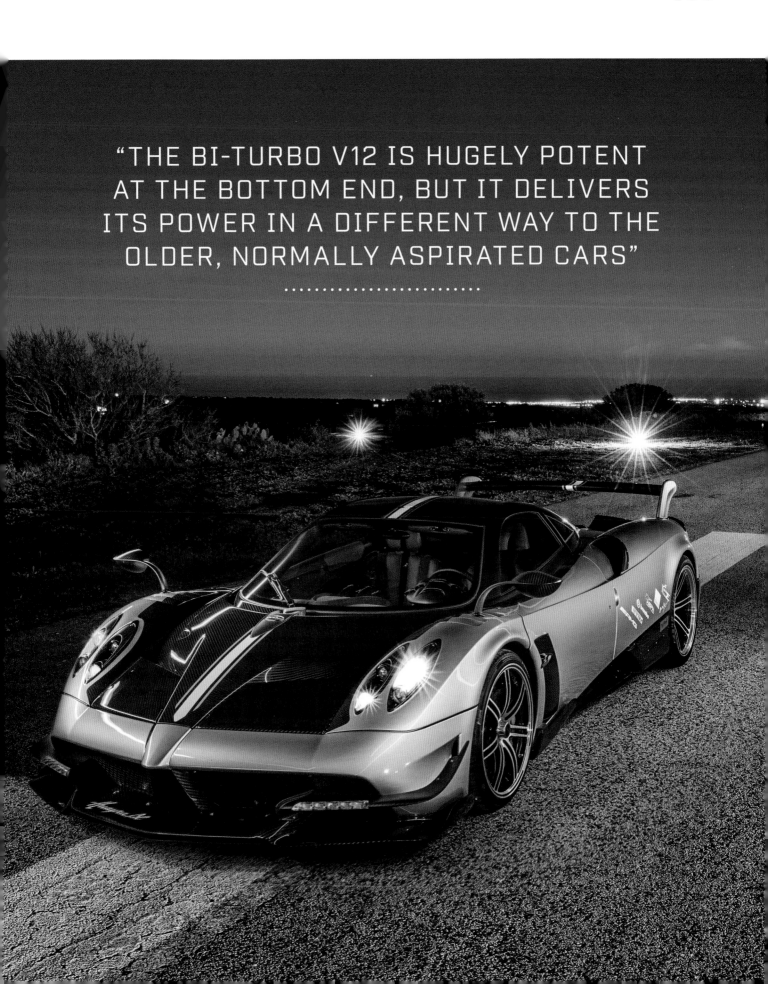

"THE BI-TURBO V12 IS HUGELY POTENT AT THE BOTTOM END, BUT IT DELIVERS ITS POWER IN A DIFFERENT WAY TO THE OLDER, NORMALLY ASPIRATED CARS"

"THE PLAN IS TO BUILD A TOTAL OF 150 BATTISTAS AT A COST OF APPROXIMATELY £2M EACH, AND PININFARINA SEES ITSELF AS A PIONEER IN THE LUXURY EV SPACE"

PININFARINA BATTISTA

Pininfarina has designed countless beautiful cars. Now it has done one of its own...

In the midst of a welter of startling facts, the folk tasked with communicating the Pininfarina Battista have plenty to draw on. It's the most powerful road-legal car ever to come out of Italy, a country that's produced its fair share of powerful road-legal cars. Thanks to a 120 kWh lithium ion battery pack and an electric motor on each wheel, it produces approximately 1900bhp and 1696 torques. Both are barmy numbers and imbue the Battista with accelerative urge to rival a Formula One car. Zero to 62mph apparently takes a tarmac-melting sub-two seconds, 186mph up in less than 12. All without the toxic haze of spent hydrocarbons. Welcome, high-net worth guilt-free zero emissions ultra-performance.

But elsewhere there's talk of creating 'the first car to make the world love electric vehicles', a tacit acknowledgement that, unless you're one of Elon's Tesla evangelists, the fast-forwarding electric revolution has yet to deliver a car you'd stick on your metaphorical bedroom wall – unless you dig Croatian start-up Rimac or China's NIO EP9. So, is the Battista 'The One'?

This is where the Pininfarina part should come in handy, because the history this name can leverage is pretty much the history of the car itself. Certainly car design. With just one exception, every Ferrari series production car to have emerged from Maranello between 1951 and 2008 wore the funky little Pininfarina imprint on its body somewhere (Ferrari's in-house Centro Stile, recently installed in an amazing new building, has been in charge for the past decade).

And there's romance. Battista 'Pinin' Farina was the youngest son in a family of 11 children, and proved precociously talented in the pioneering days of the automobile. He began working in his brother Giovanni's body shop aged just 12, and met and impressed both Fiat founder Giovanni Agnelli and Henry Ford while still a teenager.

Carrozzeria Pinin Farina was founded in 1928, and designed and made bodies for Alfa Romeo, Fiat, Lancia and many more. Banned from appearing at the 1946 Paris auto salon (Italy was still persona non grata after the war), Battista and his son Sergio drove two of their cars over from Turin, parked up outside, and stole the show. The following year, the Cisitalia 202 appeared, not just the first car with fully enclosed bodywork but one with

sufficiently sculptural form to be recognised by New York's Museum of Modern Art. To date, it's one of only nine cars in the permanent collection, and it's there, says MoMA's specialist Paul Galloway, because it represents "a specific moment where the technology, the craft, the artistry, and the cultural importance crosses the threshold into a masterpiece."

"Battista was an outlier, one in a million," his grandson, Pininfarina SpA's CEO Paolo Pininfarina tells me, paraphrasing writer Malcolm Gladwell's theory. "To succeed as an outlier, you need three things: talent, commitment, and to be born at the right moment and raised in the right place. He was born in 1893, in Turin, born with the automobile, and surrounded by other talented people who were exploring the future of the car. With these three things, success came."

Automobili Pininfarina is hoping to parlay this into big, standalone success. It's a new company, located in Munich, that sits parallel to the established Pininfarina SpA based in Cambiano, close to Turin. The project follows the company's 2015 acquisition by Indian industrial giant Mahindra, which paid around £125m. The plan is to build a total of 150 Battistas at a cost of approximately £2m each, and it sees itself 'as a pioneer in the luxury EV space'.

It uses a carbon fibre monocoque, with the batteries housed behind the occupants and along the sides in a T format. The electrical architecture is being co-developed with Rimac (itself 10 per cent owned by Porsche, and a supplier to Aston Martin, Renault, and others). It's still heavy, of course, but Pininfarina insists the layout delivers the optimum weight distribution: with four motors feeding power and torque to each wheel, it also features torque vectoring, though Lord knows 1900bhp is a challenge. Ex-F1 driver Nick Heidfeld is currently grappling with that one, along with former Porsche, Pagani and Bugatti chassis guru Dr Peter Tutzer. "Top end numbers are less impressive as they are a given these days," Tutzer says. The driving experience is key. Braking is by carbon ceramic discs and six-piston calipers, 390mm diameter at the front, 380mm at the rear. Its range is likely to be around 300 miles, 80 per cent of which can be replenished in 40 minutes on a rapid charger.

"Electrification allows us to support hypercar development with instant torque. We might even have to dial it down as its reaction time is up to 20 times faster than an ICE," the company's chief technical officer Christian Jung says. "We are trying to go to the extremes that neither Tesla nor the major OEMs are targeting as we take an absolute focus on what a traditional

hypercar customer wants in a car first, then what he or she will expect from new technologies within a new package."

The cockpit features a 'vanishing point' aspect to the main display and a futuristically driver-centric layout. The interior is covered in the finest materials, although expect to see fashionable recycleable materials rather than the usual leathery tropes. Each car can be personalised to whatever degree the client seeks to achieve; the car you see here is finished in Pura pearlescent white, whose red aluminium line in the body side is a subtle but knowing nod to the Pininfarina Modulo, a 1970 concept that reworked a Ferrari 512 S chassis to magnificently outré effect.

That the Battista is more traditional in form than a near 50-year-old concept might seem a little disappointing at first, but it's also deliberate. And the car is still a corker, replete with the sort of surfacing and detail that takes an aeon to perfect.

"We wanted to keep the form and proportion of a traditional supercar," chief designer Luca Borgogno says. "We did a lot of research, thought about how much of a spaceship it could have been, but elected to create something in line with our history, true to Pininfarina's values. The cabin pushing forward, the long tail balancing the visual weight – it's still the best configuration you can find. For us it was clear this was the way to go."

Automobili Pininfarina intends to develop the car with the right partners, rather than sinking a fortune into R&D and sabotaging the economic argument for going there in the first place. In this respect, Apple's 'asset-light' structure is a more apposite example than Porsche. Over to the man who's writing the cheques, Mahindra chairman, Anand Mahindra.

"I love Bugatti," he says, "and it was the dream of a true visionary to rejuvenate the brand. We all agree on that. But the amount of money you'd need to invest to take on the Chiron… if you choose your weapon well and you do it with electric technology, you can achieve it with a lower level of investment. I also believe electrification will lead to a new generation of more efficient petrol engines. The technologies will co-exist for some time yet."

PRICE £2 MILLION **0-60** < 2.0 SECONDS **TOP SPEED** 218MPH **NUMBER BUILT** 1,874BHP
DID YOU KNOW? THE BATTISTA'S POWERFUL ELECTRIC DRIVETRAIN COMES COURTESY OF CROATIAN FIRM RIMAC

PORSCHE 935

A £750k, 77-run limited run special doffs its cap at one of Porsche's greatest hits

Revealed to the public in September of 2018, the new Porsche 935 presides heartily over Porsche's twin fetishes for carbon-fibre composites and endless intellectual pillage of its back catalogue. Luckily, Porsche happens to have a deep, rich seam of brilliant old stuff with which to play, so neither is a particular problem. Still, the basics run to the 935/'18 being a 77-unit special that pays homage to the legendary 935 from 1978 – the one they call 'Moby Dick'. Because the new 935 isn't homologated for any race series or particular championship (though it is eligible to race), the engineers had a more relaxed brief than usual, and they went... a bit mad.

Underneath, it's basically a new 911 GT2 RS (991.2 for those who need to know the Stuttgart decimals) plumped to 700bhp-ish. It's a smidge under five metres long (4.87), and properly wide at over two metres (2.03), with extended bodywork like its grandad. There's also a bonkers rear wing that's 1.9m across and as thick as your forearm, with LED lights on endplates like small car doors. In fact, they're endplates from the 919 Hybrid LMP1 car. Similarly, the wing mirrors are nicked from the Le Mans-winning 911 RSR, the fan-style aero wheel rims a nod to the original 935/78, the machine-gun, centre-exit, titanium twin exhausts harking back to the Porsche 908 from 1968. Even the shift knob for the PDK 'box is lightweight laminated wood, just like hardcore Porsches of old, like the 917, Carrera GT and Bergspyder. To me, it just looks like a giant, boiled sweet.

In fact, there's such heavy invocation of legendary connections, it gets a bit Porsche Greatest Hits after a bit, and you start to wonder at the blur between cool and kitsch. We get it, Porsche. Cool old cars had good details. It doesn't mean to say that glueing them all onto a new thing will also equal greatness. Except for the fact that the new 935 is a proper jaw-dropper.

Just look at it. There are nostrils. There are vents and gaps packed tight with radiators. There are those delicious aero wheels, beautiful strakes on top of the wheelarches that pull the car forwards in a static caricature of speed, accentuated by the legendary swooping Martini livery. Up close, the rear wing is simply enormous, the brake lights of the 911 that got eaten by the 935's bodywork tucked up under the rear. Everything is carbon or Kevlar, apart from the exhausts, which resemble titanium gatling guns. Inside there is a full FIA 'cage, motorsport-spec dash panel and too many buttons to count. You can bias the brakes across separate front and rear circuits, set up the traction control – or switch it off entirely – disable the ESP or accidentally set off the in-built fire extinguisher before making use of the rooftop escape hatch. It is, all told, a pretty serious-feeling thing. Underneath, it's all well proved, and no less exciting. A 3.8-litre twin-turbo flat-six from the GT2, that seven-speed PDK dual-clutch paddle 'box driving the rear wheels through a rigid-mounted rear axle. It weighs pretty much the same as a GT2 RS at 1,380kg, and rocks a set of 380mm steel discs with six-pot aluminium callipers at the front and 355mm four-pistons at the back. For best effect, mix in a set of hot slicks and stand well back. Everyone should stand well back. Preferably behind a ballistic wall.

Things have been explained. I wasn't listening properly, and have very little idea of what the buttons do on the Knight Rider cut-down carbon wheel. Nerves. But too soon, the in-built air jacks thump the car to the floor, the mechanics gracefully arc away like human curtains and I'm waved out onto the Lausitzring. A race circuit I've never driven and have no idea of the layout. I plop the PDK into drive, click into manual and creep out, allowing the first few calibration rotations of the wheels along the straight ahead. Turn left, toddle out of the pits… BLAAAAAARGH. Oh yeah, pitlane speed limiter. Hit the button top right and we're off. Quite slowly.

The first couple of laps are relatively slow, to avoid shearing the surface off the brand new slicks, and to learn what I can of the circuit. There are bumps, a couple of straights, some endless corners with multiple apexes, of which I hit precisely none. The 935 feels ridiculously light for its visual heft, keen, a bit angry. But not difficult. I may not be a racing driver, but this car is not all that intimidating, once you get out of the pits. I feel a slight vibration from the rear right and pop back into the pitlane to check. Nothing to worry about, just some slight rubber pickup from not using the 'accepted' racing line… um.

Turned out once more, and I start to up the pace, everything switched on. It's quick, no doubt, but race circuits tend to dull your impression of speed, so I'm left thinking it's fast, but not desperate. Not sure of the gearing, but it's halfway through sixth on the big straight, and I can't find the mode for the speedo. The brakes are like standing on a piece of wood, and you have to leg press the pedal as hard as possible to get any reaction. Once you do, the braking is immense and bizarrely regular and fade-free – do this sort of stuff in a road car and you'd be picking brake disc out of the wheelarches within three laps, and your teeth out of the steering wheel.

It is at this point, having got a bit cocky after a few laps, that I inevitably overcook it. Coming off the main straight into a downhill left-hander, I miss my previous braking marker and end up trying to push the brake pedal through the floor. Unable to shed enough speed, there's not much for it but to turn in and maybe try to spin the car somewhere in the confines of the tarmac. The 935 does not spin. The 935 runs through the corner like a mag-lev train. I'm so surprised, the next two corners are toast. Which is when realisation hits. If you think you have experienced downforce in a roadgoing car, you haven't. Not really. Because a racecar on slicks with proper downforce is abso-bloody-lutely unmistakable. Given the epiphany, the next five laps get sketchier and sketchier: later braking, slamming the pedal and then bleeding off towards the apex, loading the car through the Lausitzring's longer corners and feeling invisible forces bullied by the 935's aero.

Driving this car is as hard as driving any 911. Driving this car to the limit of its abilities will take practice, confidence, and quite a bit of cash. By the end of the too-short session, I don't want to go back into the pits. This stuff is horribly, horribly addictive. To eke out that last mph. To brake that little bit later. To try desperately to link a perfect corner with another… without screwing it up. It's as complicated as chess on a bouncy castle, but by God I love it, come the end. And the 935 is about as perfect a thing as it gets. It makes 700bhp feel manageable, feels like a proper racecar, looks like a sculpture. It's less about pastiche than just being a bit retro and celebratory. Getting out of the car I just want to hug all the mechanics. I really do.

PRICE £750,000 **0-60** 2.7 SECONDS **TOP SPEED** 211MPH (APPROX) **POWER** 700BHP

DID YOU KNOW? WHEN PLAYING 'MOBY DICK', BONHAM'S DRUM SOLOS COULD LAST 30 MINUTES. WHAT A WEAPON…

PORSCHE GT2 RS

Know your 911s? Then you'll know that this one is the king

The GT2 RS doesn't look like a factory-built Porsche. There has always been some intangible Porsche-ness to Weissach-developed machinery, from the way it sits on the road, to the design of the alloy wheels – even the iconography of the lettering and the aerodynamic additions. You could spot it a mile off. It just looked right.

Not so this new 991-generation GT2 RS. I'm not saying it looks wrong – although I'm sure many people will think it quite foul – but that the combined effect of all that black plastic and carbon against the silver paintwork and lord-knows-what-else is to appear a little, how can I put it... aftermarket. Perhaps a darker colour would lessen the aftermarketness of the look?

There are, I suspect, two reasons why this car appears the way it does. The first is concerned with keeping a 691bhp 911 attached to the road surface as it accelerates to 211mph, a speed, incidentally, it would exceed were Michelin able to supply a tyre capable of doing just that. The rear wing is pinched from the last GT3 RS, but mounted higher, and the front scoops and troughs and chins are new for this car. The sad truth of the matter, though, is that this car exists as much to make children point as it does to zip around the Nürburgring in 6:47.3.

The effect it has on people is quite alarming. Pootle along at 20mph in town, which you can do with zero effort, thanks to the standard PDK transmission, and the world tends to get into a bit of a flap around you. Pedestrians point and stare – it has to be said with most of them smiling, not scowling – but the real curveball is the way other drivers crane necks and then need to take avoiding action when their glance lingers too long.

And unlike its mostly mute predecessor, the RS is very much audible. With the exhaust aps opened, it grumbles and fizzes unlike any turbocharged street-legal Porsche before now. And that's the first clue to how different this car is to anything that the factory (must remember that bit) has done before. Because, like all heavy artillery, the GT2 recipe has always been as simple as a Swabian pretzel. Take a series production Turbo, remove the front driveshafts, preen a little more power, add some wings 'n' stuff and ensure all new owners are aware that hideous, fiery death is a real possibility if in the wet you antagonise it. Now that appears to be a pretty extreme recipe, but this new car is way, way more angry than everything bar the very first 993 GT2. Scratch that – it makes the original widowmaker look like a palliative care nurse.

Yes, the motor is based on that of a 991 Turbo, but the blowers are bigger and many of the internal components are new. Moreover, the base character of the engine is completely different from anything we've seen from Porsche. This is a celebration of turbocharging – there is lag, the chuff arrives with an almighty wallop, then it revs to the 7,000rpm red line.

Like its predecessors, it remains rear-wheel drive, this time through a paddleshifter and Bosch's most advanced traction and stability hardware. The rear tyres are 325-sections and could probably do with being wider still. And as you digest those numbers and look at the frankly absurd thing this weird arse-engined lozenge shape, first seen in 1964, has become, it's hard to accept that most of them will be bought by speculators.

And will sit at traffic lights in Mayfair, in neutral with some Instagenius smashing the motor against its limiter. What has the world come to? The urban experiment revealed the following about the GT2 RS. The transmission is very clever and smooth at low speed. The rear steering gives a useful turning circle. The snout is way too low for snoozing rozzers and the cupholders probably should have been upgraded alongside the turbochargers to deal with the stiffer suspension. It also confirmed that I have zero interest in driving said car in an urban environment.

Michelin is on the verge of selling magic spells these days, so good are its latest Cup tyres. How they manage to make so much sense out of 691bhp, 10°C ambient temperature and a damp surface is surely beyond scientific comprehension. The slip road that takes me onto the motorway holds some interesting memories. I can remember attempting to give my own 996 GT2 the full berries here under similar conditions and realising that third-gear oversteer isn't that much fun on the public road. That first-generation 996 GT2 had more than 200bhp less than this one, yet it was far, far angrier in the wet. The old Michelin Pilot Sports were useless and the traction control apparatus had five, often sweaty, toes. I don't know if I'm in awe at how usable Porsche has made this thing in the British mid-winter, or disappointed that it has missed the chance to serve its loyal

following a slice of unfettered danger on four wheels.

It's too stiff for bumpy UK back roads, mind. The front spring rate is the same as a Cup racer uses on the Nürburgring, and the nose simply poings and deflects and generally doesn't want to engage. It's still drivable, but not what you'd call enjoyable.

At a motorway cruise, the wind noise is loud, the exhaust flaps need shutting to defeat the drone and the tyre noise is best described using the Beaufort scale. The radio attempts to make itself heard above the din, and the Bluetooth phone, which was clearly designed to operate in the hushed calm of a Carrera cabin, managed to make me sound like I'd just used the phrase "arse flaps" to a friend of mine, when I hadn't. Which was nice.

It all comes alive on a circuit. The staggering shove that demolishes 0–124mph in 8.3secs, the fizzing, angry nature of the engine. The monster traction that, with the systems on, spits this car around even a damp track at crazy speed with so little drama you have to keep reminding yourself it has more power than pretty much every racing 935 – the ultimate expression of the racing 911 – ever built. There's a little understeer, and the brakes are so strong you have to concentrate on not moving the weight forwards and backwards too violently, and leaving it in one permanently unsettled mess. And the noise – a malevolent growl that builds more intensely than any turbo Porsche I've heard outside a race circuit – is always there. Spooling, hissing, blaring.

But the RS only really reveals its full potential if you press the silly button and kill the systems. Only then do you enter a world of fourth-gear powerslides and ferocious oversteer that leaves you breathless and cackling with manic fear at the sheer fascination of a real 691bhp 911. I loved every minute of it. I wish the front was a little softer and able to bite better and the car easier to rotate on a trailing throttle, but the adjustable front roll bar would probably tweak most of that away.

People lucky enough to own one of these magnificent motor cars should only open themselves to this mayhem if they're very certain they can handle the outcome. If they can, they will have at their disposal the most exciting Porsche road car ever made, 918 included. If they don't, then maybe peacocking around town like a berk is actually a safer alternative. And I gather the cats glow red hot at night, which should keep them amused.

PRICE £209,000 **0-60** 2.8 SECONDS **TOP SPEED** 211MPH **POWER** 690BHP

DID YOU KNOW? THE GT2 RS CURRENTLY HOLDS THE NURBURGRING PRODUCTION CAR LAP RECORD... KINDA. MANTHEY-RACING TWEAKED THE RS BEFORE ITS 6M40.3SEC LAP

PORSCHE 911 R

The purist's ultimate 911?

The 911R is infused with the same sense of reverse engineering that has seen the market for mechanical chronographs boom. It's a traditional idea brought up to date by modern tech – so has an allure that's more than the sum of its parts. Over the rear axle is the same demented 4.0-litre naturally aspirated flat-six as the GT3 RS producing 493bhp at 8,250rpm, but connected to a short-throw 6spd manual – a direct response to criticism that the PDK-only GT3 and GT3 RS had lost a layer of engagement. The human-based shifting mechanism means it's a fraction slower from 0 to 62mph (although 3.7secs is enough to blow your hair back), but by

replacing the fixed rear wing with the Carrera's retractable spoiler, the top speed climbs by 8mph to 201mph. Weighing in at 1,445kg, the R undercuts the GT3 RS by 50kg thanks to a similar round of measures (magnesium roof, carbon bonnet and front wings, plastic rear windows and rear screen, no rear seats and reduced sound insulation). The chassis and body are from the GT3, barring a unique front lip spoiler and rear diffuser, while the gorgeous carbon bucket seats are from a 918 Spyder and trimmed in Pepita tartan (a nod to the very first 911s from the Sixties). The stripes and side graphics, available in red or green, draw the line between it and the 1967 911R – a road-homologated racer of which only 20 were ever made – although I'd be tempted to delete them entirely and spend my time surprising Ferraris at the lights. Carbon- ceramic brakes, 20in forged aluminium wheels and the GT3's four-wheel steering are standard. A single-mass flywheel is a £2,024 option. Your contact points to the road are Michelin Pilot Sport Cup 2s from the GT3 – 245mm wide at the front and 305mm wide at the rear – both 20mm narrower than the GT3 RS. It's that last point that gives

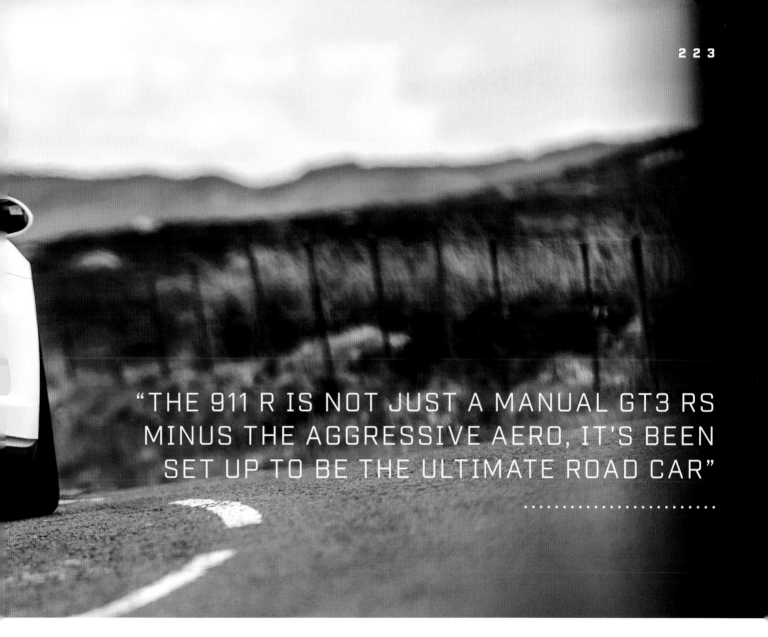

"THE 911 R IS NOT JUST A MANUAL GT3 RS MINUS THE AGGRESSIVE AERO, IT'S BEEN SET UP TO BE THE ULTIMATE ROAD CAR"

away what the 911R is really about. This is not just a manual GT3 RS minus the aggressive aero, it's been set up to be the ultimate road car, so instantly feels quite different from its track-obsessed siblings. There are buttons to control the two-stage dampers, activate the titanium sports exhaust and select Sport mode... and that's about it. Get going and the stubby, carbon-trimmed gearlever has a wonderful precision to it, so you feed it instinctively into any of its six slots. Snap shifts with your fingertips are an utter joy, although the auto-blip function isn't perfect. The steering, too, is lighter and less meaty than a GT3's. It's by no means as twirly and whipcrack-fast as a Ferrari, but it's heading in that direction. Once up to speed, though, with the suspension working hard beneath you, it still offers enough feedback as the cornering forces build and a feeling of chuckability and a sense of humour that the locked-down RS can't match. A large part of that is the spring and damper settings that have been softened off to let the car move more with varying road surfaces. In fast corners, that and the lack of aero mean it bobs and weaves like a prize fighter, keeping you busy

at the wheel, but still full of confidence that you'll exit the corner facing the right direction. The engine sounds like a gathering storm, beginning with a smooth buzz that hardens at 3,500rpm, then again at 6,000rpm, before it rips its shirt open and takes on a barely containable savagery between 7,500rpm and 8,500rpm. This is quite a powerplant to try to measure out with a clutch pedal and a lever grasped in your sweaty left palm. The perfect road-going Porsche? That title remains with the Cayman GT4. The 911R is still a wonderful thing to drive, so simple and forgiving, and that manual 'box lets you shake hands with the engine, rather than Skyping it via PDK. But, the GT4's performance is better suited to UK roads – while the GT3 RS's gearbox and aero make better use of this engine's abilities.

PRICE £136,000 **0-60** 3.7 SECONDS
TOP SPEED 201MPH **POWER** 493BHP
DID YOU KNOW? SPECULATION IS A MUG'S GAME, THEY SAY – THAT DIDN'T STOP THE R SELLING FOR £443,780... TWO MONTHS AFTER THE SELLER PAID £136K

P

PRICE £141,000 O-60 3.2 SECONDS TOP SPEED 193MPH POWER 520BHP

DID YOU KNOW? ANDREAS PREUNINGER, THE MAN BEHIND THE GT3 RS, OWNS... A RAM 1500 PICK-UP

TRUCK. ER, WHAT?

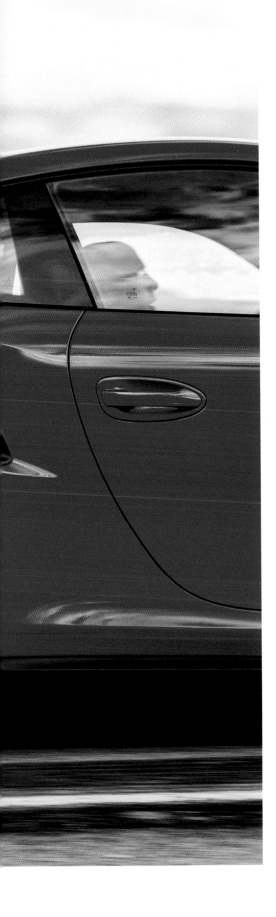

PORSCHE GT3 RS

Porsche's detail mania writ large. And fast

It has plastic windows, a sticker-for-a-badge and magnesium roof panel (30 per cent lighter than aluminium). If Porsche had stuck with a conventional aluminium roof, the car would have weighed 1,421kg instead of 1,420kg. And yet they persevered with this world first, a component that's 1mm thick, made from magnesium sourced in Malaysia, shaped in Canada and finally fitted in Germany. All for a single saved kilo. Porsche has put the same attention to detail into everything. It's highly unlikely you'll ever see the titanium con rods or the crankshaft, made of the same V361 super-high-purity steel as the 919 Le Mans car's, that had to be remelted multiple times in order to achieve the strength and grain it needs. But they're there. Likewise the dry-sump lubricated engine that now has a 4mm longer stroke, taking the 3.8-litre engine out to 4.0 litres, gaining 25bhp and 15lb ft. And the ball-jointed suspension. And the (admittedly optional) lightweight lithium-ion battery. And the titanium exhaust. It doesn't look self-conscious or visually overblown (no parody of a racing stripe here), it just looks mighty. The GT3 RS wears its motorsport background so close to the surface that occasionally it bursts through. It's the first of Porsche's naturally aspirated GT cars to use the wider Turbo body, which brings wider track widths (good for grip) and side air intakes (the ram-air effect is good for power). The broader bodyshell can't help but add weight, yet thanks to all those marginal gains, it's 10kg lighter than the GT3. And much more aerodynamically effective. In total, the GT3 RS generates 80 per cent of the downforce of the Cup racing car. Still not enough grip? Those vast 21-inch rear wheels are wrapped in comical 325/30 Michelin Pilot Super Sport tyres and, to top it all, don't forget the flat-six hangs out the back, too. Grip, frankly, is ludicrous. Traction is equally daft. You can come out of a hairpin in first gear, give it everything, and you still won't unstick the rears. Where the standard GT3 is surprisingly magnanimous, the GT3 RS is ruthless. Don't worry – it's on your side, but its take-no-prisoners attitude to roads is something to experience. that you can possibly process. It feels bombproof, both in its abilities and its mechanical robustness. It is an astonishing motor car.

ROLLS-ROYCE R-R SWEPT TAIL

Rolls-Royce creates a one-off. Like it?

The Rolls-Royce Sweptail is a bespoke one-off built for one of Rolls-Royce's "most valued customers". Inspired by the 'swept-tail' Rolls-Royces of the Twenties and Thirties – the Phantom II Streamline saloon is an influence – work began on the Sweptail in 2013, when an unnamed, exceptionally wealthy fellow asked Rolls to build him a "one-off luxury motor car like no other". So it did, before debuting at 2017 Villa d'Este Concorso d'Eleganza. The grille is the largest fitted to any modern-era Rolls-Royce. It's milled from a single piece of aluminium, before being hand-polished to a mirror shine. Further back, you've the 'swept-tail' that gives the car its name, while Rolls says the way the bodywork wraps under the car "with no visible boundary to the surfaces" is "akin to the hull of a yacht". Meanwhile, the 'bullet-tip' centre brake light and lower bumper "combine to create a greater feeling of elegance in motion". Its number plate is 08 (Rolls has given no indication where this car will live, but it's RHD...). Like the grille, the two digits are milled froma block of aluminium and hand-polished. The 'highlight' of the exterior though, says Rolls, is the panoramic glass roof. They claim it's "one of the most complex ever seen on a motor car". Inside, it's predictably opulent, with much wood, leather, metal and a 'hat shelf' with an illuminated lip. Rolls claims the dash is its cleanest to date, with a clock made from the thinnest Macassar veneer and machined titanium hands. Two panniers, one on either side, conceal bespoke attaché cases (made from carbon fibre to fit the owner's laptop/tablet). The centre console also houses a mechanism that serves up a bottle of the owner's favourite champagne (and rotates it so it's at the perfect angle to pick up) and two crystal champagnes flutes. Rolls hasn't given us any mechanical details – probably because to talk about such things as horsepower, acceleration and miles per gallon is considered a bit vulgar. However, we think it's safe to assume the Sweptail is based on an existing Rolls platform, and that under that long bonnet you will find one of its familiar V12s. The car was said to have cost approximately £10m, the most that has ever been paid for a new car – until Bugatti's La Voiture Noire arrived. Keeping pace with all this is surely the very definition of first world problems.

PRICE $12.8 MILLION **0-60** 5.1 SECONDS (EST) **TOP SPEED** 155MPH (EST) **POWER** 563BHP

DID YOU KNOW? UNTIL BUGATTI BUILT THE VOITURE NOIRE, THE SWEPTAIL WAS THE WORLD'S MOST EXPENSIVE CAR

RUF
CTR YELLOW BIRD(S)

Not one but two automotive unicorns

The Porsche 919's lap of the Nürburgring in 2018 might be the fastest of all time. But the best, most exciting, put-down-your-tea-and-just-watch lap? That still belongs to another Porsche – German tuner Ruf's 1987 promo video of its then-new CTR Yellowbird. Driven by Ruf test driver Stefan Roser, the tuned, 3.4-litre twin-turbo 911 Carrera rockets around the Nordschleife in 8 minutes and 5 seconds in clouds of tyre smoke, impossibly long skids and several dozen armfuls of opposite lock. It definitely isn't the fastest way around the circuit. But it's certainly the most entertaining to watch. Ruf only made 29 of them, but new owner Bruce Meyer quite rightly believes all his cars should be driven, not just gawped at. Even with the fuel injection doing its best to feed the engine correctly, the flat-six's lumpy tickover urges you to get on with it, press the gas and get going. So we do. First to second, second to third; the heavy clutch bites nicely and the gruff-sounding engine starts breathing more heavily. The turbos start to whistle. The thrust is surprisingly linear, not explosive. Third to... uh oh. Boy, this thing is still absurdly quick. As it should be, really, with a very conservatively measured 469bhp pushing just 1,150kg. But it's also the noise and analogue sensations, the speedo needle rushing round the dial, the gearstick slotting neatly through the ratios, every lump and bump telegraphed up through the seat and steering wheel. The Yellowbird's spiritual successor, the 2017 CTR, is also present, bringing the story right up to date. While it might look at first glance like a hot-rod version of a 964, that is very much not the case. Look closely and there are virtually no Porsche parts on this 30th anniversary Yellowbird at all. Only the front and rear screens, the door glass and frames are from the Weissach parts bin. The new Yellowbird starts with a carbon tub and spaceframe, which is then clothed in carbon-fibre panels of Ruf's own spec. The brakes and suspension are new and the engine is a heavily tuned 3.6-litre Mezger unit, as originally found in the 997 911 Turbos. The gearbox is a six-speed of Ruf's own design. The net result is an even more extreme version of the original car. Weight is 1,200kg, power now 710bhp, torque a not-inconsiderable 650lb ft. It's everything you'd expect, and hope, a next-gen Yellowbird could be.

RIMAC CONCEPT TWO

Croatian genius Rimac isn't just flogging tech to others, he's doing his own supercar

This is the C_Two, successor to the Concept_One electric hypercar. It's more powerful, faster, goes further on a charge, and terrifyingly clever. And rather beautiful, in a futuristic kind of way. Strap in, and prepare yourself for an absurd set of numbers. Rimac claims the C_Two's four electric motors develop a combined 1,914hp (1,887bhp) and 1,696lb ft – or 2,300Nm in new money. The front wheels individually use a single-speed gearbox each, while the use of twin two-speed gearboxes at the rear makes for a truly terrifying top speed. Rimac is claiming v-max at 258mph. On the way, we're told the C_Two will have cracked 0-60mph in 1.85 seconds (albeit with an American drag strip-friendly one-foot rollout), and 0-62mph, for we Europeans, in 1.97 seconds. If the driver remains conscious, the Rimac will cover off 0-100mph in 4.3 seconds. Despite a completely carbon fibre chassis (with integrated batteries), carbon crash structures and carbon panels, the C_Two is no lightweight – it's a 1,950kg machine. However, Rimac has worked to disguise this with intelligent torque-vectoring, which is fully adaptive between all four wheels. A twist of the knob inside the fabulously modern cabin shifts drive between the axles, enabling what Rimac calls "from full grip to extended drifting capability." In fact, the system is said to be so smart, the C_Two doesn't have conventional stability and traction control nannies. Instead of jabbing at the monster 390mm carbon ceramic brakes to rein in performance, it's left to the torque-vectoring tech to juggle the drive and sort out your ham-fistedness. Rimac says each hour spent in the car generates 6 gigabytes of data. This really is a laptop on wheels. Small wonder Rimac says the 72 ECUs and processors on board have the same computing power as 22 Macbook Pros…

But there's more tech. Scary tech. On-board cameras with facial recognition have not only dispensed with the need for a key – the car simply looks at your face before deciding to open the butterfly doors and start the powertrain – but Rimac says the car can also read your moods. Apparently, if you're getting ratty, the car will soften its ride and play soothing music to calm you down. Which is terrifying and yet sensible, when there's 1,900bhp under your right foot.

PRICE $2.1 MILLION **0-60** 1.85 SECONDS **TOP SPEED** 258MPH **POWER** 1,888BHP

DID YOU KNOW? MATE RIMAC'S FIRST ELECTRIC CAR WAS AN OLD BMW 323I THAT HE CONVERTED

SINGER DLS

Continuation geniuses take the 911 to another level of insane brilliance

Over the course of the past six seconds we've peeled off a slip road onto the A34 near Wantage and the noise has induced fear, mild pain and full-body euphoria... in that order. "And that's three-quarter throttle at 5,000 revs," shouts the man next to me, laughing like a bit of a maniac, because he knows there's more to come. That man is Marino Franchitti, racing driver and one quarter of a team responsible for developing the car I find myself harnessed so tightly into, I'm basically a fleshy strut brace. The car is the Porsche 911 Reimagined by Singer – Dynamics and Lightweighting Study (DLS, if you value your time). It's the answer to the simplest of questions: "What if we pursued the ultimate, no-compromise air-cooled 911? And what if we touched it with a F1 team?" That was five years ago... things have rather snowballed from there.

Singer's major partner in all this has been Williams Advanced Engineering, responsible for the suspension, aero and engine, but the list of collaborators is equally blue-chip – Brembo, Momo, Recaro, BBS, Michelin, Bosch. All needed to be fully on-board with Singer boss Rob Dickinson's vision – to restore the most advanced, lightweight, air-cooled 911 that the world has ever seen. Clearly, Singer's forensic attention to detail hasn't been lost on the world's wealthiest Beetle enthusiasts. It now has buyers for all 75 cars – at $1.8m a pop – and stands on the brink of a monumental achievement.

Restorations start in Oxfordshire in the spring next year, with first deliveries by the end of 2019, but still there's work to be done before all that. Just two early engineering mules exist with a distinct Mad Max vibe, one lurking in the bowels of the

Williams Advanced Engineering centre. Then there are two more polished EP cars, although neither is the finished article by any stretch. Marino reckons EP2, painted in Heart Attack red (the car we've been granted access to the passenger seat for a blat around Williams' home turf and Abingdon airfield) is about 75 per cent of the way there. "All the bits of the puzzle exist, now it's just about putting them together."

High on that list has to be low-speed engine calibration. At this stage (much like the half-finished interior), it's simply not worth the time and effort to finesse that final 10 per cent – as a result it's lumpier than a 15-year-old's face. I almost feel sorry for Marino as I watch him slip the clutch, trying to placate a rampant engine that has no interest in behaving below 2,000rpm. Then I remember he's the one who gets to drive this thing, I'm locked

into the Recaro on the wrong side, feet braced against the bulkhead. There shall be no sympathy here.

To the centre of Wantage, where I ask him to perform laps of the central roundabout at 12mph. Schadenfreude isn't my only motivation, this is our first opportunity to see it in the wild… experiencing a car in a perfectly lit studio is one thing, seeing it parked outside Subway next to a dog-eared Mondeo is quite another. We couldn't be further from Singer's California home, but who cares? This car brings the sunshine with it. What a thing to look at. There simply isn't a bad angle… low, high, front, back – the lens loves it. Its stance and proportions are perfect, yes, but there's an indefinable element here, a wave of Rob Dickinson's magic wand. If everyone knew how to do it… they'd be doing it.

Clutch control duly examined, we strike south and start to

wind it through the gears – we've got an airfield to mess around on later, there's no need to thrash it yet. What's quickly apparent is that there's witchcraft in these Exe-Tc dampers. Bespoke items, like pretty much everything associated with this car, they're fully adjustable via the exposed top mounts in the front and back, and just reek of quality. The lack of any sound deadening (that will be added later) and a general mechanical clamour means your ears tell you it should be uncomfortable, but the harshness never materialises.

"It would have been easy to just make a racing car, but that would be so wrong. Stopwatches did not come into this – it's about transmitting sensations," Marino reminds me as we float along in mystifying comfort. Case study: as we pull off the A34 at 70mph, I spot a nasty-looking dip up ahead. My feet instinctively brace for collision, but Marino looks completely unfazed. We impact, the chin spoiler kisses the surface and we're flat and level again immediately – no herniated discs, no nose bob, no problem. If it weren't for the engine, this would be the car's defining characteristic.

Fast forward to Abingdon Airfield, and it's time for the full hit. Marino points the nose down the runway and guns it, changing up at 8,500rpm (though it's happy to crack nine grand), and backing off only when we run out of tarmac. It's a frantic hit of g-force, as linear and relentless as anything I've been in – this is 500bhp pushing 1,000kg, remember… Veyron power-to-weight. But it's the wall of sound that shocks you. Surrounded by carbon – even the roll cage is flushly hemmed in by it – you're at the epicentre of an echo chamber with the angriest noise imaginable trying to burrow into your brain. How angry? Take 10,000 football hooligans, a few million hornets, a couple of dozen UFC fighters and pair of honey badgers, blend them up, and you're getting close. You'll note the ear protectors. Completed cars will have the sound calmed to more acceptable road-car levels.

The engine is the benchmark the rest of the car is being asked to keep up with – a 4.0-litre, nat-asp, air-cooled masterpiece built specifically for this, with input from Hans Mezger, Porsche's most celebrated engine designer. "The engine it reminds me of is the one in the McLaren F1. It's the free-revving character, the way it hits the limiter and you can't believe you're there already," says Marino. "John Magee, who did the engine development, was so nervous the first time I drove it. But I got out of the car and hugged him."

When we ask Marino to arse about a bit, more layers of genius are revealed. By his own admission, Marino isn't a "slider" but even he – a devout racing driver conditioned to consider drifting the antichrist – can cut loose in this. "God I love this car," he bellows as he tips it in, lights up the rear and keeps it nicely crossed up for the camera. "It's the precision of the throttle that lets me do it." Normally you get one, perhaps two prods to put it where you want, but with an HDMI connection between accelerator and rear tyres, your slide angle is in direct correlation with the flex of your right foot.

Marino describes the secondary steering method – that wheel in front of his face – as having just a little bit of old-school wiggle off centre so it doesn't feel hyperactive, but then supercar levels of bite and streaming feedback when you load it up more. A microcosm, then, of the car's wider ethos – to deliver modern supercar levels of grip and performance, without losing the idiosyncrasies that make an air-cooled 911 an air-cooled 911.

We'll have to wait until we drive it ourselves to confirm whether that essential old-school DNA has survived, but we're convinced that the DLS is a very sizeable achievement. To the uninitiated, $1.8m will seem like an awful lot of money for a tricked-out old Porsche. Well, consider this your initiation.

PRICE $1.8 MILLION **0-60** < 3.0 SECONDS (EST) **TOP SPEED** > 170MPH **POWER** 500BHP

DID YOU KNOW? SINGER'S FOUNDER, ROB DICKINSON, IS THE COUSIN OF IRON MAIDEN'S BRUCE DICKINSON

SSC TUATARA

American flyboys who fired the starting gun on the race to 300mph get serious

In 2007, Shelby SuperCars (SSC) stunned the automotive nobility when its Ultimate Aero set the production car speed record by hitting 255.83mph on a closed road in Washington State, taking the title from Bugatti. To add insult to injury, the Shelby record was approved and validated by Guinness – meaning America had *officially* beaten the hypercar glitterati.

"When we looked into setting the record, it became clear that there were no standards by which these speeds were validated, so we worked with the team at Guinness and agreed the parameters for an official speed run. Two passes on the same stretch of road within an allocated time. Those rules are still in place today, so, basically, we wrote the rule book," says Jerod Shelby, CEO of Shelby SuperCars.

We first set eyes on the SSC Tuatara's wildly futuristic design eight years ago, but it still looks like a spaceship. If anything, it fits into the design lexicon of 2019 hypercar far better than it did in 2011. But the design isn't focused purely on visual impact – its form has been honed by Jason Castriota (Maserati Birdcage Concept, Ferrari 599, and the one off that started it all... the Ferrari P4/5) and is driven by the unwavering demands of aerodynamics at high speed.

"At these stratospheric speeds, the aerodynamic drag of the vehicle has a huge effect on your high-end performance, and the bhp required to get to the magic number. We have a Cd (coefficient of drag) of 0.279 and the Chiron has 0.35. We've done the math and we're confident we'll do the number, with power to spare," Castriota explains.

The Tuatara is powered by a bespoke flat-plane crank, 5.9-litre, twin-turbo V8 developed by Nelsen Racing that red-lines at 8,800rpm. It delivers 1,332bhp on 'regular pump gas' or an eye-watering 1,726bhp on E85 (barrels of which have come to Monticello race track to give us the full experience today). Transferring this power to the rear wheels (yes, only the rears) is the work of a bespoke 7spd automated manual 'box, developed by CIMA in Italy and capable of delivering a flat shift in less than 50ms. SSC claims a 0–62mph time sub-2.5secs, a quarter-mile in under 9.75 and a vmax of... well, we'll have to wait and see. The Penske active suspension has three settings: Normal, Sport and Track. Transferring fire and fury to the road surface are Michelin

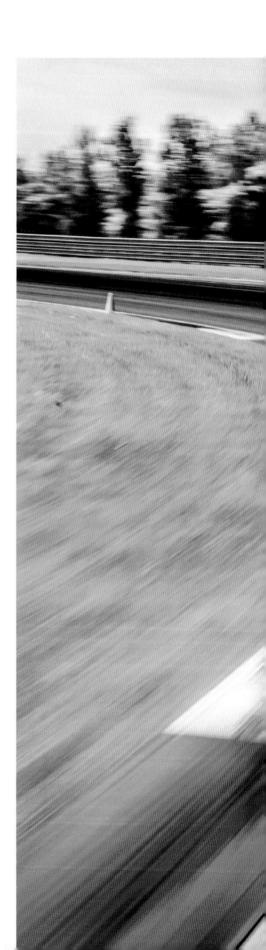

Pilot Sport Cup 2s, 245/35s on the front, worried-looking 345/30s on the rear. With all carbon bodywork and the production car featuring a bespoke carbon tub, the SSC weighs in at 1247kg, 272kg lighter than an Aventador. Open the dramatic swan wing doors and the interior has a highly bespoke feel. Take the HMI – a bugbear of most limited- series cars and a tell-tale of which OEM computer mainframe is actually keeping you on the road. SSC, and a team in Norway, has developed a completely unique system which also interacts with an app on your phone and allows you to access the car and change various parameters, including the ride height, remotely...

To truly understand the appeal of the SSC, you have to understand the clients. Today, there's a mix of ex-NFL Super Bowl winners, global business owners and big deal traders, all successful, all incredibly excited to see the car (let alone drive it) and all with a shared mentality. Each of them is on the speed-dial first-call list of every carmaker's limited-series client liaison officer, the quality they crave the most being exclusivity.

We watch each of them climb into the car and play with varying degrees of success out on the circuit. On their return, the unanimous response is shock and awe – the Super Bowl Hall of Famer exits with the broadest smile, eulogising about "limitless power" and "explosive shifts". When the VIP guests are done, it's time for me to try it. After a couple of initial exploratory laps with Shelby driving, we swap and set out to learn the circuit and see if 1,726bhp fed through the rear wheels is just an accident waiting to happen. My first four laps, learning a circuit where members are dicing in their cars, is not all kinds of fun. But contrary to my worst fears, the SSC delivers its huge power in a way no rear-wheel-drive car should.

The track is quickly swamped with a squadron of Miatas, so Jerod and I head out onto the highway to see how the SSC fares in the real world. You're conscious that excessive power is always available, and any pressure put on the throttle is accompanied by a huge inhalation then a dump of boost pressure, so you end up wafting along, barely troubling the potential under your right foot. The visibility is narrow, focused and aggressive, the ride surprisingly supple, thanks to its active Penske suspension, and the 'box shifts smoothly at these lower speeds. Our short trip showcases enough potential to prove owners could happily drive from Manhattan to Monticello.

Back at the track the following day, and after an evening to recalibrate, it's time to dig more deeply into the Tuatara's potential. With the car in Track – which drops the ride height to 60mm from the road, stiffens the dampers and makes the gearchanges whipcrack fast – we head out. With a clear circuit, I finally summon the courage to pin the Tuatara down the back straight. Second gear, full throttle... the rear of the car squats, squirms momentarily then grips and goes. It's violently impressive, but not as violent as the gearchange which is, frankly, terrifying. Every full-throttle shift is accompanied by an explosive shockwave, some of which seems to focus its energy at your elbow and feels like it's threatening to burst out.

The acceleration is brutal and, once you're in the power band with the turbos spooled up, it's linear and shows no sign of letting up until you punch a hole in the horizon. As the laps accumulate and confidence grows, the following become the headline acts. The steering is responsive, the brakes are mighty, but the pedal is currently too soft (Shelby says this has already been addressed for production). The faster you go, the more impressive the SSC's aero feels, but we need more space to truly dip into the boundaries of this car's performance. Monticello just isn't big enough to fully uncork this car. For that, we need to relocate to a very long road in Washington, close it down, point the SSC at the horizon and see where the needle stops moving.

For many, the race to break 300mph is an irrelevance, a meaningless figure already breached by many brave combatants on the salt flats. But for some, like Shelby, it's the driving force in their pursuit to build the car of their dreams. For the client base – people who have everything – having officially the fastest thing is definitely 'a thing'. There'll only ever be one production car that is the first to break the 300mph barrier, and only time will tell if the Tuatara will claim that title.

But if SSC can beat Bugatti, Koenigsegg and Hennessey to the punch, Bobby Axelrod and the real life billion-dollar boys' club will have a remarkable new item on the shopping list.

PRICE $1.6 MILLION **0-60** < 2.5 SECONDS **TOP SPEED** 300MPH (EST) **POWER** 1,726BHP
DID YOU KNOW? TUATARA'S ENGINE ADJUSTS ITS POWER OUTPUT BASED ON THE OCTANE OF FUEL YOU'VE PUT IN

TOURING DISCO VOLANTE

They junked an Alfa 8C Competizione to build this. It was worth it...

Although it looks like pure conceptual eye candy, the Touring DVS is a production car, albeit in an extraordinarily limited run: the vehicle you see here is the first in a run of six. The DVS is such a vibrant assault on the senses it may have been visible as we came into land. In fact, if we'd spied it through the window of the plane at 37,000ft it would have been apt: Disco Volante means 'flying saucer', and the car's *ceruleo blu* (sky blue) exterior colour was chosen because the sky is where flying saucers habitually spend their time.

One of the earthbound originals lives in Alfa Romeo's wonderful new museum; it's arguably the best-known example of Touring's patented 'superleggera' lightweight manufacturing technique and aluminium-beating artisanal prowess. Alfa's factory test driver Consalvo Sanesi first took to the track in a Disco Volante on June 11th 1952, eventually piloting the thing to a streamlined, aero-assisted speed of 140mph.

The DVS generates so much charisma it's difficult to know where to begin. As wide as a Range Rover, its body really is almost saucer-shaped and flaunts the basic tenets of stance and proportion so flagrantly that it simply shouldn't work. But it does, brilliantly. It's also much more than just an open version of the Touring DV coupe. The roof is a two-piece carbon fibre creation (the panels weigh 3.5kg each), the design of which necessitated a complete reworking of the windscreen. The whole top half of the car now flows seamlessly into dramatic seat fairings which are reinforced with carbon, resolving into a rear end whose volumes look almost impossibly cool. Cool or not, the sculpted taper on the DVS's rear really would be impossible if it wasn't a handcrafted, bespoke special. "It's one of the reasons I love working at Touring," the company's design boss Louis de Fabribeckers says. "I can do things like this. It's also a 360° job. We have to take care of everything, and the finished car represents 10,000 hours of engineering effort."

The DVS is well-nigh perfect in terms of its detail; although the cabin is Alfa 8C – which also donates its chassis – there are ally strips on the sills, unique body colour inlays in the doors, and even Plexiglass inserts in the seats that pulse gently with light when you unlock the car. The seats themselves are trimmed in buttery-smooth Connolly leather. There's a little wing between the fairings, inspired by the Spitfire. It's also meant to hark back to the days when Gianni Agnelli and his jammy playboy ilk genuinely did tour grandly, usually on nocturnal assignations with willowy heiresses or casino croupiers. So there's storage space inside, and a frankly huge boot under that vast, sweeping rear canopy (also made of carbon composite).

Few things are more likely to induce heart palpitations than driving someone else's multi-million pound one-off supercar onto an Italian *tangenziale* rammed with hire cars and mercenary 18-wheelers. But despite its size, the DVS is user-friendly. And fast. It's powered by the Alfa 8C's Maserati-derived, Ferrari-assembled 4.7-litre, 450bhp V8, so there's huge personality here, too, the *basso profundo* soundtrack amplified by the absence of a roof. Even the gearbox – the 8C's Achilles heel – is quicker-shifting and less lurchsome than I remember. Besides, you can drive around the torque interruption, and somehow it feels OK in this car anyway.

Over the rhythmic thump of super strada expansion joints, there's no sign of any serious or even semi-serious structural wobbles. This is a beautifully engineered motor car, underpinned by 90 years of tradition (there was a gap from '66 to '08 but let's not dwell on that). Of course, there's no reason why it shouldn't work; after all, Touring has all the CAD tools and runs all the industry-standard CFD analyses.

As we pass from Emilia-Romagna into Tuscany, and the roads tighten, our pace intensifies. It demonstrates that the Disco Volante is more than just another car – it's out of this world.

PRICE £600,000 (EST) **0-60** 4.2 SECONDS **TOP SPEED** 181MPH **POWER** 444BHP

DID YOU KNOW? DISCO VOLANTE TRANSLATES AS 'FLYING SAUCER'. OR, ROUGHLY THE BEST NAME FOR A CAR, EVER

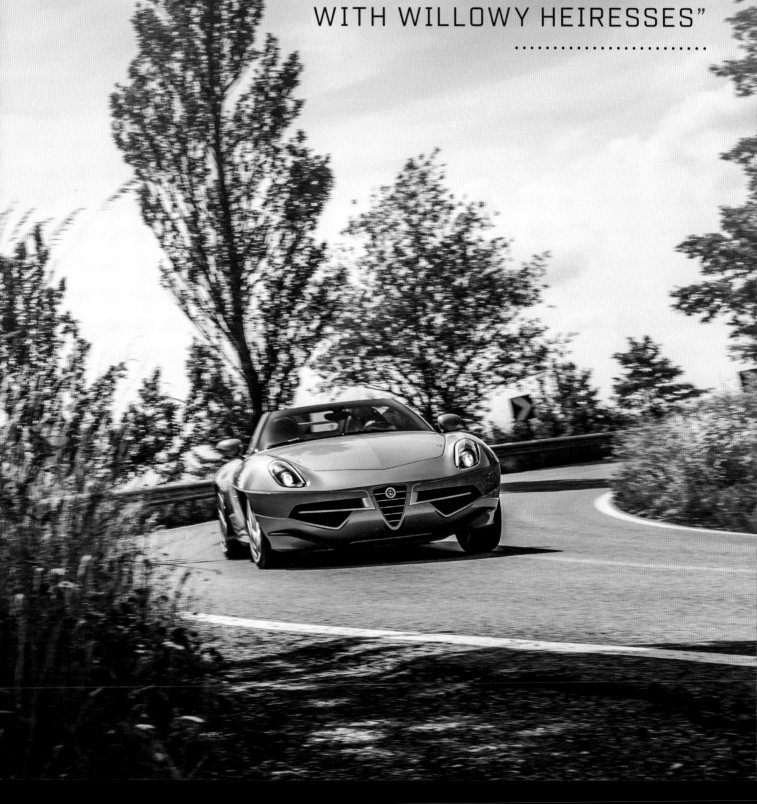

"THIS IS A CAR THAT HARKS BACK TO THE DAYS WHEN PLAYBOYS CROSSED BORDERS ON LATE-NIGHT ASSIGNATIONS WITH WILLOWY HEIRESSES"

"THE CORVETTE HAS AN INTERIOR THAT LOOKS LIKE IT COMES FROM THE COUNTRY THAT GAVE US THE IPHONE, NOT THE ONE THAT DEVISED SPRAY-ON CHEESE"

CHEVROLET CORVETTE C8

America's supercar staple comes over all
sophisticated in its 2020 form

Yes, the engine's in the middle. That engine being a 6.2-litre, naturally aspirated smallblock 'LT2' V8, sending 495bhp and 470lb ft to the rear wheels via a rear-mounted eight-speed dual-clutch gearbox. With the Z51 package fitted (which adds a sports exhaust, adjustable suspension, bigger brakes, better cooling and a spritelier final drive ratio) Chevy claims the Stingray will get from 0-60mph in around 3.0 seconds, making it the fastest 'entry-level' Corvette ever. And it's not just speedy in a straight line. The front splitter and rear wing generate a claimed 180kg of high-speed downforce for better cornering. There's a Ferrari-style electronic rear diff, optional magnetic-adaptive suspension, and a dry-sump oil system so the engine stays lubricated when the car's pulling big Gs. Chevy says this is a true supercar that can run with the European elite. Want to carry two sets of golf clubs? No, us neither. But apparently some supercar buyers do, so the Corvette Stingray has two boots. Or trunks, if you must. One in the front, and one in the back, which can also swallow the targa roof panel. Together, the trunk and frunk add up to offer 357-litres of boot space. And the cabin's roomier too. And cleverer. Look at that 12-inch digital instrument display. At last, we've got a Corvette with an interior that looks like it came from the country that invented the iPhone, instead of the country that also invented spray-on cheese. Though what's going on with that super-long strip of buttons? Did Chevy forget to put the heater controls in until yesterday? Underneath, Chevy has gone for an aluminium chassis instead of a McLaren-style carbon tub, to keep the car affordable – under $60,000 in base spec. Of course no modern sports car would be complete without an armada of modes to fiddle with. So, in addition to Weather, Tour, Sport and Track settings, the new Stingray offers two new modes to play with. There's MyMode – basically a cherry-pick-your-faves individual setting. And finally, a 'Z' mode, Chevy says "Z mode is a single-use mode activated through a 'Z' button on the wheel that takes MyMode configurations one step further, allowing drivers to adjust the engine and transmission as well".

UNITED STATES

If you can see through the tyre smoke, there are three cars here

The Dodge Challenger SRT Demon is the cockroach of the car industry – time, economics and trends just can't kill it. Based on a platform that ex-parent Daimler stopped using for the E-Class right after the turn of the century, and topping a range that starts with a V6-powered, narrow-tyred, budget model, the fervour around the Demon initially makes no sense whatsoever. Then you see it, hear it and drive it and it makes all the sense in the world. Fill it with 100-octane petrol, punch a few buttons on the dash and you are transported to a world of warm, humid Saturday night muscle-car heaven. A place where cornering prowess is secondary and all that matters is getting down the 1,320 feet as quickly, loudly and impressively as possible. And, boy, does it deliver. But only if you really know what you're doing. And you're on the right surface. Anyone can spin up the fat drag radial tyres and make clouds of smoke. But to get it to launch properly, you need real skills. For those who think that drag racing is simply holding the car on the brake, then stamping on the loud pedal when the lights go green, the Demon is here to set you straight. Set the car in Drag and it prepares for battle. You get access to the 840bhp mode, the suspension softens the front rebound damping, to help weight transfer. All the cooling from the aircon flows to the engine, so the cabin heats up. And you can engage the transbrake. In this configuration, on a prepped surface, with the skinny front wheels fitted, saving 30lb off the front axle, the Demon's 315-section Nittos will dead hook into the surface and shoot the car forward, front wheels hovering just above the track, faster than any other petrol-powered production car on the planet. Never mind one that weighs well over 1,800kg. But you have to have the reactions of a ninja to correctly sequence the release of the transbrake – by letting go of whichever shift paddle you are holding in – and then roll in the power. So it's something you need to practise and can get better at, which makes it all the more enjoyable and satisfying when you do. the width of the grin, the heart rate, the dopamine rush... The Camaro ZL1 1LE has such immediate feel within the first few rotations of the wide, special Goodyear-tyred wheels you know it's a very sorted thing. You sit low, almost stupidly low, in the car and peer, racecar style, over the instrument cluster. The competition seats hug you just so, and it's got a manual 6spd rev-matched gearbox.

So it all feels right from the off. And it just gets better and better from there. It has a set of Multimatic DSSV dampers, which can be very simply adjusted for road or track. In the latter mode, once the tyres are up to temperature, the big car gets up on its toes and dances around the track, flattering driver inputs by being responsive and forgiving at the same time. This inspires confidence which increases speed and makes you happy. Then you get out, look at your lap times and realise you've gone faster than you thought possible. The Z06 engine, which had so many heat issues in the Vette, is absolutely fine, too, as there's more space for cooling here. So you decide when you stop, not the car. But as crazy as the Camaro is, there's always crazier. Hennessey is back, with the 1,600bhp Venom F5 and some big plans. "It's to go as fast as we can... 300mph is the kind of baseline – that's where we would like to begin. Ultimately however, the tyres and the venue of where we'd run the F5 are the limiting factor." At the time of writing, he's sold 15 of the 24 cars earmarked for production (10 of 12 reserved for the US, and 5 of 12 reserved for international markets). It'll take roughly six to nine months to build one. Each car will feature a bespoke monocoque carbon tub, front carbonfibre crash structure, rear aluminium spaceframe, that monster 7.6-litre twin-turbo V8, a paddleshift gearbox, and rear-wheel drive. Yours for around $1.6m. "I think it's great what Koenigsegg did. That rivalry pushes all of us to go faster."

CAMARO ZL1 1LE

PRICE $69,995 **0-60** 3.0 SECONDS
TOP SPEED 198MPH

CHALLENGER SRT DEMON

PRICE $84,996 **0-60** 2.3 SECONDS
TOP SPEED 168MPH

HENNESSEY VENOM F5

PRICE $1.6 MILLION **0-60** 2.0 SECONDS (EST)
TOP SPEED 301MPH (CLAIMED)
POWER 1600BHP
DID YOU KNOW? AN F5-CLASS TORNADO GENERATES WINDS BETWEEN 261 AND 318MPH. AH, WE SEE WHAT THEY DID THERE

W MOTORS FENYR SUPERSPORT

Ambitious and Dubai-based, there's
a lot of serious thinking in this thing

This is the Fenyr SuperSport. Much like Tesla, W Motors' business plan appears to be based on bringing the price down and increasing the production run with each successive model, because the Fenyr is a snip at £1.4m, and up to 25 of them will be built every year. OK, not exactly mass production, but heading in the right direction. While the design is all in-house, the Fenyr will be built by Magna Steyr in Austria and places a tuned Porsche twin-turbo 3.8-litre flat-six, developed for them by RUF, just in front of the rear axle. Power and torque is quoted as 789bhp and 723lb ft, while it features a full carbon body to keep the kerbweight down to 1,350kg and the performance quite spicy. Like, 0-62mph in 2.7secs, 0-124mph in 9.4secs and a 245mph top speed, spicy. Other highlights include carbon ceramic brakes, Porsche's seven-speed dual clutch gearbox, a limited slip differential and an active rear wing with three independent moving sections. Heck, it'll even be offered in both left and right-hand drive. So, Porsche innards, European build quality and a set of performance figures that are equally as mental as the design. Question is will 25 customers a year be able to see past that rather hefty price tag? Well, you can't fault the CEO, Ralph R. Debbas', optimism. In the official press release he claims "the Fenyr SuperSport is the most incredible car ever produced so far".

PRICE £1.4 MILLION **0-60** 2.7 SECONDS **TOP SPEED** 245MPH **POWER** 799BHP

DID YOU KNOW? THE FENYR'S POWER COMES FROM A RUF-DEVELOPED 3.8-LITRE FLAT-SIX

ZAGATO ASTON MARTIN VANQUISH

Idiosyncratic Italian coachbuilder boosts relationship with British hero

Aston Martin first collaborated with Zagato in 1960, when designer Ercole Spada, just 23 at the time, re-bodied the DB4 GT to spectacular effect, following a call from Aston's then racing director, John Wyer, frustrated by the standard car's lack of pace in GT racing. Clothed in wafer-thin aluminium, Zagato made it lighter, faster, and even more beautiful. Only 19 were created, and they couldn't sell them all in period. In July 2018, one was sold at auction for £10.1m. When Aston announced a renewed Zagato collaboration back in 2016 at the Villa d'Este concorso d'eleganza, a rebodied Vanquish S coupe served as the opening volley on a quartet of Vanquish Zagatos. It was lava red with anodized bronze accents on the air vents, alloys and inside, and did the trick for a mysterious Scottish man who ordered all four versions. He only took delivery of his new carbon fibre-bodied family yesterday, and yet here we are less than 24 hours later in Dungeness, all four V12s warming up, almost 2400bhp between them and costing £2.68m in total. First up, the roofless Speedster. Theoretically a problem for the famous Zagato 'double bubble' roof, the Speedster gets round that by having a pair of what Aston dubs Speed Humps, streamlined cowls flowing back from the seats. While the other three members of the family – Coupe, Volante and Shooting Brake – number 99 in production, only

"THE SHOOTING BRAKE IS THE MOST CONCEPTY OF THE FOUR CARS, THE ONE THAT MAKES ONLOOKERS GAPE"

28 Speedsters are being made, for reasons no-one at Aston can quite explain. It's also the most expensive, at £960,000. With the DBS Superleggera and Vantage Aston's headline acts these days, it's easy to forget what a sublime piece of work the outgoing Vanquish S – on which these specials are based – still is. We make no secret of our admiration for Matt Becker, Aston's head of ride and handling, otherwise known as Mr Suspension Setting. Retuned dampers, a thicker rear anti-roll bar, revised steering, all accompanied by the bark of a 5.9-litre V12 ingesting fuel and air as nature intended: the Zagato Speedster flows down the road with ease, unfazed by the sudden dips and crests that would have less compliant cars bottoming out. Today of all days, this fluency is a treasured commodity, not wishing to shower myself in someone else's shattered carbon splitter. This is an easy, hugely rewarding car to drive quickly. And slowly. And the others? The Coupe is the most classically exact, its roof and visor-like glasshouse the elements that tie it explicitly into the Zagato narrative. The Volante feels phenomenally solid, with only the merest shimmy betraying its convertible roof. The Speedster is the loudest and most aggressive. But it's the Shooting Brake that's the most intriguing. Quite why what is effectively an estate car incarnation of a gob-smacking coupe should exert such an allure is a mystery, but maybe it's because we're a nation of dog-lovers, and you can imagine one inside. This is the most overtly concepty of the four cars, the one that makes onlookers gape. Having decided to create a family with Zagato, Aston's design director Miles Nurnberger says the original plan was to do three cars. Then three became four. "Zagatos are often polarising, but the Coupe sold out before we'd even shown it. The rear lamps are probably the most extreme thing, they're like splintered blades. Our supplier actually laughed when we first discussed them. That's a sign you're doing something right!"

PRICE £500,000 **0-60** 3.5 SECONDS
TOP SPEED 200MPH (EST) **POWER** 592BHP
DID YOU KNOW? THE ZAGATO 'DOUBLE BUBBLE' ROOF WAS ORIGINALLY MADE SO HELMETED DRIVERS WOULDN'T SMACK INTO THE CEILING

ZENVO TSR-S

Danish supercar minnow reinvents one of the aerodynamic basics

This is the Zenvo TSR-S, and it does something we've never seen before. Oh, we've heard of active aero and we've seen flaps moving and airbrakes deploying, but we've never seen anything quite like this before. Something that clearly has the Goodwood marshals in a state of some confusion. Zenvo calls it the Zentripetal rear wing. Zenvo, Denmark's only car company, has been building cars since 2007. It faces the same challenges as any other small hypercar builder. The market is in the right place now, people are buying these million-pound cars, but why should they buy yours? Pagani has its artistry, Hennessey, Bugatti and Koenigsegg their top speed battle, Rimac its e-power. Now meet the one with the maddest aero of all. As I drive around the track, it teases at the edge of my vision – I'm concentrating forwards, but I catch glimpses in the mirrors of it tilting and swinging, these very abrupt, robotic movements. It's like having a Transformer on the back deck, popping some funky moves. Can I feel the difference it makes? Not really, but aero is the unseen force in car dynamics – you only notice it when it goes. What I do notice is that the back end is more planted than the front (as you'd hope when it's the end that has to deploy 1,177bhp). The nose feels comparatively soft, the steering a little springy, so there's a sense of imbalance front to rear. But that's fine: next week this car is off to Nardò for chassis maestro Loris Bicocchi to work his magic. But I'm getting into it, summoning up the courage to deploy ever greater chunks of the twin-supercharged 5.8-litre V8. Troels Vollertsen, ex-race mechanic and engineer, is the man behind Zenvo: "The TSR track car had a fixed rear wing, but I'd been thinking that maybe we could alter the downforce so we could put more pressure back across to the unloaded inside wheel while cornering, so you not only get downforce, but also create an effect like an anti-roll bar. So we took the standard wing and tried it at different angles in the simulation, and we could see there was a massive impact." This is a more carefully considered and innovative car than I'd expected, full of race thinking but in need of the final polish to make it that bit more usable. Zenvo has made less than 25 cars in its history so far, and as Troels points out, "Our customers are not buying a car, they are investing in the company."

PRICE $1.5 MILLION (EST) 0-60 2.8 SECONDS TOP SPEED 202MPH POWER 1,117BHP

DID YOU KNOW? THE TSR-S IS THE STREET-LEGAL VERSION OF THE TSR, WHICH IS THE TRACK-ONLY VERSION OF THE TS1